T0305270

ANONYMOUS AGENCIES,
BACKSTREET BUSINESSES,
AND COVERT COLLECTIVES

ANONYMOUS AGENCIES, BACKSTREET BUSINESSES, AND COVERT COLLECTIVES

Rethinking Organizations in the 21st Century

Craig R. Scott

Stanford Business Books
An Imprint of Stanford University Press
Stanford, California

Stanford University Press
Stanford, California

Special discounts for bulk quantities of Stanford Business Books are available to corporations, professional associations, and other organizations. For details and discount information, contact the special sales department of Stanford University Press. Tel: (650) 736–1782, Fax: (650) 736–1784.

Printed in the United States of America on acid-free, archival-quality paper

Library of Congress Cataloging-in-Publication Data

Scott, Craig R. (Craig Richard), author.
    Anonymous agencies, backstreet businesses, and covert collectives : rethinking organizations in the 21st century / Craig R. Scott.
        pages cm
    Includes bibliographical references and index.
    ISBN 978-0-8047-8138-1 (cloth : alk. paper)
    1. Communication in organizations. 2. Comparative organization. 3. Secrecy—Social aspects. I. Title.
HD30.3.S377   2013
306.3′4—dc23

                                                    2012033111

ISBN 978-0-8047-8563-1 (electronic)

Contents

Acknowledgments

I have benefited from many sources of inspiration and support throughout this project. Much of this has come from my academic colleagues. I wish to thank my mentor, Steve Corman, who encouraged me to explore anonymity and identification issues in organizations and whose work with extremist groups has inspired me to think more broadly about organizations. I thank Cynthia Stohl, whose comments about clandestine organizations at a conference we both attended several years ago—and in other helpful conversations since then—have helped to focus some of my own interests in issues of organizational anonymity and member identification. Several other colleagues have provided valuable reviews of the book that have helped to keep me on track (George Cheney, Hans Hansen, Vernon Miller, and Tracy Russo) or joined me on conference panels specifically examining hidden organizations (Jack Bratich, Kevin Corley, Paul Godfrey, Bryant Hudson, Dennis Schoeneborn, Michael Stohl, and Angela Trethewey)—all of which helped to clarify my thinking and motivated me to continue with work in this area. In a broader sense, I am grateful to several former colleagues at the University of Texas at Austin who encouraged me to write a book related to anonymity and also to my current colleagues at Rutgers University who have been equally supportive of my efforts (listening to me ramble on about my ideas and picking up the slack when I took a long-awaited sabbatical to write this book). I wish to specifically thank my colleague Brent Ruben for his unwavering support and for pointing out connections in this work that even I did not see initially.

I am grateful to all the good people at Stanford University Press who have guided me through this project—most notably Margo Beth Fleming, who not only recognized the importance of this topic but also provided the perfect mix of praise and feedback in helping me craft this work. Closer to home, I'd still be writing were it not for the tremendous logistical support of my research assistant and doctoral student Muge Haseki. Later on, Ph.D. students Chris Goldthwaite, Katie Kang, and Surabhi Sahay provided valuable help with final revisions and figures. Closer still, I want to acknowledge my family. My incredible kids Parker and Mikyla were patient (even when I was not) and regularly asked how my book was coming. My wife and colleague Laurie provided me with not only useful advice for writing a book but also good ideas for this project. More than that, her undying faith in me and my work provided inspiration even when I doubted myself.

Preface: Necessary Disclosures

On certain days, I take a back route to the Rutgers University campus where I work. Part of that journey takes me past a business park that I never used to notice, but which one day began to strike me as a bit odd. The lot houses two somewhat similar multistory office buildings with dark windows but no identifying information on the structures at all. In fact, the only real signage to be found is along the road where two address markers read 45 Knightsbridge Road and 53 Knightsbridge Road. The occasional appearance of a delivery truck and the rare sighting of people entering/leaving suggest to me that the complex is not abandoned. The presence of a few dozen cars in the back of the buildings, several with state government tags, seems to confirm the existence of one or more organizations. An online search of the addresses reveals at least a management company and a law office in one building; moreover, the other seems to include a state youth and family services office, a church, a children's learning and skills development center, a business intelligence software company, an IT company, a religious foundation, and the office of a registered nurse—though few of these have their own websites (and most of those that do seem to downplay the location). As a result, this place and the organizations inside are essentially invisible. Most people would never drive by these addresses, and even if you did there are few clues as to what organizations may reside there.

For me, this obscure office park began to symbolize an entire range of organizations that are hidden by their own design and circumstances—tucked away in unmarked buildings, well off less-traveled roads, and with minimal online presence. We often hear that we live in an age of transparency and we are regularly bombarded by various corporate branding efforts; but amid all that exists an alternate reality that the hype about openness and image management may, in fact, mask. Organizations like those in my emblematic office park represent only the tip of the iceberg as we start to consider the many hidden collectives in our society. This book is about these hidden, anonymous, backstreet, and/or covert organizations and how we should think about them relative to the more familiar and visible collectives on which we often set our sights.

My basic argument in this book is reasonably straightforward. Many organizations and their members devote extensive resources to promoting themselves and being known to others—and as a result it is easy to simply assume that all organizations wish to be highly visible and easily identified. But that assumption is fundamentally flawed because not all organizations want or need their identity to be recognized and not all organizational members want to have their membership or affiliation known by at least certain others. When we inadvertently privilege organizations that wish to be seen, we are taking an overly narrow view of the collectives in society. As we proceed to consider secret societies, anonymous support programs, hate groups, terrorist cells, covert military units, organized crime, gangs, parts of the underground economy, front organizations, stigmatized businesses, and even those hidden enterprises tucked away in quiet office parks, we have to question what we think we know about the identity goals of organizations and their members. The concealing and revealing of identity by these organizations and their members to relevant audiences can vary substantially—demanding that our thinking and theorizing about organizations expand to encompass these anonymous, hidden organizations.

This book is not intended as an exposé or investigative reporting, even though much of the material may be unfamiliar and even provocative to many readers; instead, its primary goal is to offer a framework for thinking about how a wide range of organizations and their members communicate their identity to relevant audiences. Considering the degree to which organizations strategically make themselves visible, the extent to which members express their identification with the organization, and whether the relevant audience is more mass/public or local, we can describe various "regions" in which these collectives reside—ranging from transparent and only somewhat shaded to more shadowed and dark. Importantly, organizations operating in these spaces differ in how they and their members communicate identity to others. So much of our current thinking and research has been around relatively transparent organizations and those operating only somewhat in the shadows, but the perspective offered here helps draw attention to more shadowed and dark collectives as important organizations that must also manage identity communication issues (sometimes with very different goals). The framework developed here is not meant to replace other typologies, models, and categorization systems for classifying organizations—but it can help us fundamentally rethink the contemporary landscape by focusing on the communication of identity along a much broader spectrum.

This particular reframing is timely. We find ourselves in an era in which the desire for organizational disclosure looms large around the globe. The work of collectives like WikiLeaks and the impact of the Occupy movement suggest deep concerns about overly secretive institutions. At the same time, we have seen an increase in the use of hidden political donors, a rise in the prevalence of anonymous organizational sources, and growing terrorist and underground movements in many parts of the world. These forces and the efforts to counteract them seem to regularly involve clandestine actions and at least partially hidden organizations. Add to this the rapid development of communication and information technologies that may on the one hand help organizations and their members to hide their existence while on the other hand provide traces that identify them to relevant audiences.

All this matters because there are real consequences associated with the successful and unsuccessful efforts of these organizations and their members to conceal and reveal their identity to key audiences. Organizations and/or members who remain hidden may continue to commit terrorist and criminal acts without punishment. Yet, anonymous support groups and stigmatized businesses protect their legitimacy and their members' safety by remaining hidden. Substantial embarrassment and even casualties can occur when covert intelligence operations are revealed; but people may be spared substantial harm and misinformation when the operations of front organizations are exposed. Beyond that, the financial and mental resources required to conceal or reveal identity can be enormous for certain organizations and their members. For these reasons and more, we as citizens/consumers, policymakers, and scholars need models and frameworks that can provide us with ways to better understand hidden organizations relative to those about which we know more. The goal here is not only to shed some light on these consequential collectives but also to better understand and appreciate the various degrees of darkness in which they may operate.

Although the need for this framework may be current, my own interest in these issues began years ago. My love of James Bond was partly due to a fascination with MI6 and covert British intelligence operations—as well as the secret organization (SPECTRE) that he sometimes battled. One of the many lures of the television show *Charlie's Angels* was the mostly unidentified Charlie, who owned the Townsend Detective Agency but never appeared to the detectives or the viewing audience. The secretive organizations on *Star Trek* (e.g., Obsidian Order, Section 31) and *The X-Files* (the Syndicate) were, for me, some of the most fascinating aspects of those cult classics' mythologies. In another sense, I was playing with issues of anonymity and identity even before online tools made it relatively easy to do so. For example, I published a column in our college newspaper under the pseudonym "Papa C," and my secret camp counselor identity at Camp Cahito in San Diego was "Bronco."

As formative as some of those early experiences were, they are not what best position me to talk about anonymous organizations. Admittedly, this book is not an ethnographic account, drawn from my own vast experiences spent underground or in various clandestine operations. In fact, my direct experience as a member of a hidden organization is limited. I am not a former street gang member, have never worked for military intelligence, and went to a small college without secret societies—at least to my knowledge. However, I have firsthand experience with different aspects of the informal economy, have worked part-time for what I would describe as essentially a front organization, and have belonged to a couple of organizations that I would probably never admit to others. I have also encountered several companies that I describe in the book as mildly or moderately shaded organizations, and I worked behind the scenes for a public relations firm that was regularly hidden from at least certain others as we worked to promote the image of our client organizations. While you may also consider yourself to be someone who is generally open with few secret affiliations, I am willing to bet that most readers can claim at least one comparable experience—along with a similar fascination about those organizations operating in at least some degree of darkness.

More notably, as part of my intellectual interest in organizations and communication, I have been examining anonymity and related topics in that context for over twenty years. In that time, I have published dozens of theoretical and empirical articles and book chapters about organizational identification, anonymity, and organizational communication generally. This book has afforded me a unique opportunity to pull together those scholarly strands. As an added bonus, this project has also provided a wonderful excuse for me to make repeated trips to places like the International Spy Museum, to visit some of these hidden organizations in person, and to rewatch all my favorite Bond classics.

With those admissions on the table, it is time to more formally begin our explorations. I begin the book by more fully setting the stage for our journey by highlighting the significance of this issue and the need for a new classification of organizations (chapter 1). In order to provide the necessary background, the next two chapters cull research literature across multiple disciplines to paint a picture of what we know already about various types of hidden organizations (chapter 2) and to highlight key topics pertaining to organizational identity, reputation, image, branding, identification, anonymity, secrecy, and stakeholders (chapter 3). Building on this foundation, chapter 4 presents my own theoretical framework, which is truly the heart of this book. That model allows us to describe the transparent, shaded, shadowed, and dark regions in which organizations operate on the basis of three key dimensions: organizational visibility, member identification, and relevant audience. Chapters 5 through 7 delve into that framework to talk about specific characteristics and organizations operating in both transparent and dark regions—as well as every shaded and shadowed space in between. It is in these chapters that we really begin to get a feel for many of the similarities and differences across hidden archetypes as we consider detailed examples of each. Finally, chapter 8 draws conclusions, discusses implications, and suggests directions for the continued exploration of this topic. By this point, I hope that the reader will see the need to rethink organizations to better emphasize the problematic nature of communicating one's identity—especially for the anonymous agencies, backstreet businesses, covert collectives, and other hidden organizations found (and not so easily found) in our world today.

ANONYMOUS AGENCIES,
BACKSTREET BUSINESSES,
AND COVERT COLLECTIVES

1   To Name or Not to Name, *That* Is the Question

Even after working in what are essentially the suburbs of New York City for over six years, I still marvel at Times Square with every visit to uptown Manhattan. My amazement is driven not only by the people and the buildings but also by the mass of multistory neon advertisements promoting a vast range of organizations and products. A recent effort to document every ad appearing in one day in the few blocks that make up Times Square (see http://www.flickr.com/photos/ironicsans/sets/72157594496838152/) inspired me to do something similar. Standing in the middle of Times Square one summer afternoon, I observed in less than thirty minutes what I consider to be the following organizational names seen only on the stores and buildings along Broadway and Seventh: Disney, LG, Forever 21, Swarovski, Planet Hollywood, Swatch, Pepsi, Spike TV, NASDAQ, Clear Channel Advertising, Fox News, TGI Fridays, TD Bank, Ambassador Theater, Walgreens, Wilson Theatre, Sbarro, Tad's Steakhouse, Neil Simon Theatre, (Doubletree) Guest Suites, Eugene O'Neill Theatre, Lamar Advertising, Broadway Theater, Barclays, 47th Digital, The Change Group, ABC, Budweiser, Dunkin' Donuts, TDK, Toshiba, Sony, Hard Rock Cafe, WGN America, Levi's, Aéropostale, Thomson Reuters, Marriott, Kodak, Hankook (tires), McDonald's, Facebook, Twitter, Bank of America, UFC, American Eagle Outfitters, T-Mobile, Roxy Deli, Grand Slam New York, W Hotels, Prudential, CNN, Blue Fin, New York Police Department, Morgan Stanley, Allianz, Aerie, Corona (beer), Coca-Cola, Crowne Plaza Hotel, Hyundai, Xinhua News Agency, H&M, Times

Square Visitor Center, Lunt-Fontanne Theatre, Olive Garden, Hershey's, Duane Reade, TKTS, Times Square Alliance, Merrill Lynch, Sunglass Hut, Sabrett, and Viacom. If you include the organizations mentioned on taxis, buses, trucks, shirts, bags, camera straps, handouts, garbage cans, and other handheld signs, we could add Century 21, LAN Airlines, Super Shuttle, Under Armour, American Girl, Aerosoles, Hollister, Nike, Sony, M&M, Crate & Barrel, Lamborghini, United States of America, Toys "R" Us, JC Penney, Nikon, RBK, Quicksilver, Birkenstock, Grayline, Moishe's Self Storage, Broadhurst Theater, City Sights Tours, Boston Bruins, Boston Red Sox, New England Patriots, Cincinnati Reds, Chicago Blackhawks, Rutgers University, and seemingly every New York sports team—as well as several different comedy clubs and taxi companies. Many of these names are known globally while others are well known only locally.

Even if Times Square and its $70 million annual advertising business (Times Square 2005) is in many ways unique, it is also something of a microcosm of the extreme lengths some organizations take to promote themselves. Many of the companies we know and often love spend incredible amounts of time and money in efforts to ensure they are highly visible. Chief communications officers and other professionals in corporate communication, public relations, and public affairs are tasked with activities such as managing the image, branding the organization, maintaining a positive reputation, and ensuring proper visual identification. The multibillion-dollar public relations industry provides some evidence for the magnitude of this effort. Organizational communication and identity experts note the corporate communication function has expanded dramatically in recent decades as a variety of organizations attempt to closely manage communication—and as organizations brand themselves to various audiences (Christensen, Morsing, and Cheney 2008). As a society, we regularly celebrate visible organizations— seeking employment with them, purchasing their products and services, and praising them as good corporate citizens.

But this focus on what is visible and known can sometimes lead us to overlook what is less visible and less known. We become so enamored with the high-profile companies and the glitzy ad campaigns that we forget about those organizations that may be more discreet and/or not blitzing us with various commercial messages. Even when all that is interrupted by messages about important issues in our society—terrorist attacks, financial backing of political candidates, human trafficking, anonymous donations to a troubled school system, and so on—we too often fail to think of these issues as fundamentally organizational ones as well. Returning to my opening example, it is easy enough to see the millions of dollars worth of corporate names in Times Square—but what do we *not* see? What do we have to look harder to notice? In Times Square itself we see knockoff products pretending to be from a certain manufacturing organization and vendors whose organization is not clear. We also see the big screen and camera that shows people in the square, which can be a reminder that there are numerous other surveillance cameras (with security organizations watching). It even occurred to me that one might think I was a criminal or terrorist making detailed notes of organizations in the area—which suggests that other terrorist or criminal organizations could also have a hidden presence here as well. In fact, one could see from my vantage point the approximate spot of the failed car bomb attempt in Times Square in 2010.

Much of what we cannot readily see is somehow behind (or above or below) the scene also. In this area, also known as the "theater district," this is what we might think of as somewhat backstage. On the immediate side streets one quickly sees doors with only a street number and an incomplete/outdated directory of obscure-sounding businesses; large garage doors that only open on appointment to reveal some company and its goods; and spray-painted information that sometimes reflects a temporary address for some organization and at other times is likely to signify graffiti from a gang. As you look above the street level and behind the advertising signs, there are what appear to be offices for otherwise unmarked businesses—and even higher up in the skyscrapers are the numerous organizations whose existence to most is found only in a small directory on a first-floor lobby. The subways that run underneath are perhaps symbolic of what are surely multiple underground clubs and other organizations kept largely out of public sight. Beyond all that, would we even begin to recognize elements of a criminal organization, shadow economy, counterintelligence agency, or secret religious movement operating amid everything else? Unfortunately we as citizens, consumers, and students of organizations have failed to adequately consider these various forms of hidden organizations—creating both missed opportunities and potential dangers. Our focus on the familiar organizational foreground of predominantly large for-profit businesses, easily recognized governmental agencies, and a few high-profile nonprofits and NGOs contributes to a lack of vision on what may be an even larger arena of other less visible collectives.

It is not especially difficult to imagine how this happens. After all, you do not need to be in Times Square to know we live in a world where too often the name of the game is the name game: being known and identifiable to all the appropriate audiences. We teach our MBAs about branding and identity creation, our professional associations conduct training workshops to improve our skills in reputation and image management, and we draw primarily on these recognizable organizations in our teaching and consulting. Furthermore, there is a general bias in much of the world for openness and transparency—while anything hidden or kept secret arouses suspicion and feels less than democratic. Thus, it should be of little surprise how powerful these forces related to organizational identity have become. Consider a few examples illustrating this organizational need for visibility and recognition.

Reputation

McKinsey & Company's recent international survey of executives argues that reputation now matters more that it has for decades (Bonini, Court, and Marchi 2009). Considering that claim, we should not be surprised to find reputational studies ranking everything from the top colleges/universities to the best steakhouses on the planet, or from the world's top 10 golf courses to America's top 100 Teddy Roosevelt Terrier breeders. One of the best-known reputation lists is *Fortune*'s "World's Most Admired Companies" (World's Most Admired Companies 2012). The 2012 top 20 list is not surprising and reflects the success of the identity efforts of these organizations (ranked in order): Apple, Google, Amazon.com, Coca-Cola, IBM, FedEx, Berkshire Hathaway, Starbucks, Procter & Gamble, Southwest Airlines, McDonald's, Johnson & Johnson, Walt Disney, BMW, General Electric, American Express, Microsoft, 3M, Caterpillar, and Costco Wholesale.

The Reputation Institute, a global private consulting firm, recently conducted a survey of consumers in fifteen different global markets to assess the global reputation of the world's most recognized companies. Organizations were rated on their products and services, innovation, workplace, governance, citizenship, financial performance, and leadership, and the list was then published in *Forbes* (Smith 2012b). BMW (Germany), Sony (Japan), Walt Disney (United States), Daimler (Germany), Apple (United States), Google (United States), Microsoft (United States), Volkswagen (Germany), Canon (Japan), LEGO (Denmark), Adidas Group (Germany), Nestlé (Switzerland),

Colgate-Palmolive (United States), Panasonic (Japan), Nike (United States), Intel (United States), Michelin (France), Johnson & Johnson (United States), IBM (United States), and Ferrero (Italy) comprise this more international listing. Similar lists even exist for nonprofit organizations. The American Institute of Philanthropy grades nonprofits as part of its charity watch (Top Rated Charities 2011), though the names here are often somewhat less recognizable.

Individual countries may publish their own organizational reputation studies. New Zealand, for example, rates a wide variety of organizations (Birchfield 2010)—noting not only Air New Zealand (most reputable business) but also Kiwibank (most reputable state-owned enterprise), New Zealand Police (most reputable government department), and the Salvation Army (most reputable nonprofit). Of course, having a reputation does not necessarily mean it is a good one, which can affect the degree to which one wishes to push their name at certain times (and the need to improve reactions associated with a given identity). The reputation institute and *Forbes* (Smith 2012a) published a similar study identifying the least reputable U.S. organizations in 2012: Freddie Mac, Fannie Mae, Goldman Sachs, Halliburton, Bank of America, Citigroup, AIG, News Corporation, ExxonMobil, and Altria.

The names on these lists are relatively well known to many of us. But what about all those organizations that do not have a very strong or very weak reputation or that perhaps have little reputation at all? Consider the vast majority of businesses without an expensive public relations or corporate communication arm to constantly engage in image/identity management. How important is reputation for those organizations that do not produce a product or service relevant to most of the public? Consider all the nonbusiness and even nongovernmental organizations (NGOs) for whom having a reputation of any sort might even be problematic. For obvious reasons, one is quite unlikely to find a list of those organizations published in *Fortune* or *Forbes*; but perhaps such a list would be useful. Of even greater concern is the obsession with reputation without the recognition that reputation is not a driving force for all organizations.

Organizational Naming

An organization's name is not only the first impression we have of it but also a central part of the collective's identity. Perhaps that is one of the reasons why organizations regularly change their names—a phenomenon often referred to as "corporate rebranding." According to one of the many corporate-naming firms, a company changes its name approximately every hour of each business day in the United States alone (Strategic Name Development 2007). That is close to 2,000 name changes every year because of some challenge or opportunity in the environment—ranging from mergers and changes in an organization's focus to spectacular successes or scandals for the company in question. According to companies like Strategic Name Development, the changes range from mild (Amerada Hess Corp. to Hess Corp.) to wild (Citisource, Inc. to China Shuangji Cement Corp.) but often focus on trends such as going green (Radiant Technology Group to GreenBridge Technology, Inc.), going global (Yellow Roadway Corp. to YRC Worldwide), and finding short/catchy names (America Online, Washington Mutual, and Outdoor Life Network to AOL, WaMu, and Versus, respectively).

Although the frequency of and reasons for name changes are noteworthy, the costs of such alterations reveal the incredible importance we place on naming. It is difficult to find an exact estimate, but industry experts typically put the cost of planning and conducting organizational rebranding between $75,000 to $455,000 per change depending on the extensiveness of the effort—and that does not even include costs for announcing/launching the change, new signage/stationery/cards, and other needed realignment (see Dawson 2011; Shalit 1999; Spaeth n.d.). At that rate, the $70,000 spent by US Air to become US Airways was quite a bargain, especially compared to the more than $1 million Hewlett-Packard eventually paid to come up with Agilent for its spinoff company (Shalit).

This naming business may be sizable, but what about the millions of organizations whose names do not communicate identity information? Some names simply reference a largely overlooked owner/founder (e.g., *Akai*, a consumer electronics brand founded by Saburo Akai in Japan), a product/service that may no longer be primary (e.g., England's *WPP* stands for Wire and Plastic Products, but it is now one of the world's largest global media companies), the geographic location of the original company or other key facilities (e.g., *Lexmark*, which references a production facility in Lexington, Kentucky), or perhaps little at all that may be recognizable to most (e.g., U.S. retailer *Pamida*, whose name is formed by the first two letters of the cofounder's three boys). More important, what about organizations that change their name to escape negative public attention (e.g., Anderson Consulting rebrands itself as Accenture;

ValuJet merges with and takes the name of AirTran; the large private security contractor Blackwater Worldwide becomes Xe Services) rather than attract it? Consider also the hidden organizations who do business as (d/b/a, also known as "operating as" or "trading as" in certain countries and sometimes referred to as "assumed business names" or "fictitious business names" in the United States) some other company or who create front organizations and shell corporations so that their name is not easily known. None of this necessarily includes criminal organizations or underground collectives that are largely nameless to most. Names are an important part of most organizations' identity; but being strongly identified by a powerful moniker—regardless of its cost—is not a goal of all organizations.

Visual Identity

Efforts to brand organizations extend well beyond names to include a variety of visual elements related to logos, trademark symbols, various graphic standards, colors, fonts, and emblems—which may appear on buildings, letterhead, emails, uniforms, trucks, business cards, promotional items, websites, custom signs, and so on. The relevance of corporate visual identity (CVI) efforts extends to various types of organizations. "The importance of CVI is quite obvious for organizations that operate in a competitive environment. But it may be equally important for governmental organizations that . . . still need to be recognized as of use to society" (van den Bosch, de Jong, and Elving 2006, 140). Indeed, a variety of for-profit and nonprofit organizations have highly recognizable logos (without the name): for example, United Way's supporting hand, the Michelin Man, Apple's apple, Nike's swoosh, Playboy's bunny ears, the Red Cross's cross, Shell Oil's shell, and the Olympics' rings.

Other evidence suggests the importance and scope of these efforts. The U.S. Patent and Trademark office reports 1,655,542 total active trademark registrations on the federal register as of the second quarter of 2011—a number that is steadily growing even though one is not required to register such marks with the federal government. The U.S. sign industry reports that manufacturing of signs has steadily increased even while other forms of manufacturing have steadily declined. The sign industry had shipments of $50 billion in 2006 alone according to industry statistics (International Sign Association 2008). Of course, the most visible place of all for such visual information is online. It is difficult to find a Fortune 1000 company without a website today, and

70 percent of the largest small businesses have one as well (Campbell 2009). Additionally, among Fortune 500 companies in 2012, you will find 73 percent using Twitter and 66 percent with their own Facebook page (Barnes, Lescault, and Andonian 2012).

It becomes easy to think of all major organizations as having these recognizable logos and the corresponding signage and online tools on which to display them—and the failure to have them is typically seen as exactly that, a failure. But what about all the organizations that lack a logo or graphic emblem to help identify them? What about the smaller businesses and other organizations that do not have, or need, a public website or a presence through social media—or are not readily located in any sort of phone or address directory? Even more extreme, some organizations have no signs noting their existence—relying on a simple address or location description if there is a physical existence to the collective at all. Despite the sizable attention given to visual identity, there is substantial variation in how identified various organizations may wish to be.

Not Playing the Name Game

Many organizations dedicate extensive resources toward providing a highly recognizable name and reputation-enhancing visual identities, which helps reinforce the assumption that organizations wish to be prominently identified to various audiences. That assumption may seem reasonable to most consumers and citizens, because this is what is done by the large global financial corporation as well as the nonprofit community healthcare clinic and even the state government task force, along with various other generally recognizable collectives that readily come to mind when we talk about organizations. Much of our theory and research about organizations tacitly accepts this assumption in that most of our definitions, frameworks, and methods have privileged these easily recognized and highly visible forms of organization.

We need to seriously question that assumption.

Indeed, the complex society of the twenty-first century is characterized by increasingly diverse organizations. This is more than just the first-order expansion we see as we move from a focus on large corporate businesses, governmental agencies, and universities/colleges to also consider nonprofits, small community businesses, and nongovernmental organizations. The second-order expansion presented here begins with greater recognition of the hidden organizations in our communities and our world. Interest in such organizations is too often linked to the fringe and marginal or thought to be little more than conspiracy theories. While such a critique is not entirely incorrect, we will see that hidden organizations are far more common, more important, and more consequential than we have typically allowed ourselves to admit. As a result, they also need to be better integrated into thinking about organizations by scholars, policymakers, and everyday citizens. Organizational identity expert and communication scholar George Cheney (2000) notes there have been periodic calls to move beyond mainstream organizations, but the answers have rarely included the hidden organizations of interest here. As Cheney notes, "We do not know those who are out of view. . . . Thus, we must make extra efforts to break our own seclusion and isolation" (138). Reinforcing this, others have observed, "We live in a complex world, characterized by interaction with a lot of different people, organizations (*of whom most are barely known*), and production processes" (Alvesson 2004, 168, emphasis added).

Hidden Organizations

Perhaps ironically, the word *corporation* has been defined in the U.S. courts as an "invisible" being and the terminology used for certain corporations in Europe translates to "anonymous society" or "anonymous venture." Yet, even though there is a link between such organizations and ideas of limited visibility, corporations and companies are not usually what we would consider as invisible or anonymous today. So what are these anonymous agencies, backstreet businesses, and covert collectives alluded to in the book's title? Most exotic among these more hidden organizations are various shadow governments, clandestine groups, terrorist cells, crime cartels, undercover units, and other dark networks. We can likely supplement that list with a variety of brotherhoods, sects, cults, enclaves, certain fraternal orders, and various secret societies. Perhaps less fascinating, but similarly hidden from view, are various clubs, establishments, parlors, and other groups—some of whom front for criminal organizations or parts of the shadow economy and all of whom benefit from reduced exposure to certain audiences. We can also add a variety of backstreet, behind-the-scenes, underground, unmarked, and/or unpublished businesses that remain nearly invisible not only to the public but also to most organizational scholars. We will explore a more formal framework for classifying these organizations in subsequent chapters and will review research about many of these collectives in the next chapter, but for now it is informative to briefly describe some of the many different overlapping forms hidden organizations may take.

Secret societies and fraternal orders

Secret societies are organizations whose activities—and sometimes whose members or very existence—are largely or completely concealed from outside members (and whose actual existence is itself sometimes disputed). Though difficult to distinctly define, we know them best (though not necessarily most accurately) via pop culture portrayals. Actual secret societies have appeared in a number of fictional novels, comics, popular video games, and especially mainstream films: Freemasonry in *National Treasure*, the Illuminati in *Angels and Demons*, the KKK in movies such as *Mississippi Burning* and *A Time to Kill*, the Order of the Dragon in *Bram Stoker's Dracula*, the Knights Templar in *Indiana Jones and the Last Crusade*, and Skull and Bones in *The Good Shepherd*. A number of fictional secret societies have also emerged (e.g., the Brethren Court in *Pirates of the Caribbean: At World's End*, the Dead Poets Society in the movie by the same name, and the Syndicate in *The X-Files*). Many of these groups are religious in nature or trace beginnings to religious issues (e.g., Rosicrucians, Opus Dei); others are student societies (e.g., Pitt Club at Cambridge, Speculative Society at University of Edinburgh); and some are more about politics (e.g., Bilderberg Group, The Fellowship).

Many of these societies are also known as fraternal orders, which may range widely in terms of how secret the organizations are. One online listing of all fraternal organizations (Hartzog 2010) suggests over 1,000 such groups ranging from the Ancient Order of the Nobles of the Mystic Shrine to Zonta International. Although some of these groups could be described as hate or racial supremacy groups, far more are better classified as benefit societies. The various Krewes commonly associated with Mardi Gras represent another form of secret society where member identity is hidden and that has historically included the wearing of masks at public parades. At least one website devoted to these groups claims over 120 such organizations in New Orleans alone (http://www.krewecentral.com/home) and another 60-plus in Mobile, Alabama—where I first encountered colleagues widely rumored to be in a Krewe. Finally, new religious movements (sometimes referred to as cults) might fit here as well for some. The growth of these organizations in the 1960s and 1970s in the United States has made some of these names familiar: Moonies, Hare Krishna, Scientology, and so on (see Eyre 1994). Other such movements are largely unknown until some media event brings them to our attention (various doomsday cults, Branch Davidians, Heaven's Gate, etc.).

Organized crime

Another set of hidden organizations are those involved with various criminal activities. Criminologist Paul Lunde (2004) notes that gangs of pirates and bandits, the Thugs of India, African drug-trafficking rings, and various criminal groups in Japan and Italy date back centuries. Then, like now, such organizations emerge when government and society are disorganized, weak, or not viewed as legitimate. One of the best-known criminal organizations today—thanks to popular media depictions through *The Sopranos* and *The Godfather* series—is the Mafia; but other well-known collectives include the Irish Mob, Chinese Triads, Russian Mafia, Aryan Brotherhood, and Japanese Yakuza. The Yakuza's main families combine to form the largest criminal organization in the world—and one that is potentially unique. The organization itself is not as secretive as other crime organizations, though sometimes members will dress in such a way as to hide identifying tattoos. Most criminal organizations have to keep a relatively low profile to avoid law enforcement.

Another element of organized crime includes street gangs or youth gangs such as the Nortenos, Crips, Bloods, Vice Lords, and Gangster Disciples. Estimates put the number of distinct gangs in the United States in 2008 at approximately 27,900, which is a 28 percent increase from 2002 (Egley, Howell, and Moore 2010). Other reports claim over 1,000 gangs in the United Kingdom (Wheeler and Brooks 2010), nearly 200 in Northern Ireland (Warning Over Number 2011), and 225 gang organizations within U.S. Navajo country (Gang Violence 2009). Gangs are interesting in part because members may wear certain colors, display tattoos, or dress certain ways to indicate membership; conversely, they may also use code words, secret greetings, and hand signals known only to organizational members. Similarly, some gangs and members may actively use various Internet tools for recruitment, for glorifying the gang, and for members to openly express their activities; yet they also operate largely out of the spotlight. As one Florida law enforcement officer noted, "while gangs thrive on being feared in their communities, they don't go out of their way to draw attention outside of their circle for fear of being identified by law enforcement" (Kitzmiller 2011, 2).

Terrorist organizations

Although terrorist organizations are regularly engaged in criminal actions and criminal organizations sometimes use terror to impose their will, we tend to treat and confront terrorist organizations and groups as something different from organized crime. Though terrorist organizations are not new, they today tend to be collectives united by causes related to social revolution, nationalist/separatist movements, religious extremism, right-wing or left-wing terrorism, and even groups centered around a single issue (e.g., ecoterrorism). The U.S. State Department classifies foreign terrorist organizations based on three key criteria: (1) it must be a foreign organization, (2) the organization must engage in terrorist activity or terrorism or retain the capability and intent to engage in terrorist activity or terrorism (as defined by U.S. law), and (3) the organization's terrorist activity or terrorism must threaten the security of U.S. nationals or the national security (national defense, foreign relations, or the economic interests) of the United States. Based on that there are forty-eight such organizations listed at the time of this writing, including al-Qaeda, Al-Shabaab, Army of Islam, Basque Fatherland and Liberty, Communist Party of the Philippines/New People's Army, Continuity Irish Republican Army, HAMAS, Hizballah, Islamic Jihad Union, Liberation Tigers of Tamil Eelam, Libyan Islamic Fighting Group, National Liberation Army, Palestine Liberation Front, Revolutionary Armed Forces of Colombia, and Shining Path (see Foreign Terrorist Organizations 2012).

The Global Terrorism Database operated by U.S. Homeland Security and the University of Maryland lists over 2,100 known terrorist organizations that have made attacks since 1970 (Global Terrorism Database 2011). Of the over 65,000 attacks they have documented in the past forty years, the terrorist organization responsible is unknown in over one-third of those cases—and even when the perpetrating group is thought to be known, only some of those cases are confirmed. These organizations operate both locally and internationally and vary in size/structure. Many are divided into smaller cells that carry out tactics—and who may not even be aware of other cells or other members. Though terrorist organizations may engage in their activity for publicity, other efforts are made by these groups and their members to hide their identity to law enforcement and much of the general public.

Counterterrorism/intelligence organizations

From James Bond's British Secret (Intelligence) Service to Jack Bauer's Counter Terrorist Unit (CTU) on the TV series *24*, most of us have some familiarity with this form of hidden organization. Not surprisingly, the rise of organized crime and especially of terrorist groups has resulted in various organizations to counter those efforts—and many of these agencies and other units sometimes operate in secretive, clandestine, and/or covert ways. *Covert* operations are those conducted to hide the identity of the sponsoring organization, whereas *clandestine* primarily refers to concealment of the operations themselves (Best and Feickert 2006). Traditionally, many of the clandestine and covert operations in the United States have been run through the Central Intelligence Agency (CIA). The CIA was established in 1947 and its mission was quickly seen as including a range of covert actions overseen by the Directorate of Operations. Journalists David Wise and Thomas Ross (1964) detailed the sizable growth of what they called "the invisible government" during much of the Cold War era—claiming CIA employment rolls were classified, its activities were top secret, and agency budget appropriations were concealed from the public. A few years after the events of 9/11 both clandestine and covert operations were overseen specifically by the National Clandestine Services, which is one of four main parts of the CIA (Clandestine Services: FAQs 2010). The Joint Special Operations Command (JSOC), run through the Department of Defense, is not necessarily covert—but much of their work is shielded by a veil of secrecy as well (here you will find groups like Delta Force and SEAL Team 6). Across the globe, numerous other intelligence agencies and defense programs are doing similar work (see List of Intelligence Agencies 2011).

However, today this counterintelligence work is also performed by private companies who often operate with some degree of concealment. Journalist Jeremy Scahill's (2009) investigation for *The Nation* points to the work of Blackwater (now Xe Services) and its affiliate organizations as vital to efforts in countries like Pakistan despite deniability by several parties that the organization is even working there. As an interesting side note, the organization does most of its work under an affiliate's name because of problems with Blackwater and Xe's names (Scahill). Misconduct by private contractor organizations MZM and ArmorGroup North America have exposed otherwise hidden organizations. More significant is a *Washington Post* investigation on the emergence of top secret organizations here in the United States in response to other covert collectives. The findings are somewhat startling: 1,271 government organizations and nearly 2,000 private companies work on top secret programs related to counterterrorism, homeland security, and intelligence in 10,000 locations across the United States; in the Washington, D.C. area thirty-three building complexes for top secret programs have been or are being built since September 11, 2001; Homeland Security depends on 318 outside organizations for various services; and NSA works with nearly 500 civilian firms (Priest and Arkin 2011). Although the biggest names (e.g., General Dynamics) are largely recognizable, many of these organizations are largely hidden given the nature of their top secret work.

Informal economy/sector
Whether you call it "shadow," "parallel," "twilight," "underground," "black," "hidden," "unregulated," "nonobserved," "unrecorded," "subterranean," "irregular," "second," or any of the other numerous terms that can be found (see de Grazia 1980; Hart 2007; Mulinge and Munyae 1998; Quintano and Mazzocchi 2010), this *other* economy represents the organizations and activities that are not monitored, not taxed, and not part of any official estimates of GNP or employment (i.e., not the *formal* economy). Economists have paid substantial attention to this area even though measuring a system that operates off the books or under the table is challenging. Recent estimates (Schneider, Buehn, and Montenegro 2010) confirm that the informal economy is especially large in regions the World Bank defines as developing (over 40% of total economy in sub-Saharan Africa and Latin America/Caribbean, for example) and smaller but still clearly present (17 to 23% of total economy) among what it defines as "high-income regions." Although criminal to the extent that this economy may include efforts at tax evasion and may engage in exchanges of illegal substances or services, the work and organizations in the informal economy are qualitatively different from criminal organizations— and a number of definitions exclude criminal activities.

Many of the businesses involved are quite small in order to avoid detection, but that also makes these microbusinesses or microfirms less able to obtain needed credit and attain economies of scale (Ferreira-Tiryaki 2008). While it is common in less-developed countries for firms to operate entirely underground, in more industrialized regions a single enterprise may engage in both formal and informal efforts (e.g., an established garment manufacturing organization that also secretly employs workers in makeshift shops to produce additional goods—without the tax burden or the higher costs of formal employees; see Gerxhani 2004). Thus, the hidden organizations in the informal economy could be cottage enterprises, street traders, small manufacturers, service providers, and distributors (Becker 2004) as well as those facilitating certain forms of prostitution and gambling, barter of goods and services, and unreported work related to legal activities (Schneider 2002).

Backstreet businesses
Clearly not all businesses even in the formal economy are entirely visible to others. In some cases there is a strong benefit to disguising certain stigmatized or marginalized operations. A reasonable example is found in the sex industry—which includes organizations engaged in the creation and distribution of pornography, sex shops, businesses that provide escorts and adult entertainment, strip clubs, bathhouses, sex clubs, spa/sauna/massage parlors offering erotic services, and brothels. This continues to be big business, though most of us would not be able to identify the actual organizations often employing the sex workers (despite the widespread availability of sex advertisements online and in various publications). Many men's bathhouses, sex clubs, and erotic massage services are discreetly marked and thus nearly invisible to the general public. As a different example, some organizations choose to be anonymous in part by doing business under a fictitious name—which is designed to attach a person/owner to a business entity that does not include that person's name but can also serve to help disguise certain companies operating another business under a different name. For example, you may know your bank as Colorado Mortgage Alliance of North Colorado, Keyes Mortgage, or Brady Home Loans—but you may not realize that each of those is a fictitious name for a different operating subsidiary of a common parent company: Wells Fargo (National Bank Operating Subsidiary List 2009). In general, though, it can be difficult to identify companies doing business under a different name in many U.S. states and in other countries.

   In other cases, backstreet businesses are functionally hidden because they are not on a more visible main street or on any of those lists of highly recognized organizations. This actually characterizes a substantial percentage of businesses that either lack the resources to heavily promote themselves or do not need to do so given their relations to various audiences. These organizations are typically part of the small businesses (less than 500 employees in the United States) or small-medium enterprises (less than 250 employees in the European Union) that represent over 99 percent of all employing firms (Frequently Asked 2010). Despite their sizable numbers, these organizations may remain hidden when they are located off the beaten path, poorly identified by signage, or part of the 44 percent of such companies that have no website (Leggatt 2009). In fact, other estimates have suggested that 55 percent of small businesses that have annual revenues under $500,000 lack their own website (Campbell 2009). A useful resource in thinking about the nature of organizations in our world is Manta, the world's largest online community for promoting and connecting small businesses—listing sixty-four million company profiles as of May 2011 (All U.S. Companies 2011). Based on their data, if we focus on the highly visible, larger organizations (over $1 billion in annual revenue and 10,000-plus employees), we have barely over 1,000 such businesses in the United States; yet, there are 12,624,723 public U.S. companies with fewer than ten employees, under $500,000 in revenue, and in a single location. That is over half the twenty-four million total U.S. businesses. Although they do not provide similar breakdowns for the more than sixty-four million organizations listed worldwide, a similar majority of smaller and lesser-known organizations seems likely. So, pretty much randomly selected organizations like Complete Tanning Supply in Aurora, Colorado (two employees, four years old, in Consumer Electronics and Appliances, and no website listed), Allen Research Corporation in Huntsville, Alabama (six employees, in the aerospace business for twenty-seven years, and a two-page website indicating they are a subcontractor for Boeing), Meditrack in Hudson, Massachusetts (fifteen employees, nine years in the medical instrument manufacturing business, and with a website under construction), and W R Cold Storage Business in Wisconsin Rapids, Wisconsin (a warehousing company in business for four years with no webpage and nine employees) not only are going to be unknown to most people but arguably do not need to be visible to more than a few very select audiences.

Anonymous support groups

Another form of hidden organization would be those that provide various forms of social support through either confidential means or via groups facilitating anonymity of members. The best known of these is Alcoholics Anonymous (AA), founded in 1935 in the United States and with over 115,000 groups worldwide as of 2010 (Alcoholics Anonymous 2012). Alcoholics Anonymous has a twelve-step program and twelve traditions as part of its treatment philosophy. Two of those traditions speak directly about anonymity (Alcoholics Anonymous 1952, 192):

11. Our relations with the general public should be characterized by personal anonymity. We think A.A. should avoid sensational advertising. Our names and pictures as A.A. members ought not be broadcast, filmed, or publicly printed. Our public relations should be guided by the principle of attraction rather than promotion. There is never need to praise ourselves. We feel it better that our friends recommend us.

12. And finally, we of Alcoholics Anonymous believe that the principle of anonymity has an immense spiritual significance. It reminds us that we are to place principles before personalities; that we are to practice a genuine humility. This to the end that our great blessings may never spoil us; that we shall forever live in thankful contemplation of Him who presides over us all.

It is common in AA meetings to use first names only and what is said in meetings is intended to be kept confidential (though there is no legal requirement for this). This philosophy has been extended to numerous other twelve-step support groups: Co-Dependents Anonymous, Debtors Anonymous, Gamblers Anonymous, Narcotics Anonymous, Overeaters Anonymous, Smokers Anonymous, Sex Addicts Anonymous, Workaholics Anonymous, and dozens more.

A different type of anonymous support group can be found online. These growing groups—found in chat rooms, social media sites, Second Life, discussion boards, and elsewhere—function similarly to face-to-face meetings but with the possibility of much greater confidentiality. Online groups can provide greater privacy and anonymity for users (Galagher, Sproull, and Kiesler 1998). In many cases, such groups are run by various advocacy organizations, professional health services, and/or nonprofit organizations; however, many of these organizations are themselves quite visible and transparent. The organization providing the support may be relatively hidden if they are promoting what may be illegal or immoral as judged by society (e.g., International Pedophile and Child Emancipation, Canada's white supremacy group Northern Alliance). A final type of hidden support organization can be found in the various shelters and safehouses for victims of domestic violence and other abuses. Comprehensive lists of such facilities are often difficult to attain publicly because these organizations help ensure the safety of residents by remaining unlisted with no visible markings on the facility itself in many cases. One group notes that in England and Wales, there are 7,500 refuge facilities for women and another 60 for men (Campbell 2010)—and chances are most people have no idea where these shelters are.

Other

Obviously, a fully or mostly hidden organization may be so obscured that most of us are neither aware of it nor able to find any information about it. Even after discounting those organizations that are little more than creations of conspiracy theorists, no doubt such entities exist. But even beyond that, there are a handful of additional hidden organizations we do know about that do not seem to fit neatly into any of the above categories. In addition to online support groups, there are other organizations that exist mostly or entirely online but yet remain largely anonymous. These could be ones that operate in places like Second Life, but more likely they use a range of new media to coordinate their online and offline efforts. A key example of this kind of organization goes by the name Anonymous. This decentralized collection of unidentified individuals who must remain anonymous to maintain membership have coordinated multiple disruptive attacks on individuals and especially various organizations that limit Internet freedom and/or free speech. This secretive organization has taken down White supremacist Hal Turner's website, targeted Tunisian and Egyptian websites during the political revolutions of 2011, attacked Sony Corporation as well as the Westboro Baptist Church, and sided with Julian Assange and WikiLeaks with denial of service attacks on several corporations and government groups seen as working against Assange. Most famously, this group organized multiple attacks on the Church of Scientology because of what Anonymous labeled "Internet censorship."

Another example not easily classified are 527 and 501(c)(4) organizations (named as such because of the sections of the Internal Revenue Code that exempt them from paying taxes), as well as Super PACs, which can influence the election of candidates to political office. Not only do many of these organizations help hide other groups who fund them, but they may also appear less than transparent because their names sound neutral even when their ideology is not. Among the biggest "givers" in the 2012 U.S. elections were names like Restore our Future, Club for Growth, Americans for Job Security, Priorities USA Action, Patriot Majority USA, and EMILY's List. If you are unfamiliar with these names, just know that the first three clearly lean Republican and the last three are decidedly more Democratic in their views.

One related final example is the existence of various generic *front* organizations. In organized crime, such fronts (or shells) may help to legitimize an organization and/or hide its criminal activities. The growing niche of "shelf" organizations (which are created on paper and then set aside until someone claims a then-established company) and "paper businesses" (with little more than a post office box and stand-in corporate officers) represents ways to legally conceal organizations and their ownership. Organizations "operating as" or "doing business as" another are using a type of front as well; but other examples of fronts abound. The CIA used Air America not so much as a civilian air charter company but as a way to supply covert operations during the Vietnam War. More recently, Russia's Aeroflot was used as a front for Russian intelligence work. Investigators have also noted multiple front organizations operated by the Church of Scientology, pro-Israel groups, and the Communist Party. As the Center for Media and Democracy's *PR Watch* warns, front organizations often have misleading names that disguise their real agenda (Landman 2009).

Summary

Given what we know about organizations generally and the dynamics surrounding the use of anonymity and secrecy, it is not surprising that these various hidden collectives may seek this reduced visibility for a wide range of purposes (some of which are seen as socially admirable and others that will be viewed by most of us as morally or legally unacceptable). These hidden organizations range in their political and ideological views as well. The role of new information and communication technologies is worth mentioning here also. On the one hand, Internet-based tools help provide cover for these organizations as they seek to avoid identity detection; on the other hand, they afford the means for promoting identity, often to a very broad audience.

The more important argument for our purposes here is that these hidden organizations do exist—in multiple forms and in significant numbers. Table 1 lists the general types we have examined here and provides an example of each. These organizations are, by most measures, becoming more prevalent and important. However, their somewhat hidden nature often makes accessing information about them challenging.

TABLE 1. Preliminary List – Key Types of Potentially Hidden Organizations

General Type	Example
Anonymous support/hate groups	Narcotics anonymous
Front organization	Get Government Off Our Backs
Gangs	Gangster Disciples
Fraternal orders	Freemasonry
Government intelligence agencies	Central Intelligence Agency (CIA)
Hackers/Hacktivists	Chaos Computer Club
Informal economy organizations	Sweatshop
New religious movements/cults	Church of Scientology
Organized crime groups	Yakuza
Political fundraising organizations	527s
Secret societies	Skull and Bones
Select small businesses	W R Cold Storage Business
Stigmatized/backstreet businesses	Men's bathhouse
Terrorist organizations	al-Qaeda

Organizing Hidden Organizations

Considering the various hidden organizations just described, we would be wise to do all we can to better understand these collectives and how they compare/contrast with one another and with less hidden organizations. To that end, it is useful to consider possible ways of characterizing different types of organizations—with an eye toward frameworks that help us to organize these collectives in ways that account for issues of identity and anonymity. One of the many methods of classifying organizations is to develop typologies, which use two or more dimensions to theoretically categorize these collectives (McKelvey 1982). Since they provide a form of theoretical shorthand for not only classification but also prediction of causal relations, these have been popular in various organizational literatures for providing more holistic understanding (Fiss 2011). Though similar to more empirically based taxonomies and classification schemes, typologies "provide a means for ordering and comparing organizations and clustering them into categorical types without losing sight of the underlying richness and diversity that exist within the type" (Rich 1992, 758).

Before going further, it is important to note two brief, but important, points about the relevance of an organizational typology or similar framework for classification. First, while it is somewhat true that typologies, taxonomies, and the like are perhaps most associated with a paradigmatic approach no longer considered in vogue in many circles, the desire to classify is a familiar one to laypersons and social scientists alike. Having the language to talk about different types of organizations serves a variety of theoretical and practical endeavors. Second, the emphasis here on organizations, more so than the underlying organizing processes that give rise to them, is meant for ease of reading and for consistency with how most of us talk about these collectives. There is no question that hidden organizations partly result from organizing that has worked to conceal parts of their identity and that these organizations continue organizing in ways that may make them more or less hidden. Yet, rather than potentially confuse readers by talking about classifying organizing processes, I will refer to efforts that help classify organizations based on identity-related regions in which they generally operate.

This desire to organize organizations is nothing new, as various classifications for specific types of organizations already exist. For example, self-help groups have often been classified based on the type of help provided (for alcohol abuse, narcotic abuse, etc.); however, some have classified self-help groups primarily in terms of external dependence and internal authority, producing five types: unaffiliated, federated, affiliated, managed, and hybrid (Schubert and Borkman 1991). Similarly, professional service firms have been classified on the basis of knowledge intensity, low capital intensity, and workforce professionalization—resulting in four types of firms: technology developers (e.g., biotech), neo–professional service firms (e.g., consulting), professional campuses (e.g., hospitals), and classic or regulated firms (e.g., law, accounting; see Von Nordenflycht 2010). Other typologies are for a wider range of organizations, but they offer rather basic distinctions: public and private, product and service, agricultural/industrial/service, profit and nonprofit, governmental and nongovernmental, newer/older, small/large, and organizations in developed versus undeveloped countries. Practically useful but equally limiting are classifications based on various sectors and industries. For example, the North American Industry Classification System (formerly the Standard Industry Codes) lists twenty sectors including the following: educational services, utilities, construction, manufacturing, wholesale trade, retail trade, transportation and warehousing, and information. The six types of organizations defined by the IRS (sole proprietor, corporation, partnership, S corporation, trust, and nonprofit organization) provide yet another way of classifying organizations.

Organizational scholars William Carper and William Snizek (1980) along with noted management expert Bill McKelvey (1982) offer insights into several of the many organizational typologies/taxonomies found in the organizational studies literature. Thus, it is not necessary to describe all existing typologies here; however, it is worth mentioning the major ones to provide a feel for what currently exists. Among those cited in the two works are Woodward's (1958) typology based on production technology (small batch, large batch, and continuous process); Parson's (1956) functional types (economic, political, integrative, and pattern maintenance); Katz and Kahn's (1966) variation on Parson's functions (productive, maintenance, adaptive, and managerial or political); and Burns and Stalker's (1961) distinction between mechanistic and organic organizations. Also listed are Etzioni's (1961) work, which recognized that organizations tend to emphasize one of three compliance relationships (coercive, utilitarian, and normative); Blau and Scott's (1962) model suggesting organizations differ in terms of the beneficiary they emphasize (owners, members, clients, public); and Emery and Trist's (1965) classification of organizational environments (placid random, placid clustered, disturbed reactive, and turbulent fields), which helps describe organizations that find themselves in those environments. Other well-known work cited by either Carper and Snizek or McKelvey includes Thompson's (1967) examination of differences in core technology (long-linked, mediating, or intensive); Miles and Snow's (1978) typology of organizational configurations (prospector, analyzer, defender, and reactor); Mintzberg's (1979) variations that include simple structure, machine bureaucracy, professional bureaucracy, divisionalized form, and adhocracy; Perrow's (1967) distinctions between craft, routine, nonroutine, and engineering organizations; and Meyer's (1977) typology of insular, oligopolistic, competitive, administrative, and composite organizations. McKelvey himself offers a fascinating examination of organizational lineage and evolution that results in a taxonomy of organizations past and present.

Considering the rather sizable number of existing category systems, another framework of organizational types may initially seem unnecessary. But Carper and Snizek's (1980) review allows one to observe some significant limitations (as well as strengths) in the existing work, two of which are important to the arguments here. First, many of these efforts are developed primarily with production/manufacturing organizations in mind—and sometimes they are built on the basis of studies of industrial organizations (almost exclusively in the United States or Britain). Even those that extend to service and other nonproduction organizations still have an understandably limited view of organizations. Second, these typologies focus on a variety of topics—but most regularly around issues of the type of (production) technology needed, the function of the organization, or the environment in which the organization operates. Again, it would seem that a very narrow set of issues is foregrounded that may have been relevant to the dominant organizations of the day but that are not necessarily able to understand the wide range of organizations found in the contemporary landscape of the twenty-first century.

As one might expect, other work has emerged in the past thirty years related to organizational classification, and it partially addresses some of the limitations of prior models. This would include, for example, work to better understand and classify nonprofit organizations (Frumkin 2002) and the civil society sector (Lewis 2005). At least one typology distinguishes between uncivil actors (e.g., terrorist groups), business actors (corporations), and civil society actors (NGOs) and further divides the last type into four subcategories of civil society (Costoya 2007). Interest in network organizations (Podolny and Page 1998; Powell 1990) and other emergent forms (see McPhee and Poole 2001) has also better accounted for existing organizations and organizational configurations. Attention to such forms has even produced a typology of networks related to just-in-time manufacturing (Kerwood 1995). Scholarly work on metaphors of organizations (Morgan 1986) and of communication (Putnam, Phillips, and Chapman 1996) can also be viewed as efforts to describe and classify with attention to issues of audience and language in mind. For example, we can classify organizations as machines, brains, cultures, and prisons as well as those where communication functions as conduits, linkages, performances, and voice.

An Expanded View of Organizations

Despite these efforts and the often very useful classification schemes they have produced, two primary problems still exist. First, we have relatively few typologies that consider organizations in a diverse sense beyond business organizations. Those that do incorporate government, civil society, and, in at least one case, uncivil society still fall short in accounting for the various hidden organizations introduced in this chapter. Given the growing prominence of these hidden organizations we need approaches that allow for this expanded view of organizations and that facilitate comparisons across organizational types. Second, the issues that would seem most central in describing these hidden organizations and comparing them to more visible counterparts is the communication (or lack thereof) of identity by the organization and/or its members to various audiences. Yet a focus on the communication of identity is largely absent in these prior classifications. Even those typologies recognizing the environment and its importance do not adequately address identity management issues with various others. Cheney and Christensen (2001) have argued persuasively that identity has become the central concern for organizations today, and "the issue of identity is closely tied up with the ways organizations organize their 'world' in terms of communication" (241).

In short, our inattention to these other types of agencies, businesses, collectives, and so forth and what communication of their identity might mean for them has left a critical gap in our understanding of organizations today. There is a need for a contemporary framework that captures key communication and identity issues at play for a range of organizations—including, but not limited to, those where members or entire organizations remain largely hidden to at least certain key audiences. It is this challenge we will attempt to address in this book.

2 Unmasking What We Know about Hidden Organizations

I t should come as no surprise that research about organizations, like any other topic, is biased. For example, we know more about organizations in the West than we do of those in other parts of the world, especially less developed regions. Another important bias is the overwhelming focus on sizable corporations relative to other types of organizations. A quick keyword search of major databases in this area (e.g., Business Source Premier or Academy of Management archives) leads to the same conclusion: we have researched "corporations" extensively (with "Fortune 500," "Fortune 1000," and "small business" turning up as relatively prominent also). This attention given to corporations dwarfs even the combined scholarship in organizational studies about secret societies, terrorist organizations, counterintelligence agencies, fraternal organizations, criminal organizations, the sex industry, the informal economy, front and shell organizations, 527 organizations, and new religious movements. The linking of organizations with business and management indexes accounts for some of this bias, of course; to correct for that, the research presented in this chapter comes from a wide range of disciplines examining various hidden organizations. Even considering that, it is safe to say there has been a clear lack of focus on anonymous agencies, backstreet businesses, and covert collectives in mainstream organizational research.

One potential reason for the seeming inattention to these hidden organizations is seen in broader critiques about our continued reliance on outdated organizational theory even amid recognition of widespread changes.

Gerald Davis (2009), professor of management and organizations in the Ross School of Business at the University of Michigan, offers an informative critique in arguing that large corporations have lost their central place in American social structure as we move from an industrial to a postindustrial economy where finances are a more critical factor. As he argues:

> In a postindustrial economy, the applicability of several of our existing theories is called into question. Some scholars have jibed that organization theory is, to a large extent, the "science of General Motors." . . . But GM's declaration of bankruptcy in June 2009 also signified the bankruptcy of the corporate-industrial model that has been the basis of much of our theory and research. Theories that rely on evidence based in manufacturing may have limited application in a service economy. (41)

Although Davis ultimately moves toward a different sort of solution, his critique here is important because it suggests the benefit of an approach that differs from the common focus on formal corporate organizations. In a related vein, Swedish scholars Ahrne and Brunsson (2011) have recently argued that the study of organization and organizations is still highly useful, but only if it is "defined somewhat more broadly than students of organization have usually defined it" (84). This broader focus for them includes what they call *partial organizations,* which lack at least some element of formal organizations. Our explorations here also echo Renate Mayntz of the Max Planck Institute for the Study of Societies, who is critical of the fact that "organization studies have come to concentrate increasingly on one specific type: economic organizations, or firms. . . . As a consequence, organizations that live and act in the underworld . . . will not attract special attention" (2004, 5).

Thus, a contemporary view of organization, organizations, and organizing has to look beyond the large corporation and the formal organization to consider other types. These large formal corporations are not the only ones to organize themselves; a wide range of collectives not usually seen as formal or even corporate can be usefully examined as organizations. Furthermore, if issues related to transparency and identity—which are among the many topics we will examine in the next chapter—are important for formal corporate collectives, they are potentially even more relevant as we explore organizations significantly defined by their lack of transparency and concealed identity.

The purpose of this chapter is to examine relevant research about these less apparent and less examined organizations as it has emerged in various disciplines. We will focus specifically on these collectives as organizations, which means that scholarship examining invisible work and workers, individual whistleblowing, and the dark side of organizational member behavior (e.g., bullying, harassment) is largely outside our immediate interest. Invisible colleges, the invisible hand of the marketplace, and even the study of company/trade secrets (unless they relate closely to the identity of the organization) will generally not be examined here, either. Furthermore, we will not focus on those organizations that want to be discovered but have not yet been noticed (e.g., an underground musical band still trying to attract attention) or those that have been ineffective in their planned efforts to promote themselves (e.g., a new enterprise that fails to advertise enough to create name recognition among potential customers). Instead, we will highlight work that begins to help us talk about the strategic communication of organizational and organizational member identity along with other communicative processes in these more hidden organizations.

Secret Societies

Despite our contemporary fascination with secret societies, these organizations date back centuries. Scholarly attention to these societies also has a long history of examining a wide range of groups across the globe (see Chan 2004; Erickson 1981; Heckethorn 1965; Klement 1984; Little 1949; Nosco 1993; Ownby and Heidhues 1993; Simmel 1906; Tefft 1992; Wedgewood 1930). *Life* magazine discusses "chthonic" organizations (meaning "under the earth" in Greek) dating back centuries B.C., which helped establish the basis for other secret societies that would follow throughout much of recorded history (*Hidden World of Secret Societies* 2012). Current scholars claim modern secret collectives began in the eighteenth century (Anheier 2010). Some of these societies are very localized (Fong 1981) or only existed for a short while; yet others have persisted over time and spread across countries. Some are indeed linked to what we might call primitive societies with nonliterate members, while others are located in very developed countries with highly educated citizens. Furthermore, some groups are linked to criminal/subversive activities, whereas several are engaged in underground resistance to illegitimate power, and some are more social and apolitical in nature.

In certain historical periods these groups have flourished. Despite the difficulty in making accurate counts when organizations failed to keep complete records or denied access to them, Harwood (1897) reported as many as one of every five men were in some sort of fraternal order in the United States in 1896. Other scholarly estimates note that between 1870 and 1910 Americans joined more than 3,500 various fraternal orders (Palmer 1944) and by 1927 thirty million persons in the United States were in secret societies (Gist 1938). Sociologist Lawrence Hazelrigg (1969) noted a decline in the number of "visible" secret organizations since the early part of the twentieth century and a lack of serious attention to those that had survived. Yet, even with these declines, studying such organizations remains important given both their potentially extreme nature and their possible similarities to other contemporary organizations that attempt to hide either their own identities or those of their members.

"The study of secret societies . . . is, in general, a hard one, since the very secrecy that distinguishes these societies obscures them, especially when disclosure is truly dangerous" (Erickson 1981, 204). Nevertheless, scholars have begun to offer useful insights into these groups. In many respects these societies are essentially organizations engaged in organizing processes. They may structure themselves in familiar hierarchical forms (in part to help maintain and enforce the organization's secrecy), though they can take on other structures as well (and may even move away from hierarchical forms over time). Furthermore, like most organizations, they are typically formed in response to a perceived need or gap in the existing social structure that individuals alone cannot address. Issues of selection, power, control, and effectiveness matter in these societies as well.

Perhaps somewhat more uniquely relevant to our concerns here, these organizations are defined substantially by the high premium they place on secrecy.

> What unites them is not any one purpose or belief. It is, rather, secrecy itself: secrecy of purpose, belief, methods, often membership. These are kept hidden from outsiders and only by gradual steps revealed to insiders, with further secrets always beckoning, still to be penetrated. (Bok 1982, 46)

Indeed, one of German sociologist Georg Simmel's (1906) claims is that the control of information and knowledge about one's secrets is fundamental for these organizations. For him, much depends on trusting a member not to endanger the organization by revealing the group's identity and/or its activities. Others have argued a secret society, by definition, must have both secret activities and recurring patterns of relations among members (Erickson 1981); furthermore, the power of these collectives depends heavily on their ability to control information (Tefft 1992). "Secret societies prevent or restrict communication, and distribute information and knowledge in ways that create nuanced structures of knowing and not knowing, of awareness and ignorance" (Anheier 2010, 1356).

Notably, these societies are not all alike structurally or in the degree to which information is restricted. Though all share some common structural similarities, they can also be classified into functions that are rather different: philanthropic, revolutionary and reformist, patriotic, professional/occupational, mystical/occult, religious orders, military, collegiate social and recreational, honor, criminal, and so forth (see Gist 1938). Hazelrigg (1969) suggests secret organizations take two forms: those where everything (including the organization's existence) is secret and those in which only some aspects (membership, goals, etc.) remain concealed. Additionally, Palmer (1944) claims two types: active (goal-driven like the KKK) and ceremonial (most lodges and fraternal orders). All this suggests not only the importance of function but also the relevance of the motive for secrecy.

MacKenzie's (1967) *Secret Societies* offers what is essentially a classification of organizations based on degree of secrecy: *open* organizations have no secrets from anyone; *limited* organizations select their own members, but outsiders know the organization's activities; *private* organizations restrict membership and activities are mostly concealed; and *secret* organizations have very strict limits on membership and make strong efforts to hide organizational activities from public scrutiny. David Ownby (1993), whose work has largely examined secret societies in Southeast Asia, argues for more of a continuum of organizational forms, with secret societies as one form of nonelite practice. These organizations range broadly from mutual aid groups and corporations to criminal groups and rebels; thus, he contends some brotherhoods have more in common with a working-class European institution than with other secret groups. In short, these secret societies vary substantially—not only in the degree of secrecy employed but also in the motive for that secrecy.

Criminal Organizations and Organized Crime

For obvious reasons, research into many aspects of organized crime is quite difficult due to the largely underground nature of so much of this work and the potential threat (for both members and victims) associated with revealing information to outsiders. But the development of organized crime is nothing new, having existed in some form or another for centuries. Criminal organizations have historically been involved with a range of illegal activities including drug trafficking, human trafficking, money laundering, counterfeiting, gambling, prostitution, weapons, and stolen goods. Today, criminal organizations are also involved in cybercrime and markets for organs, antiquities, and wildlife. In a complex world filled with global competition, network access to varied markets, and differing legal regulations/enforcement, it is not surprising that organized efforts are needed.

Defining organized crime can be challenging, but two key issues are relevant to our discussion here. First, organized crime may take many different forms of organization. For example, one study reported that drug trafficking enterprises are of four types: corporations, communal businesses, family businesses, and freelance (Natarajan and Belanger 1998). Chinese criminal organizations have been described as traditional hierarchies, hermit-crab hybrid organizations (which take over shells of legitimate entities), and criminal networks (Xia 2008). In fact, efforts to address organized crime can encounter legal problems when traditional conceptualizations of criminal organizations as hierarchies inadequately apply to contemporary forms. Form is important here because network structures provide a chance to operate with less visibility as these configurations are inevitably harder to detect (see Michael 2008; Williams 2001).

It is also worth noting that organized crime may not always be especially organized—and may even be disorganized as criminology and public policy professor Peter Reuter (1983) has argued. Law enforcement and popular culture have sometimes made organized criminal entities, especially the Mafia, seem more prominent than they perhaps are. For Reuter, the underworld and illegal markets are not a mythical notion—but the role of organized crime may be exaggerated. Nevertheless, it seems clear that organizations are clearly involved in the coordination and execution of various criminal activities—in fact, many smaller and less permanent organizations may be involved rather than simply a few large criminal organizations (see also Southerland and Potter 1993).

Second, an examination of definitions reveals that "identity" issues have not been seen as central. Nevertheless, there is a recognition that these organizations can operate in very hidden ways. In fact, some work has even linked secret societies with criminal organizations, arguing that secret societies initially created to resist/overthrow unpopular governments or provide protection to others (e.g., the Mafia or Chinese Triads) may later develop interests in other criminal activity. A prime example of this is Chinese criminal organizations that still resemble secret societies (Xia 2008). Others have drawn parallels between Bernard Madoff's organization (or his special division of it) and secret societies. His people were separated from most others physically and received special privileges, helping to ensure they would keep secrets, and information flow outside the organization was tightly controlled as well (Van de Bunt 2010). But Madoff was also successful for so long because he was not isolated but established—thus blending in as normal and thus trustworthy. Thus, the criminal organization succeeds in staying at least somewhat hidden in part because it has a legitimate face or aspect as well, which helps keep the criminal part largely invisible to most.

Whether they are secret societies or not, secrecy remains vital for many criminal organizations (Paoli 2002), with information about rituals/oaths and organizational activity withheld from nonmembers (which also creates a special loyalty bond among organizational members). These rituals, along with secretive gestures and signs of recognition, help convey a criminal group's collective identity (Paoli 2002; Xia 2008). Criminologist Paul Lunde (2004) suggests Colombian drug cartels have gotten smarter by becoming smaller and less visible over time—with some organizational leaders even going so far as to have plastic surgery to change their looks and fingerprints as a further form of disguise to others. As another way of only vaguely concealing their activities, Lunde also notes organized crime groups even go by different names in different parts of the United States: The Outfit (Chicago), The Arm (Buffalo), and The Office (New England) are but some examples. Criminal organizations are often difficult to locate physically—disappearing into the communities in which they operate through efforts to "have no precise physical presence and to avoid drawing unnecessary attention" (Thorne 2005, 599). Key to remaining at least somewhat hidden is not only the existence of these secrets but also silence about them. As a prime example, "omerta" refers to a code of silence found in Mafia organizations. In this extreme form of loyalty, silence shows commitment (and being an informant represents extreme disloyalty). For organizations involved in criminal activities, members cannot risk revealing secrets publicly even when conflicts surface between cartel members (Van de Bunt 2010).

Perhaps the most relevant examination of communication in organized crime is Diego Gambetta's *Codes of the Underworld* (2009). Even though it is more about criminals than their organizations, several key ideas are relevant. Gambetta highlights three critical concerns stemming from the inherent secrecy of organized crime. First, the *communication problem* is the need to interact with known colleagues without unwanted others (rivals, law enforcement) intercepting and understanding the message. Second, the *identification problem* concerns the need to identify other organizational members (and be identifiable to them) without being recognized by a third party. Third, the *advertising problem* suggests most criminal organizations cannot promote their goods and services in traditional ways despite the need to attract interested others and relevant resources (though he recounts an amusing tale of an individual seeking various illegal services who actually used the Yellow Pages to contact what she thought was a criminal organization). Insightfully, Gambetta suggests names and trademarks are relevant for organized crime because they help establish a reputation among customers/clients and other criminal organizations. These reputations are likely difficult to establish, especially for criminal organizations; furthermore, no outside entity can protect a criminal organization's use of trademarks or other identifying information (allowing other organizations to potentially borrow or mimic one's identity). Yet, Gambetta contends the Mafia name matters in the "protection" market (though use of the term "Mafia" is very rare even by its own members). Organized crime is also filled with the use of nicknames that have been linked to increased secrecy about one's identity.

Research into a couple specific forms of organized crime offer some additional insights as well. When something like trafficking in human organs is made illegal and/or a market for such items emerges beyond what a formal market can provide, organizations emerge to fill this gap (Meyer 2006). Efforts to control such activities or make them illegal have the effect of moving these businesses further underground, creating a vicious circle of even greater need for regulation and oversight. Not surprisingly, a report from the National Human Rights Commission, Institute of Social Sciences, and United Nations on human trafficking notes these organizations "usually operate underground and do their best to remain unnoticed" (Sen and Nair

2004, 141). As a result, many criminal organizations try to build their business around "victimless" activities (loans, wholesale drug distribution, etc.) that help them avoid public scrutiny (Kopp 1999). As another criminology scholar explains:

> All illegal market actors risk imprisonment and the seizure of their properties by law enforcement agencies and must take precautions against such events. Thus . . . each entrepreneur will try to structure his relationship with employees and customers, reducing the amount of information available to them concerning his own participation. (Paoli 2002, 65)

Another useful example is to look at research on street or youth gangs. Researchers have classified types of gang organizations in several ways. This includes classification by activity (social, cultural, criminal, delinquent, party, etc.), level of organization (loosely knit to highly hierarchical; emergent to formal), stage of development and organizational history, membership types, and extensiveness of rules/rituals (Valdez 2003). "Some gangs place high importance on monikers, colors, symbols, and hand signs, which are used for self-identification. Although this type of gang may be involved in illegal activities such as drug dealing, its primary goal is to protect the gang's honor, turf, and solidarity" (Valdez 2003, 15). Others have also found that gangs may keep the identity of organizational leaders compartmentalized to minimize damages if law enforcement attacks part of the gang (Ayling 2009). Some of the most insightful work in this area comes from communication professor Dwight Conquergood (1994) and his ethnographic studies of Chicago street gangs. He describes gang communication as deliberately opaque and relying extensively on cues that are incomprehensible to outsiders. Written manifestos and charters are carefully kept hidden from outsiders and "the need for silence, secrecy, and circumspection is intensified because the line between insiders and outsiders is slippery and shifting" (29). This secretive communication, which serves to shield members from outsiders, also enhances bonding between gang members.

Informal Economy

The informal economy involves those entities that are hidden for tax and/or welfare purposes (but are otherwise legal) or are part of the gross domestic product that either is not reported or is underreported officially (see

Habibullah and Eng 2006; Williams and Windebank 2004). Although the informal economy is sometimes linked to and confused with organized crime—because of potentially illegal activities and the common need for secrecy—there are also clear differences as will be described below. As noted in the opening chapter, the informal economy is a significant aspect of all countries, though there are sizable regional variations (see Schneider, Buehn, and Montenegro 2010; Schneider and Enste 2000). Much of the research seems to be by economists tackling the challenge of measuring the size of this economy. Not surprisingly, this analysis is typically at the country/nation level of analysis. It is not difficult to find research on many specific countries, various regions, and across nations (for example, see Heinonen 2008; Kinyanjui 2010; Martins and Ligthelm 2004; Mulinge and Munyae 1998; Peña 1999; Thießen 2010; Toth and Sik 2002; Walsh 2010; Williams and Windebank 2004). Research tends to show that increases in regulation grow the shadow economy (see Enste 2010).

Beyond the extensive efforts to measure this economy, research is understandably lacking. "Given that so many members of the informal sector are hidden from official scrutiny, it is not surprising that comparatively little useful information on how the sector works is available and there are gaps in locating the relevant activities within a theoretical framework" (Walsh 2010, 161). More specifically, there is relatively little organizational research related to the informal economy. Indeed, management scholars have recognized that "little research has focused on organizations operating outside of laws and regulations in different societies or on how institutions can encourage ventures to transition from the informal to the formal economy" (Webb et al. 2009, 506). Perhaps this is due in part to the fact that the informal economy is filled with entrepreneurial activity that may be preorganizational (Williams and Nadin 2010). Much of the activity in this other economy concerns individual workers as what is hidden, more so or rather than relevant organizations. In other cases, organizations may emerge to aid workers or to give voice to those in the informal sector—but these organizations are not themselves hidden.

Yet management scholar Paul Godfrey (2011) argues "the informal economic activity represents a significant new frontier for management scholarship and investigation" (233). Godfrey reviews literature across disciplines to create a model of the informal economy. His framework suggests there is substantial activity involving firms/organizations at work in both the informal and semiformal parts of the economy (though he does not elaborate on specific firms).

Sociologist Alejandro Portes and colleagues have made a couple of useful distinctions relevant here. First, there is a difference between formal, informal, and criminal arrangements based on the legality of both the production/distribution process as well as the final product—with criminal being illegal for both but informal producing a legal final product (see Castells and Portes 1989). Second, Portes and Haller (2005) note three types of informal activity: (1) *survival*, which is individual/family sale of goods/services for survival or added income; (2) *dependent exploitation*, which is off-the-books hiring/subcontracting by formal-sector firms; and (3) *growth*, which refers to accumulation of capital by small firms through various relationships. The last of these may best represent a hidden organization and can be seen in Central Italy's enterprises in textiles, ceramics, and other goods. The second category also suggests that formal-sector firms sometimes engage in the informal economy as well. "Formal businesses increasingly sub-contract stages of production to employers who employ off-the-books workers under degrading, low-paid and exploitative 'sweatshop-like' conditions" (Williams 2008, 111).

Another useful framework is presented in the management literature (Webb et al. 2009). If we consider both the *legality* and the societal *legitimacy* of means and ends, the formal economy (where both means and ends are both legal and legitimate) stands in sharp contrast to the renegade economy (where both means and ends are both illegal and illegitimate); comparatively, the informal economy is viewed as socially legitimate—but either the means or ends (or both) are viewed as illegal. Webb et al. point to pirated software, counterfeit products, and employment of undocumented workers as examples of this sort of activity. Emphasizing informal organizations, these scholars argue that cooperative groups form between entrepreneurs in these areas. Those involved may share a common identity, but little is said about the communication of that identity to others. Indeed, other comparisons between formal and informal organizations do not tend to distinguish them based on anything related to the communication of identity or visibility of the organizations involved (see Mulinge and Munyae 1998).

Yet, the nature of what these organizations do necessitates them being less visible to various audiences. The various names given to this sector, or at least to parts of it ("shadow," "twilight," "underground," "black," "hidden," "nonobserved," "unrecorded," "subterranean," etc.), illustrate this lack of visibility. Existing research reinforces this point. For example, Portes and Haller (2005) argue that the success of informal organizations in highly regulated environments depends heavily on avoiding detection by authorities; in other words, in more developed areas where regulations are more extensive, those engaged in such activity have to do more to conceal themselves. Periodic rites of solidarity, trust, and community enforcement help to maintain these secrets (e.g., entirely clandestine factories). Research sponsored in part by the Aspen Institute (Losby et al. 2002) argues that "the viability of informal enterprise relies considerably on being able to operate under the regulatory radar screen" (10).

A few more specific examples also illustrate the importance of visibility and identity issues in these organizations. Eric Schlosser, perhaps best known as author of *Fast Food Nation,* offers a compelling look at three industries in the vast informal economy in his compilation titled *Reefer Madness* (2003). He begins by noting "if the market does indeed embody the sum of all human wishes, then the secret ones are just as important as the ones that are openly displayed" (9). With regard to the marijuana industry in the United States, he notes that an underworld has emerged that is hidden to outsiders. Marijuana growers are "extremely secretive" and farms may remain small or even decrease in size to avoid detection; however, it is unclear if secret organizations are operating here (as opposed to individual entrepreneurs growing the plants). In the strawberry industry with its use of migrant farm workers, Schlosser notes a different type of hidden organization. The Strawberry Workers and Farmers Alliance was created by a public relations firm on behalf of growers. Although it seemed to call for farm workers' rights, the actual goal of this alliance and the organizations secretly behind it was to discourage and confuse members considering joining the United Farm Workers.

Schlosser's most fascinating study is of the pornography industry created primarily by Reuben Sturman, a Cleveland salesman who turned his small magazine business into a multicompany international media conglomerate. Among his tactics were secret alliances, disguised ownership of businesses, use of multiple aliases, and a general lack of communication with the media. In some ways, the development of this industry has entered the mainstream and is not primarily about secret organizations at all, but Schlosser's tale reveals at least two types of hidden organizations (one of which is relevant here and one that we will examine later in the chapter). To avoid government control and taxation, Sturman would hide ownership of his businesses by linking them to other companies that often were outside the United States (e.g., in Lichtenstein or Panama) or in states with few regulations about such practices (e.g., Nevada). Schlosser concludes his book by noting the tension between public and private morality: "The underground is a good measure of the progress and health of nations. When much is wrong, much needs to be hidden" (221).

The sex industry is a complex one. Its characteristics include a formal/legal and highly visible component (not of interest here), a formal/legal aspect that seeks to avoid attention (to be discussed later), the already examined illegal side of human sex trafficking and prostitution often connected to organized crime, and a more informal aspect that seeks to avoid taxation and regulation that is of relevance as part of the informal economy. These various organizations may include escort services, strip clubs, go-go bars, peep shows, after-hours clubs, hourly motels, hotel parties, adult theaters, massage parlors, health clubs, bathhouses, brothels in various establishments, and organizations that front for various sexual services (see Raymond, Hughes, and Gomez 2001). Some of these organizations advertise widely, but others keep a relatively low profile to avoid undesired attention and some even take extensive measures to remain completely under the radar of authorities and the general public.

A few other examples of informal economy organizations and their somewhat hidden nature can be found in the research literature. A report from the United Nations Research Institute for Social Development notes that in Kenya some businesses in the market operate anonymously though legally (Kinyanjui 2010). These are temporary businesses that appear and disappear in the marketplace. In Liberia largely invisible rotating credit associations known as *susu groups* operate in secrecy to avoid market officials and empower women economically (Cruz 2012). Clandestine abortion clinics are still found in parts of the world where abortions are illegal or considered highly immoral, which forces such organizations to be very discreet. Sneakers bought and sold in unmarked urban buildings known only by word of mouth are yet another example.

Terrorist Organizations

As we begin this section, it is useful to remind ourselves that terrorism can be domestic, regional, and/or international; it may be state-sponsored or not; and, despite the growing attention to terrorism following the events of 9/11 in the United States, terrorism has a long history. Although we will not directly engage in this debate, it is reasonable to assume that the negatively valenced labels "terrorist" and "terrorism" are often attached by others (and not necessarily the actors perpetrating such acts); thus, the research discussed in this section may not be seen as terrorism by some parties (just as the work on counterterrorism and intelligence in the next section may be viewed by some as involving terrorist groups). Indeed, all the subcategories we are using in this chapter are very permeable; clearly, terrorist organizations, organized crime, and shadow economies can sometimes overlap. We have already seen how organized crime may get involved in the informal economy. Furthermore, organizations in the shadow economy or those that are engaged in criminal activities may use business fronts and other tactics that allow them to remain hidden while earning funds to support a range of activities, including terrorism. Clearly, most terrorist acts are seen as criminal ones.

One of the most important shared characteristics among these overlapping organizations is their secretiveness:

> Terrorists and international organized criminals depend on secrecy as a foundational concept for their organizations. This includes secret membership, secret locales, secret leadership, and secret communications. The organizers of their activities are hard to identify, and both groups use all forms of modern information technology to execute their operations with minimal risk of disclosure. (Shelley and Picarelli 2002, 3)

Like other somewhat hidden organizations we have examined, terrorist organizations are not completely secretive. Hamas, for example, has some elements that work openly in mosques and social service sites whereas other aspects of the organization operate in very clandestine ways (Zanini and Edwards 2001). International terrorism and national security expert Steven Emerson's (2002) testimony to the U.S. Congress about the embassy bombings in Kenya and Tanzania also shows that terrorist organizations partner with other for-profit and nonprofit organizations—knowingly and unknowingly—in part to help conceal their identity. In fact, the International Islamic Relief Organization has tried to hide its identity as a source of funding for terrorism by working through two differently named organizations (the International Relief Organization and the Success Foundation) that all report a common address and phone number. Al-Qaeda has also used legal businesses to legitimate its activities while camouflaging its actual existence and location.

Communication scholars Michael and Cynthia Stohl (2011) define clandestine organizations, such as terrorist groups, based on three characteristics clearly related to their concealment: members agree to keep their own and others' affiliations secret, internal structures operate outside public knowledge, and external traces of the organization only become visible over time. These organizations may be illegal or legal, working for or against the state, and their secrecy can serve to maintain freedom of action, disguise relations with others, and/or enhance organizational effectiveness. Other scholars have responded to Stohl and Stohl by suggesting it is both the visibility (of planning and execution of terrorist acts) and the invisibility (of governing structure) of terrorist organizations like al-Qaeda that differentiate them from more legitimate private businesses; furthermore, rather than being clandestine and hidden, organizations such as this depend greatly on a high degree of visibility—though that visibility may come more from media attention than from specific communication strategies of the organization itself (see Schoeneborn and Scherer 2012). Key to the arguments in this book, terrorist groups and other clandestine organizations vary in terms of how recognizable they wish to be to certain groups and how known/unknown their members may wish to be.

Although the research on terrorist organizations has rarely come from organizational studies, it is quite clear that we often characterize these groups as organizations. David Whittaker's *Terrorism Reader* (2001) includes organizations with an identifiable chain of command or some type of conspiratorial cell structure as a defining element. An analysis of the 2008 attacks in Mumbai, India, concludes that organizations still matter greatly in terrorist studies—despite discussions of homegrown and leaderless jihadism (Acharya and Marwah 2011). Other international terrorism scholars have claimed that "Al Qaeda, first and foremost, exists as a formal organization with a solid structure even if it is not based in a fixed or identifiable territory" (Gunaratna and Oreg 2010, 1044). They claim terrorist organizations are similar to other types given the concern for structure, roles, leadership, and goals. Similarly, Jones (2006) draws on organizational theory to describe the flexibility and adaptability of the al-Qaeda network—depicting Osama bin Laden as a terrorist CEO of a group that once operated much like a centralized organization (but is now a loose network of networks). However, despite a growing interest in large-scale networks, we still know relatively little about the dark networks of terrorist organizations and other covert groups (Xu and Chen 2008).

Stohl and Stohl (2011) note that too often similarities are drawn between terrorist organizations and familiar "corporate" models—with repeated mention of terms like "franchises," "corporate takeovers," "umbrella networks," and "brand names" (in addition to hierarchy, top leadership, and/or decentralization) well documented. Such a critique does not suggest that an organizational perspective is inappropriate but rather serves as a call to expand our notion of organization beyond corporations to recognize such differences. Other work also suggests the need for expanded classification efforts. For example, Randol (2003), a fellow at the World Policy Institute, offers a model of terrorist organizations that includes publicity/propaganda and clandestine groups/members as two of seven key variables; interestingly, terrorist organizations may need both publicity and recognition for their actions along with an ability to conduct actions in covert and clandestine ways. In a series of white papers and books, the Center for Strategic Communication at Arizona State University has also called for new models and ways of thinking about battling extremism (see Corman, Trethewey, and Goodall 2008). In this spirit, we shall examine one such classification in chapter 4.

Some of the terrorist research has looked at communication issues. A group from Tilburg University in the Netherlands modeled the relationships between network structures and the ability to both maintain secrecy and share information efficiently, noting, "Terrorist organizations, and more in general covert organizations, constantly face the dilemma between secrecy and operational capability" (Lindelauf, Borm, and Hamers 2008, 3). They found that centralized information flow was best for inexperienced covert organizations operating in a hostile environment; however, all-to-all communication was better in a friendly environment, and more established covert networks did best with cellular networks in more hostile environments. Related to this, others have suggested network structures "limit connections and communications in order to enhance operational security, mission execution and organizational survival" (Drozdova and Samoilov 2010, 65).

Other research about these organizations has examined issues of visibility and awareness. Al-Qaeda even changed its name several years ago as part of its effort to strengthen itself globally and increase public awareness while also maintaining its local connections (Marret 2008). Some experts have used the notion of social visibility to describe the degree to which interests and actions are known (though this work is more about internal conflict; see Morrill, Zald, and Rao 2003). Notably, most terrorist attacks are anonymous. Since 1968 64 percent of attacks worldwide have been conducted by unknown groups; furthermore, that percentage has increased since September 11, 2001, with three of every four attacks now done anonymously (Abrahms 2008). The identity of the sponsor of terrorist acts is a key issue, but sponsorship may less often be clearly linked to various states/nations today (see Arquilla, Ronfeldt, and Zanini 1999).

Professor Philip Jenkins, in his book *Images of Terror* (2003), argues that attribution is key in understanding terrorist actions. In some cases, multiple groups will claim responsibility while the actual attackers remain hidden. These "false flags" are used for various reasons. One such motive Jenkins calls "deniability," where a terrorist organization creates a separate front organization to carry out its terrorist activities (e.g., the use of the Izz al-Din al-Qassam brigades by Hamas) or to negotiate with an enemy state (e.g., the use of Sinn Féin by the Irish Republican Army), or where a bogus front group can be blamed for unpopular acts (e.g., the use of Black September by the al-Fatah). Another type of false flag is known as "stigmatization," where a heinous crime is committed and then blamed on an enemy organization. False flags may also be used for destabilization, which Jenkins describes as violence to disrupt a hostile state or other enemy.

Sometimes the so-called veil of anonymity is necessary for these organizations—as when one sees organizational members with faces covered in videos or hooded/masked members such as those of the Black Bloc during the protests in Seattle in 1999 (Armond 2001). But that veil can make it difficult for terrorist groups to spread their message beyond certain groups relatively close to home (Arquilla and Ronfeldt 2001). This tension also surfaces in the use of communication and information technology, which is seen as both facilitating and threatening an organization's anonymity (Caiani and Parenti 2009; Zanini and Edwards 2001). In many ways, however, these organizations

have been able to use these tools while obtaining adequate amounts of anonymity—through password-based websites, stenography, private chat rooms,
encrypted CMC and cell phone messages, and prepaid phone cards. Indeed,
rather than viewing the Internet as a target for cyberterrorism, most terrorist organizations have used it for what Thomas (2003) calls "cyberplanning."
Reviews of existing research note that the Internet has been used by extremist
groups to recruit, to reach a global audience, and to foster a common collective identity (Caiani and Parenti).

Despite operating in hidden ways, these organizations use various
online tools to promote themselves and their identity. Interestingly, extremist groups were some of the first to use early computer bulletin boards to
promote their views (Zhou et al. 2005). Today, they use parts of the Internet
for image management by highlighting certain aspects of the organization
over others (Caiani and Parenti 2009; Zanini and Edwards 2001). For example, a study of Hamas (see Mozes and Weimann 2010) revealed that some of
their migration online used the Hamas brand found offline; however, for
the Palestinian Information Center website Hamas crafted a new brand that
concealed the link to Hamas offline (at least in non-Arabic language sites).
Indeed, the relationship between the offline organization and its online
presence is complex.

New technology also plays a role in recruiting and retaining members in
these organizations. However, the research suggests some real limitations
here. A decision to join a terrorist organization depends greatly on the network and the organization; that is, it is not an individual decision. These
organizations cannot recruit openly via ads in the media—they must turn
to those they trust (e.g., kinship ties) in their network (Stohl and Stohl 2007;
Tucker 2008). This recruitment and retention is based on a strong sense of
identification with the terrorist organization and/or its cause. Mayntz (2004)
concludes that ideologically based organizational identification is vital to terrorist organizations, even if not unique to them. Clandestine groups regularly
seek ways to facilitate organizational identity/solidarity (Zhou et al. 2005).
However, that sense of identity and identification may be harder to instill in
a network organization than in the more tribal/clan or hierarchical form of
terrorist organization (Ronfeldt and Arquilla 2001).

Secret Government Agencies

In this category the research encompasses state intelligence agencies, covert and clandestine counterterrorism and counterintelligence operations, secret police, and other hidden organizations (both public and private) working against various enemy groups. As noted earlier, the determination of what makes one organization's efforts terrorism and another's counterterrorism can be controversial, but it is not a debate central to our efforts here—as the categories are merely to help group research on different types of hidden organizations. The nature of the work in these agencies may involve the establishment of fake organizations and falsified work histories as part of establishing covers for organizational members. It may also require the organization and/or its member(s) to "go dark," where the member cannot reveal his/her ties to the investigating agency and even the organization itself may remain unidentified. These actions provide the organization behind them with a degree of plausible deniability.

Like other areas of research on hidden organizations, this research can be difficult to conduct; moreover, the addition of classified information and mis/disinformation in these organizations creates an additional challenge. In general, this is an area where very little research appears about the organizations themselves and their communication. As one business scholar advocating such linkages observed:

> Agencies relating to intelligence, counter-terrorism, warfare, defence procurement, policing and so on can be understood as organizational apparatuses which could be studied in similar ways to any other organization. In fact, such studies are rare when compared to almost any other sector. (Grey 2009, 311)

Even though covert intelligence and secret government groups have existed in many parts of the globe throughout much of our recorded history (e.g., Sparta had secret police in the fourth century B.C., and the Culper Spy Ring played an essential role for the United States during the Revolutionary War), it is the more sophisticated efforts during and following World War II that have received special attention—especially in book-length treatments of specific organizations. Great Britain's Bletchley Park, as described in Michael Smith's book *Station X* (1998), provides one interesting example of a secret organization not substantially revealed until decades after it ended. Bletchley Park was a war station for MI6 and the Government Code and Cypher School as they worked to break German codes during WWII. Its designation as "Station X" meant "station ten" using a Roman numeral and not something more secretive—but the organization was quite secretive, with a hidden location and members told not to reveal what they were doing. The work of this secret organization is credited by Smith with reducing the time needed to defeat Hitler by up to three years. Another example is examined in Jennet Conant's book *The Irregulars* (2008), an examination of the British Security Coordination, which she describes as one of the most successful covert campaigns in the history of espionage. This shadow organization engaged in secret propaganda to encourage U.S. involvement in World War II. It was led by the equally secretive and mysterious William Stephenson, who worked undercover as a Canadian businessman but eventually was heading "nine distinct secret organizations in the United States and throughout North and South America" (77) as well as a secret Canadian training camp.

Still today, many nations have extensive intelligence organizations that operate in part as secretive government agencies (see Thomas 1999), including the United Kingdom's GCHQ and MI6, China's Ministry of State Security, Israel's Defense Forces and Mossad, and secret police units within Russia's Federal Counter-Intelligence Service (an updated version of the former KGB). In the United States one of those organizations is the Central Intelligence Agency (CIA), whose creation following World War II led to a sizable increase in the use of secret government operations and covert actions (Gross 2009). Interestingly, analysis of CIA covert operations during the Cold War suggests that because covert operations were used somewhat indiscriminately, the reputation of the CIA as the organization behind them ultimately suffered (Del Pero 2003).

We of course know the names of some of these organizations like the CIA and MI6, yet we do not know all that much in specifics. Journalists David Wise and Thomas Ross (1964; 1967) provide several insights into what they describe as invisible government—noting, for example, that CIA cover names and pseudonyms are used internally and that even ex-members often cannot list the CIA as a former employer. They also note that MI6 has a number of secret buildings and the identity of its leaders are kept secret from the public. Furthermore, there are organizations within these and other agencies that may be very hidden. For example, Bamford (2001) describes several of them: an assassination unit within Division D of the

CIA that operated in great secrecy (until it was discovered and banned); the 303 committee of the National Security Agency (NSA), which reviews covert operations; the Special Collection Services (alternately led by the CIA or NSA) that plants eavesdropping equipment and recruits key foreign communication personnel; and the Joint Functional Component Command for Network Warfare, which is a very secretive hacking organization within the U.S. Strategic Command. These hidden internal organizations are found elsewhere as well (e.g., the ultrasecret "S Wing" of Pakistan's Inter-Services Intelligence; see Lieven 2011).

In addition to intelligence, another form of sometimes secret government work concerns counterterrorism. Here we also see named but not well-known organizations, engaged in what are sometimes merely clandestine operations but also covert affairs (where the organization itself is hidden). For example, Special Air Services (SAS) provides Great Britain with covert military capabilities (King 2009). However, members of groups like SAS are not always as silent as one might expect. As the BBC's Mark Urban reports in his book *Task Force Black* (2010), individual egos and public intrigue about these elite solders and their operations leads to substantial leaking of information.

Additionally, U.S. Joint Special Operations Command (JSOC) is itself very secret, and branches within it such as the Strategic Support Services are even more hidden (see Scahill 2009). As the primary covert operations force within the U.S. military, JSOC controls covert groups like Delta Force and SEAL Team 6. According to investigative research reported in *The Nation,* the Strategic Support Branch (SSB) was created by a handful of people in the George W. Bush administration and operated "outside the military chain of command and circumvented the CIA's authority on clandestine operations" (Scahill 2009, 17). Best and Feickert (2006) note that U.S. Special Operations Command (USSOCOM) was created in 1987 as another part of counterterrorism efforts. Several other examples of these hidden counterterrorism efforts in the United States are known to exist, including the Office of Special Plans, which has been described as a "Pentagon-within-the-Pentagon," and the National Counterterrorism Center, which remains hidden amid high-rise office buildings (Schmitt and Shanker 2011, 49). Of course, perhaps the biggest example today is the ultrasecret National Security Administration, whose acronym "NSA" is described by those working there as "No Such Agency" and "Never Say Anything" (Bamford 2008). Dana Priest and William Arkin's *Top Secret America* points to the NSA as the capital of this alternative America. They describe it as a place where "many are forbidden from providing a job title in public. Most are prohibited from telling outsiders what they are working on" (160) and "silence and avoidance are everyday practices" (163).

Changes in terrorist and crime organizations (e.g., network forms, decentralization, smaller units) have also resulted in changes in law enforcement to use more flexible approaches (Kleemans 2007); indeed, it may well be that such organizations have to match their counterparts in terms of communication about one's identity as well (matching hidden approaches with equally hidden ones). Another change concerns the partnering with private organizations to secretly conduct counterterrorism work. Although there have been largely hidden organizations like the Security Affairs Association (SASA) to serve as a bridge between the intelligence and industrial communities since 1980, those partnerships have taken a different form in the so-called War on Terror. For example, Blackwater allegedly works for the CIA at hidden bases in countries like Afghanistan and Pakistan (Scahill 2009). Within it are allegedly even more secret organizations such as Blackwater SELECT.

Other secretive government organizations may extend beyond counterterrorism and intelligence to include policing and other activities. For example, Schlosser (2003) discusses the use of Drug Enforcement Agency undercover operations to identify illegal marijuana growers. Jenkins (2003) describes the secret Defenders of Democracy as a death squad trained by police and federal authorities in Puerto Rico. Kleemans (2007) describes covert policing in dealing with criminal organizations. Blauvelt's (2011) analysis of the Cheka and other secret police in the Soviet Union suggests that loyalty was maintained among members by recruiting those about whom compromising information was known—but loyalty was also provided by those in charge as long as one did his tasks faithfully. Political science professor Jacqueline Stevens (2010) found that in recent years immigration organizations have been known to hold residents in unlisted and unmarked subfield offices (or ambiguously marked ones with signs saying "Service Processing Center") in sparsely populated areas; furthermore, they may use nonuniformed agents driving unmarked vans and working in hidden offices or in office parks with no signs (even though other businesses there are fully signed). As a director of immigrant rights commented about one such detention center, "without knowing where you were going . . . it's not clear to me how anyone would find it" (14).

Other Hidden Organizations

In the opening chapter we saw several other examples of potentially hidden collectives beyond secret societies, organized crime, the informal economy, terrorist organizations, and various secret government agencies. Scholarly research on these other organizations exists—but again, rarely does it examine the hidden and secretive nature of these organizations in detail. For example, when it comes to support groups a sizable body of research exists on Alcoholics Anonymous and other twelve-step groups modeled after it, though the role of anonymity appears to rarely be a focal point of scholarly interrogation. Other work on an HIV support group in Zimbabwe observed that meetings were held in unmarked building to avoid stigma and members were like undercover agents as they lived double lives in a society where they could not disclose their illness to others outside their support unit (Engell 2011). That anonymity may also protect small and/or private foundations who wish to make gifts but do not wish to be in the public eye or easily contacted by those seeking support. The organized efforts of the Underground Railroad—which helped move thousands of slaves to freedom via cover of night, coded messages, disguises, and a network of secret hiding places—would represent another example where concealment of the organization and its members was vital. Although this informal network was at times barely organized (a fact which may have helped conceal it), the development of coded signals recognized by railroad members and not outsiders, and the establishment of helper roles (called "agents," "station-keepers," and "conductors"), was crucial to the success and continuation of this effort (Siebert 1898).

Anonymous hate groups represent another type of hidden organization. Today, many of these use the Internet to spread their views and recruit members as well as to hide certain aspects of their organizations, including the identity of their members. Considering that they have grown by over 50 percent in the first decade of this century (Hate Group 2009), they deserve examination. A conglomerate of such sites in France, for example, not only spread hate speech but also carried out attacks on people and buildings. Although the initial conglomerate was eventually shut down, most members remain unknown and have reorganized online to continue this work (see Tirreau and Kerforn 2004). Others have claimed that prosecution of organizations and their leaders has led to leaderless groups without formal organization when it comes to hate groups—though organizations may also simply change websites

and names as they continue their extremism (Selepak 2010). Although little
has been written in the communication literature about online hate speech
and hate groups, they are using online communication tools (especially visual
capabilities) to build the community of members (Barnett 2007).

Business professor and consultant Hermann Simon's *Hidden Champions*
books (1996; 2009) also reveal a whole range of formal businesses that pas-
sively or actively seek to remain obscure even as they perform quite well.
Simon's own words capture this group:

> They shy away from publicity, some through explicit policies of not dealing
> with the press—or, by the way, with academic researchers! As an executive
> of a leading manufacturer of material processing equipment said, "we are
> not interested in revealing our success strategies and helping those who have
> recently neglected their business." Another hidden champion CEO wrote,
> "We don't want to be on your list. We strongly prefer to remain hidden." And
> the chief of the world market leader in a critical component for vibration con-
> trol equipment remarked, "We want neither our competitors nor our custom-
> ers to know our true market share." The young chief of a service company
> commented, "We have cherished our anonymity for years and feel very com-
> fortable about it. Nobody has noticed our niche." (1996, 3–4)

The companies' invisible or low-profile products typically not provided
directly to consumers further allows for this. Despite the obvious importance
of their hidden nature, Simon's work more strongly emphasizes the fact that
these organizations are not megacorporations. Related to this, the Aspen
Institute notes that very small enterprises (fewer than ten employees) and
microenterprises (fewer than five employees) account for three-fourths of all
U.S. establishments and are an enduring feature of the organizational landscape (see Losby et al. 2002). "These enterprises are largely invisible or operate
at low levels of visibility" (36).

As a different type of example, front groups help the collectives behind
such entities remain hidden to various audiences. These fronts may be most
common for organizations and industries whose image is damaged (e.g., the
tobacco industry). Health scholars Dorie Apollonio and Lisa Bero (2007)
report on a case study of one such front organization: Get Government Off
Our Backs. This group was heavily funded by R. J. Reynolds to try and influence government regulation in general and smoking legislation in particular. Apollonio and Bero noted that neither scholars nor media at the time

made the links between this front group and the tobacco industry—which was unfortunate, because such attention can often help expose questionable industry links. Other scholars have noted additional front organizations for this industry (Solet 2001): The Advancement of Sound Science Coalition (TASSC) began as a tobacco industry front group and was controlled by an international public relations and lobbying company; the Center for Indoor Air Research (CIAR) tried to promote its independence, but its budget came almost exclusively from the four largest U.S. tobacco companies; and Citizens for the Integrity of Science, which may have had only one actual member and was registered at the home address of the executive director of TASSC. More recently, shadowy corporate front organizations such as the Center for Medicine in the Public Interest and Americans for Quality and Affordable Healthcare were backed by some in the pharmaceutical industry (though other backers were never clearly revealed) in an effort to defeat healthcare reform in the United States (Fang 2009). These more visible front groups help conceal the actual corporations and other interests behind their efforts, making this an important area where organizational scholars should be involved.

As another form of hiding, organizations may engage in partnerships with silent partners who remain unknown to all but the other partner(s) and have limited liability. In Japan these are known as *tokumei kumiai*, or anonymous partnerships. In such cases, the public face of the organization can be rather different than who is really behind that face financially.

Another type of hidden organization is found in U.S. politics. Boatright (2007) notes that many of the organizations organized under Section 527 of the U.S. tax code "adopted names that gave little indication of the issue focus, the partisan leanings, or the membership base of the groups" (1). His examination of these organizations suggests they act somewhat as interest groups, but also as the "shadow party" of the political party network (16). Others have noted that 501(c)(4) organizations, like 527s, may have equally unclear names and can engage in campaign activity (as long as it is not their primary activity)—and in fact attract political donors primarily because there is no disclosure of donor names (Aprill 2011).

Schlosser's (2003) work about the pornography industry reveals another type of hidden organization. In Los Angeles County alone, "hundreds of businesses in the sex trade—sound stages, editing facilities, printing plants, sex toy factories—are tucked into middle-class and working-class neighborhoods, amid a typical Southern California landscape of palm trees, strip malls, car washes, and fast food joints" (167). Business scholars Bryant Hudson and Gerardo Okhuysen (2009) have examined men's bathhouses as a core-stigmatized organization (a collective whose central outputs, processes, or customers violate social norms), finding that patrons often attempt to hide membership. Furthermore, their research found that these organizations often used discreet locations, limited signage, and other boundary management conditions—which we can describe as identity management efforts—designed to make "bathhouses nearly invisible and anonymous" (141).

Although the list of organizational types suggested here is almost certainly incomplete, we will close by mentioning one final type of organization. There is an emerging research interest in hacker—and later hacktivist (i.e., hacker activists; see Taylor 2005)—organizations, such as the Legion of the Underground, Chaos Computer Club, Cult of the Dead Cow, Phrack, and Pulhas (Denning 2001). Members of these loosely organized communities typically operate pseudonymously, because as one hacker website somewhat playfully puts it, "Their real names cannot be made public, as doing so would place them in great mortal danger"(Cult of the Dead Cow 2011, team bio page). Scholars have started to analyze these hackers as actual organizations and have found social network analysis appropriate for doing so (Lu et al. 2010). One particularly notable organization with ties to the hacker community goes by the name Anonymous and uses the image of a faceless entity to represent itself. This group lacks identifiable leaders or members, and yet names itself and seeks recognition for its efforts; there are no membership dues, pledges, charters, or official code of conduct. Yet, it still exhibits shared cultural values that allow a separation of insiders from outsiders (Underwood 2009). We will examine it in more detail in chapter 7.

Recognizable Conclusions

The research examined in each of these areas suggests several conclusions that seem to apply to multiple hidden organizations. First, it is apparent that there is substantial use of organized collective efforts in each of these areas, making an organizational analysis appropriate. Clearly, these organizations often do not follow more bureaucratic forms or other models associated with large corporations; indeed, their smaller size, more decentralized nature, and sometimes network form facilitates less visibility for these organizations.

Second, even though identity and visibility issues are not always explicit in the research on these organizations, they clearly emerge in forms such as the following: hidden locations, members, and leaders; communication about the organization and its activities is restricted to various degrees; there is a substantial use of various signs, rituals, and codes by members as enforced by the organization; the use of aliases in various forms is found; identity and reputation issues may still matter, but the goal is not always being transparent; and new information and communication technologies are used primarily to enhance connectivity while maintaining substantial anonymity.

Third, these organizations may use a variety of other organizations to help remain at least somewhat hidden. Sometimes this involves the creation of a front organization engaged in legitimate work that helps hide the primary organization; in other cases, the front organization carries out certain tasks while providing plausible deniability to its funding organization. Some organizations may partner with other established organizations for similar results, create hidden organizations within their more visible organization, or actually operate in both hidden and visible ways as a single organization.

Several other conclusions also seem to emerge. The motives for being hidden may be socially acceptable or unacceptable: providing support to a stigmatized group or spreading hate messages, protecting one's freedoms or avoiding accountability for one's actions. Recruitment takes on special significance when one cannot typically advertise openly and widely but must instead look to trusted networks for members and support. Similarly, issues of loyalty and solidarity matter greatly in these organizations, where part of that commitment typically involves not revealing information about the organization and/or its members. Additionally, issues of accurate attribution matter as organizations potentially deny responsibility for actions, falsely take credit for others' actions, and seek to pin blame on other organizations.

One final point is to take Gambetta's (2009) description of the three problems he sees as stemming from the secrecy of organized crime and then noting the relevance of that for most hidden organizations. After reviewing the research, it would seem that most hidden organizations are faced with the *communication problem* (the need to interact with known colleagues without rivals or law enforcement intercepting the message), the *identification problem* (the ability to identify organization members without being recognized by a third party), and the *advertising problem* (the inability to promote one's goods/services in traditional ways despite the need to attract interested others). These are concerns not widely addressed by research examining transparent organizations, but they are of substantial importance as we talk about shadow organizations, secret societies, organized crime, terrorist groups, secret government agencies, and several other hidden collectives. To these problems, we may also wish to add challenges related to identity, image, and reputation, which also take on different meanings as we expand our notions about organizations. We turn to an examination of these identity-related issues—along with associated areas of research on organizational anonymity and secrecy—in the next chapter.

3 Revealing Research
on Organizational Identity
and Related Issues

Without question, identity issues have become central for organizations today (see Albert, Ashforth, and Dutton 2000). Organizational identity scholars George Cheney and Lars Christensen (2001) contend that amid the explosion of communication in our world there is a growing problem with being heard; thus, many organizations have become seduced into what they call the "corporate identity game" and various professional roles have emerged to help manage identity issues in the ongoing "quest for visibility" (241). Additional pressures promoting organizational transparency and full disclosure of information also create an environment where issues of identity are highlighted. The development and manifestation of organizational identity is very tied to communicative efforts to promote (or hide) identity information. As Majken Schultz, Mary Jo Hatch, and Mogens Holton Larsen claim in their book *The Expressive Organization* (2000), "increasingly organizations compete [for customers and members] based on their ability to express who they are and what they stand for" (1).

Unlike the research about various hidden organizations that rarely comes from organizational scholars, substantial literature from fields such as management and communication have examined a range of organizational identity issues. These include work on organizational and corporate identity, branding, reputation, and image, as well as research examining the sense of identification organizational members may experience for an organization. Also included here is a smaller body of research examining issues of organizational secrecy, privacy, transparency, and disclosure as well as work on anonymity as it pertains to organizations. Finally, the work on organizational stakeholders is relevant here, given that most, if not all, of these identity constructs are ultimately negotiated via interactions with various audiences. We will explore each of these topics in this chapter, which will help provide the basis for a fuller examination of how identity is both concealed and revealed in the subsequent chapter.

Before analyzing existing research, it is important to note that much of this work reflects an orientation that identities, brands, images, and reputations can and must be managed for key audiences, which may regularly involve the clear and transparent communication of information about the organization to relevant stakeholders (and the avoidance of secrets and anonymity). As we have already argued, such assumptions may work well for some organizations but certainly not others. Moreover, identity issues arguably carry even greater relevance for more hidden organizations and their members. Crafting identities that only reveal certain organizational characteristics, communicative choices about withholding identity information, decisions about which audiences receive what messages, managing efforts by various groups to identify and hold accountable an organization, and issues related to the expression of belonging by members all point to key identity- and communication-based processes important to organizations and their members. Thus, even though the existing organizational identity literature appears to assume a rather narrow range of organizations, that research provides us with a number of very useful ideas and concepts that can help us think about various identity issues in more hidden organizations as well. The goal here is not to provide exhaustive reviews of each of these areas but rather to present general background on each. In doing so, we will borrow some of the relevant ideas as well as critique some of the current work in terms of its applicability to a wider range of organizations—all of which will inform the model presented in the following chapter.

Organizational Identity

Organizational identity is defined by management scholars Stuart Albert and David Whetten (1985) as that which is central, distinct and enduring about the collective. At its most fundamental level, questions of identity ask, "Who are we?" or "Who is _____ (fill in organization)?" Organizations traditionally identify themselves through their name, their products or services, their physical location, and/or the people they employ (see Cheney et al. 2004). Furthermore, an organization's visual identity (which includes names, logos, colors, fonts, slogans/taglines, and even architecture and product packaging) "symbolizes the organization, it provides visibility and recognizability . . . and it may enhance the extent to which employees identify with the organization" (Van den Bosch, de Jong, and Elving 2006, 140). This "quest for visibility" guiding much of the work on organizational identity assumes all collectives seek visibility. With various types of more hidden organizations that do not benefit from widespread recognition, that wish to keep membership and meeting times secret, or that seek to avoid accountability for their actions, assumptions about the quest for visibility have to be questioned.

In a complex environment, organizational identity management has focused on communicating such information consistently and frequently. Clearly, this identity construction is very much a communicative one for organizations—both in the practical sense that various communication vehicles (advertising, public relations, marketing, etc.) are used to disseminate identity features and in a broader constitutive sense where identities are constantly negotiated, shaped, and reshaped based on our many interactions with relevant others (see Cheney and Christensen 2001; Czarniawska 1997). Thus there may be both a preferred identity based on management strategies and a more emergent identity that results over time from the involvement of many others assessing the organization and who it seems to be. While this more constitutive and negotiated nature of organizational identity seems applicable to a wide range of organizations, the idea of consistent and frequent communication may actually mean something quite different in a hidden organization. In these collectives, identity information may be consistently and regularly withheld by the organization and/or its members. In other words, the identity is managed by carefully concealing some aspects or parts of the organization's identity.

Other work in this area has attempted to list dimensions of organization identity, such as intensity, complexity, content, context, abstractness, and homogeneity (see Whetten and Godfrey 1998). Although useful, such a scheme says little, if anything, regarding decisions about how *expressed* an identity will be or how *visible* it is to others—suggesting an assumption in this work that of course organizational identities would be made known to others. We will elaborate more on how organizations conceal and reveal their identities in the next chapter. For now, we note that just as individuals may hide some identities from others, so too do certain organizations.

Like individuals, organizations also have multiple identities to reflect different aspects of who they are. This often occurs when there are different views about what is central, distinctive, and enduring for the organization (Cheney 1991; Pratt and Foreman 2000). Views of organizations and identities as ultimately fragmented, fleeting, and conflicting further reinforce the utility in adopting a multiple identities perspective on organizations. These multiple identities are viewed as manageable by the organization. Management scholars Michael Pratt and Peter Foreman offer a useful framework for how multiple and sometimes conflicting identities are managed—and one that could be adapted to fit certain hidden organizations (though that was clearly not their goal). As they describe it, *compartmentalization* is when the organization and its members choose to retain all identities but to keep them separate. This could be what a criminal organization with a legitimate business front does as it keeps one identity largely secret and allows a more legitimate and legal one to be reasonably transparent. We examined other examples in chapter 2 of front groups that could fit here as well. A *deletion* strategy where some identities are abandoned could happen as a secret society with both a private and public organization that becomes more public and open to all over time. An *aggregation* response to multiple identities, where all identities are maintained and integrated together, could occur when several different aspects of an organization are all kept reasonably hidden and may even work together to reinforce that secretive nature. Perhaps several clandestine units within a larger terrorist or intelligence organization might all communicate in such ways to reinforce the hidden nature of each group's identity. But the most important point here is that organizations regularly have multiple identities; thus, it seems reasonable to conclude that some identities may be communicated actively and openly while other identities of the same organization can remain partly or completely hidden from various audiences.

Although some scholars have noted useful distinctions between organizational identity and corporate identity—which focuses more specifically on how management represents the organization symbolically to external audiences primarily through mediated channels (see Hatch and Schultz 2000)—these ideas are highly interrelated in that corporate identity efforts are typically based on underlying aspects of the organization's identity (Cornelissen, Haslam, and Balmer 2007). Management professor John Balmer (2001) distinguishes between an organization's actual, communicated, and conceived identities, noting the desire for alignment between all of these. Other influential work (Brown et al. 2006) has suggested a need to think about four related constructs: organizational identity (who we are as an organization), intended image (what does the organization want others to think about it), construed image (what does the organization believe others think about it), and reputation (what do stakeholders actually think). Similar linkages have been made in discussions of identity as it relates to branding, image, and reputation (see models of these relations in Dukerich and Carter 2000; Gioia, Shultz, and Corley 2000; Hatch and Schultz 2000, 2003; Whetten and Godfrey 1998). Thus, we briefly examine each of those areas next.

Corporate branding

In today's global arena, corporate branding has become even more important than product branding. Corporate communication experts Paul Argenti and Bob Druckenmiller (2004) note *corporate* branding is when the company itself is marketed as a brand—which the American Marketing Association defines as a "name, term, sign, symbol, or design, or a combination of them intended to identify the goods and services of one seller or group of sellers and to differentiate them from those of the competition" (368). These experts distinguish organizational identity (which asks, "Who am I?") from the corporate brand (which asks, "Who do I say I am and who do I want to be?"). "A strong corporate brand allows a firm to express itself in terms of 'who it is' and 'what it is about'" (Keller 2000, 133). Not surprisingly, company names are intimately tied to corporate brands. The name may even be a link between the company identity and its image (Muzellec 2006). Sometimes the corporate name is also the brand used for a product—but in other cases (e.g., Toyota's use of Lexus for its luxury brand) the corporate name is hidden.

The research to date on corporate branding has tended to focus on large corporations; only in more recent years has attention turned to small- and medium-sized firms (Abimbola and Vallaster 2007). Branding of the organization name has not usually examined more hidden organizations. On one hand this may make substantial sense given that such organizations wish to avoid the visibility and recognition that comes with brand awareness. On the other hand, brands also increase trust and reduce risk—which may be quite desirable to some hidden organizations. As we saw in the previous chapter, the terrorist group Hamas has something of a brand. Communication and terrorism expert Steve Corman (2011) has even argued that al-Qaeda also has a brand, but one that has become toxic (which may require rebranding). As other examples, one could argue that certain anonymous twelve-step support groups market their brand and that the Mafia represents a recognizable brand in the world of organized crime—suggesting the potential relevance of branding even among these hidden organizations.

Image

As suggested above, image in this context typically refers more to how we want others to think of the organization (projected image) and how we think others view the organization (construed external image). This makes it different from identity, which is more about who an organization believes it is. Management, communication specialists, and various other organizational members intentionally create images based on this core identity and assess their perceptions of others' views against that identity. Identity and image issues have regularly been linked to Erving Goffman's (1959) dramaturgical views about the masks we use to make impressions and the facework we engage in as we manage how others see us. Thus, the image that is presented to certain others may or may not reflect what the organization is and/or who it wishes to be. In this sense, all organizations may hide their identity or parts of it to some degree. In fact, management scholars Dennis Gioia, Majken Schultz, and Kevin Corley note that this projected image, which actually resembles corporate identity, "could be a bona fide attempt to represent essential features of organizational identity to others"; but, as they go on to argue, "projected image, however, might also encompass attempts to convey a socially desirable, managed impression that emphasizes selected aspects of identity; it could even conceal or misrepresent identity" (2000, 66). This insight is critically important, because it allows for the complete or selective concealment of one's identity as it gets communicated to others.

Image and identity experts Jane Dutton and Janet Dukerich (1991) focus more on the construed external image as what organizational members believe outsiders see when they look at the organization—describing image as a mirror for the organization. Image matters greatly because it represents our assessment of what others see when they look at the organization, which may very well encourage the organization to adapt its identity in response. Again, this is important for hidden organizations to the extent that they may adjust how their identity is or is not communicated based on perceptions of how they believe others see them (including the possibility that others are literally able or unable to identify the organization).

Of relevance to our topic, recent work has begun to examine core-stigmatized organizations, which suffer from a type of tainted image. Hudson (2008) notes that this sometimes refers to episodic events such as bankruptcies, industrial accidents, or product defects where organizations have to work hard to repair their image. However, he notes there are also core-stigmatized organizations (e.g., bathhouses, abortion service providers, swingers clubs, tobacco industry) where who they are and what they do results in a negative image that perhaps cannot be repaired. As a result, Hudson predicts these organizations will often operate as small, specialized businesses to reduce exposure to a stigmatizing audience or diversify operations into a non-stigmatized arena. Of special interest are what he calls "hiding strategies," which involve discreet locations, nondescript signage, and limited advertising. Another study of an AIDS service organization in Canada revealed that a stigmatized organization might also manage impressions to certain audiences by concealing part of its identity through promoting a non-stigmatized (non gay) board of directors, acting as professionals even though few held such degrees, and hiding stigmatizing symbols (Cain 1994). Some of the hidden organizations we have examined would seem to be core-stigmatized, making the strategies Hudson and others outline relevant to these organizations as well. Others have also suggested such stigmas sometimes produce favorable outcomes, such as when they unite those stigmatized to give them a shared identity or provide an opportunity to challenge the stigma itself (see Paetzold, Dipboye, and Elsbach 2008). Of course, much of this stigma comes from the actual assessments of what the organization does, which takes us nicely into the topic of reputation.

Reputation

Reputations are the perceptions of outsiders about the organization's core characteristics. They tend to develop and persist over some period of time rather than exist as a short-term impression (see Fombrun and Rindova 2000; Spittal and Abratt 2009). These perceptions are revealed to the organization and various others in a number of ways, such as company rankings, comments by analysts, media coverage, and feedback provided directly by consumers. A number of experts have written extensively about the importance of reputation for creating positive organizational outcomes (see review by Walker 2010); thus, it is of little surprise that management values it greatly and substantial attention has been given to attacks on or threats to one's reputation.

Economics scholar Steven Tadelis (2003) suggests a firm's name symbolizes its reputation—reminding us of the close connection between identity and reputation. Thus, negative reputation feedback can threaten one's core identity, creating great concern and high likelihood of response (Dukerich and Carter 2000). Without question, organizational members and other stakeholders will link any reputational assessments to the organization's identity(ies)—illustrating the processual nature of identity development as an organization and its members communicate with various others. Additionally, many organizations will have more than one reputation that is assessed by various audiences (see Padanyi and Gainer 2003).

Reputation is frequently linked to how well an organization communicates with others, which typically translates into being very transparent with and expressive to stakeholders (see Fombrun and Rindova 2000). Some work has explicitly linked favorable reputations to transparency, even in collectives where bureaucratic secrecy is a source of power (Moffitt 2010). What is unclear is how this reputational literature applies to organizations whose identity is so secret that few if any efforts are made to project an image to which various others might respond. Is a reputation formed at all in situations where there is an absence of identity-related communication? In the complete absence of information about the organization, there is nothing to perceive positively or negatively. But how is the reputation affected by an organization's hidden nature when we are at least partially aware of its existence? We could speculate that in societies that value openness and transparency, the lack of identifying information would lead to negative assessments of those organizations by many. Conversely, the ability of a hidden organization to successfully hide its identity from certain others could also lead to a positive reputation among those who value or benefit from that secrecy.

Identity summary
Identity, brand, image, and reputation are related ideas linked to the dynamic process of communicating the organization's identities (including the possibility of concealing those identities) to various others. Regardless of the type of organization, "who we are" is always a very relevant question—as is the degree to which we think others know who we are. However, this literature does not address degree of visibility as a key dimension of identity (a task we will undertake in the next chapter). It does examine multiple identities, which allows for the possibility that some identities of an organization are hidden even while others are rather openly revealed. Organizational branding may

not be used to increase visibility for hidden organizations, but it may still be relevant as a way to establish trust and respect with certain audiences. The image conveyed may not always match the organizational identity, and when the image is tainted, organizations may use different strategies to manage it. The organization's identity, especially as revealed in its name, is linked to reputation. Reputation is complicated for organizations that are unknown; for those where there is awareness, limited identity information may lead to negative reputations except among audiences who value the organization's secrecy.

As we have seen, organizations regularly seek to manage this entire identity/brand/image/reputation process. Sometimes this is done with what might be called "integrated marketing communications," which seeks to create a unified impression via a single voice for the organization. This, of course, can be difficult when an organization has multiple identities and/or is in a complex environment. Furthermore, communication scholars such as George Cheney have noted that "identity management is carried out not only by managers with communication responsibilities but also by rank-and-file members who identify with the organization" (Cheney et al. 2004, 126). Thus, we turn to a discussion of identification by organizational members next.

Organizational Identification

The theory and research on organizational identification commonly defines it as "the perception of oneness with or belongingness to [a collective], where the individual defines him or herself in terms of the [collective] in which he or she is a member" (Mael and Ashforth 1992, 104). When that affiliation is with a highly regarded organization, it reflects quite positively on the organizational member (though the inverse is true as well). Organizational identification scholar Jim Barker (1998) argues identification "is not just a Western phenomenon; instead, it is *a characteristic of any organizing practice*" (261, emphasis in original). Scholar Michael Pratt (1998) also contends that organizations encourage identification of their members as a key task of organizing. Without question, our organizational identification is a key part of who most of us are—revealed most clearly by how often people mention their work or who they work for in initial encounters with others. In general, strong identification has been linked to a wide range of benefits for organizations and their members.

This work on organizational identification comes primarily from two different traditions. Management scholars (e.g., Dutton and Dukerich 1991;

Mael and Ashforth 1992, 1995; Pratt 1998, 2000), usually drawing on Social Identity Theory (Tajfel and Turner 1986), have highlighted how individuals come to see themselves in terms of the organization's identity; thus organizational identity and organizational member identification are closely linked. Often the emphasis here is on a more cognitive view of identification where the focus is on a member's beliefs and knowledge about the organization's identity. Additionally, just as organizations may have multiple identities, so too may individuals have multiple identities (see Ashforth and Johnson 2001).

Some of the research and theorizing in this area has linked organizational identification to image and reputation issues. Of special relevance here is work suggesting that the link between attractiveness of an organization's image and the strength of member identification depends on visibility of affiliation. Organizational identification researchers Jane Dutton, Janet Dukerich, and Celia Harquail (1994) proposed that visible/public roles heighten one's awareness of the organization and thus typically increase organizational identification. Furthermore, when people have highly visible affiliations with an organization or there is public knowledge about that affiliation, behaviors and attitudes may more closely conform to organizational goals as part of impression management efforts—again strengthening organizational identification. What is unclear from such theorizing, however, is how such predictions might change in a more hidden organization where visibility is less normative or even restricted.

Management scholars have also paid attention to the dark side of member identification, which may be especially relevant. Janet Dukerich, Roderick Kramer, and Judi Parks (1998) are among those who have examined disidentification, apathetic identification, deidentification, underidentification, overdisidentification, and schizo-identification. Although this work tends to frame these other forms as pathological, there are also benefits associated with not being overly attached or not expressing that attachment at certain times. For example, they define *schizo-identification* as simultaneously identifying with and disidentifying with the same organization; seemingly this may provide a way to manage one's identification with a hidden organization when that identification would not be viewed favorably by others. Another important branch of this work has examined identification among members engaged in "dirty work," where the tasks have a physical, social, or moral taint associated with them. Management scholars Blake Ashforth and Glen Kreiner (1999) report that, surprisingly, some of these workers (e.g., corrections officers) have very favorable identification to at least their occupation; however, it is unclear if those engaged in the very dirtiest types of work—such as might be found in certain hidden organizations—would as proudly express their involvement. Related work suggests that in the most stigmatized occupations, members may both identify and disidentify; but, if the dirty work is central to what the organization does, stronger identification may occur as compared to organizations where the dirty work aspects are less central to the overall identity (Kreiner, Ashforth, and Sluss 2006).

The second primary research tradition examining organizational identification comes from organizational communication, where identification has frequently been traced back to the rhetorical strategies of Burke (see especially Cheney 1983a, 1983b; Scott, Corman, and Cheney 1998; Tompkins and Cheney 1983, 1985). In this view we use specific communication strategies (unified "we" terms, talking up the organization, uniting against a common enemy, statements about who we are, statements indicating one's membership or belonging, etc.) to create and reflect that sense of connection we feel. These communicative expressions are largely verbal but may also be nonverbal (e.g., wearing of company logo, items displayed with company name); they may be directed internally to others in the organization or externally to friends/family and even competitor organizations.

Especially relevant to the arguments made in this book is some of my own work, published with communication scholars George Cheney and Steve Corman, where we suggest a more situational and communication-based view of organizational identification. As we argue, the "most important indicators and expressions of identification are found in language. Thus, communicative manifestations of identification are emphasized as they occur in social interaction with others" (Scott, Corman, and Cheney 1998, 305). Thus, expressions of belonging or positive statements of membership represent important forms of member identification with the organization. Additionally, our situational view allows for strong identification displays to some audiences but not others—and in some contexts but not others. It also recognizes potentially conflicting/competing identifications given multiple organizational attachments (which are sometimes managed by expressing identification with one target instead of others).

Although generally useful to take a communication-based view of identification that emphasizes expressions of attachment, such a view is complicated by more hidden organizations. As we have already seen in earlier chapters, in some hidden organizations members may show loyalty and identification through an absence of communication, that is, by not talking up their organization or noting their membership in it. Furthermore, even though most organizations are thought to encourage—if not demand—member identification, we also know that some organizations discourage such attachment from certain individuals (for example, see Gossett 2002 and her research on temporary workers). In a similar way, it is possible that hidden organizations may manage their visibility in part by limiting the degree to which members should express identification with the organization.

Organizational identification issues do surface in some of the research on secret societies. For example, Hazelrigg (1969) suggests for secretive organizations/societies, more than others, a very strong sense of identification that is totally encompassing may be best to help ensure attachment. Discussions of related constructs (loyalty, commitment) also exist, usually reinforcing the notion that identification is key to helping ensure an organization's secrecy. Far less often has any of the organizational identification scholarship directly addressed hidden organizations—and for the most part, connections are largely dismissed. For example, identity scholars Susanne Scott and Vicki Lane (2000, 50) predict that organizational legitimacy is a prerequisite for organizational identification. While admitting people do sometimes identify with illegitimate organizations such as the Mafia or a gang, these authors attribute that to inadequate socialization (maybe driven by fear or by family pressures). Yet, across the range of hidden organizations we have already begun to discuss (many of which are not viewed as entirely legitimate by certain societal standards), identification issues would seem very relevant in describing the extent to which members feel a sense of oneness and the degree to which they express that oneness to others.

This need for identification likely applies to a wide range of organizations—though specific motives may vary. *Why* do we so naturally seem to want not only to belong to certain organizations but also to tell others about it? Michael Pratt (1998) suggests this stems from needs for safety, affiliation, self-enhancement, and more holistic (almost spiritual) goals. Extending this work to the topic at hand, desires for affiliation and safety could indeed be met by identification with less visible organizations. Identification with some secret organizations (e.g., new religious movements, various anonymous support groups) may provide for more transcendent needs, especially when those needs cannot be met by more mainstream organizations. In most cases, the self-enhancement motivation—which largely depends on others' recognition of organizational prestige—may not readily explain identification with a more hidden organization; however, if the recognition one seeks is entirely internal to the organization, then such identification based on this motive remains possible.

Identification is also thought to benefit greatly from communication with relevant others. For example, the size of one's organizational network positively influences organizational identification by encouraging communication with others (Jones and Volpe 2011). In a previous study of the Cooperative Extension Service in the United States, I found that in decentralized, geographically dispersed organizations members identify more strongly with local offices with whom they almost certainly have greater interaction than with the larger organization (Scott 1997). This could suggest some barriers to identification in a secretive organization that reduces network size and operates in smaller units that have little contact with others in the organization. We will elaborate on this idea of communicating one's sense of identification (i.e., belonging, affiliation) in much greater detail in the next chapter as we examine differences between expressed and silent forms of identification.

Anonymity, Secrecy, and Related Ideas

Ideas about anonymity and secrecy clearly link to a broader interest in issues of identity; however, terms such as these start with an assumption of concealing, rather than revealing, who we are from others. Whereas so much of the organizational identity research has focused on being visible and known, the work on anonymity and secrecy foregrounds that which is hidden and unknown. In some ways, allowing for organizational anonymity and secrecy is consistent with other work critiquing our unquestioned acceptance of ideals such as openness in organizations (see Eisenberg and Witten 1987). Indeed anonymity and secrecy may be seen as quite appropriate when they are used to protect the rights of the organization or others it serves from unjust attacks or discrimination. For example, privacy and freedom of speech may both be protected in part through anonymity. Of course, anonymity and secrecy may be viewed quite negatively when they allow an organization to escape responsibility for its actions, especially when those behaviors are consequential to others. As another illustration, we generally find it socially unacceptable for an organization to secretly use its profits to support its involvement in organized criminal activities. We examine here relevant work in these areas where it is the identity of the organization that is kept anonymous or secret.

Anonymity

To be anonymous is literally to be "without name." When it comes to anonymity and communication, I have argued elsewhere that anonymity is partly based on the degree to which a message source is unknown (Anonymous 1998)—which relates not only to knowing the source's name but also to knowledge of other identifying characteristics. Sociologist Gary Marx (2004, 2006) has offered a rather useful list of identity types that can be readily applied to organizations (even if Marx intended them for persons defined more biologically). For him, identity can be about individual identification (legal name, nicknames, ancestry, etc.), shared identification (e.g., industry, physical characteristics, demographic makeup of members), geographical/locational information (e.g., mailing address, telephone number, website URL), temporal data (when one exists), networks (e.g., partner organizations, neighboring groups), objects (e.g., equipment, communication devices, buildings), behaviors (content of communication, economic activity, etc.), beliefs/attitudes/emotions, various measurement characteristics (credit ratings, reputation rankings, etc.), pictures/images of oneself, and trace information (nonverbal and other cues that make us unique). As more identity information becomes known to others, the organization is less anonymous. Conversely, organizations we consider secret or hidden are able to conceal more of that identity information from relevant others. Clearly, names are among the first listed and represent an important indicator of an organization's identity; yet they are clearly not the only aspect of identity—which would also include various addresses, physical characteristics, beliefs, and behaviors. Although Marx's list of identity information is perhaps so expansive that it leaves little about an entity *not* linked to its identity, the broader significance here is that there is a sizable range of information about an organization that can be identifying (and that must be concealed if one is to remain hidden).

Additionally, communicative definitions of anonymity emphasize not only the degree to which the source is known but the degree to which it can be specified (Anonymous 1998). This pertains directly to differences between more circumscribed groups (within which an anonymous source is less anonymous given fewer possible source options) and more dispersed possibilities where the organizational source could be any of some rather sizable number.

Thus, a hidden organization that is one of several similar types (e.g., a terrorist group amid many terrorist groups in a region) may be less easily identified when compared to a secret organization that is the only one of its kind or the only one that could have performed a certain action.

Another aspect of the definition of anonymous communication is the *degree* of knowledge about the message source—which can range from completely anonymous to completely identified with many forms of partial anonymity in between (Anonymous 1998). Two forms of partial anonymity involve the use of pseudonymity (a false name understood to be false that is linkable to various behaviors) and confidentiality (where one is anonymous to many, but the identity of the source is known to a few who agree not to share it with others). Sometimes the partial anonymity is a function of choices made by the communicator in question (e.g., a full name with a descriptive picture is more identifying than use of a pseudonym and limited contact information, which is more identifying than no name with no published address). In other cases, the anonymity is seen in degrees because of how it is perceived by those receiving such messages (who may have other knowledge of the organization or who may vary in their skill and motivation to identify an organization). Applied to organizations, we should expect them to vary in the degree to which they are anonymous. Although Simmel (1906) notes it is possible for entirely secret societies to be unknown to all but their members, *relatively* secret societies seem more likely. We will further develop ideas about degrees of anonymity as we present the theoretical framework in the next chapter.

A few other types of anonymity deserve mention here as well (see Anonymous 1998; Bronco 2004). *Physical anonymity* is when we cannot sense the presence of a message source (e.g., it is not visible); *discursive anonymity* is when specific comments/behaviors cannot be attributed to a specific source (e.g., no name is attached to a message). Thus, an organization that cannot be seen is different than one that cannot be named—and one that is neither visible nor identifiable by name may be especially anonymous. Additionally, there is *self-anonymity* (a sender's perceived anonymity when interacting with others) and *other-anonymity* (anonymity attributed to the source when we receive a message from that source). An organization trying to be anonymous may initially assess how anonymous it feels when communicating; but the anonymity that others attribute to it may be even more important in ultimately remaining invisible/unidentified. Information and media scholar

Jacquelyn Burkell (2006) identified three distinct types of anonymity in the research literature that influence behavior in different ways. Anonymity in name and anonymity as being seen are very similar to discursive and physical types. She also describes anonymity of action, where people feel known by their actions and history of past behaviors (even if those are only connected to a pseudonym).

Models of anonymous communication have attempted to better understand communicator decisions to be anonymous and receiver reactions to that anonymity. Again, even though these focus on individual persons, they provide insights into organizational choices and reactions to those choices related to revealing/concealing identity. I have argued that any communication source can attempt to be anonymous or identified (see Anonymous 1998). Decisions to anonymize may be based on having suspect information, being in a less powerful position, having low credibility, or simply having the means to easily be anonymous; conversely, decisions to be identified are based on having power, having accurate information, high needs for recognition, and ease of being identified. These ideas start to provide a rationale for organizations who choose to communicate about themselves anonymously (including the possibility of not expressing much communication at all) and those who seek to be readily identified as they communicate about themselves. In that same work, I also examined how message receivers might react to anonymous or identified sources (either accepting or rejecting such attempts). Furthermore, I described just how effective such efforts by message initiators and recipients might be—noting that effectiveness depends substantially on the message channels used (and their ability to provide tracking information) and actual cues revealed in the message content itself.

Steve Rains and I (2007) examined receiver responses to anonymous communication in greater detail. Such responses seem relevant because they ultimately shape efforts to maintain anonymity when a communicator desires it. As we note about our model, the message receiver's perception of the sender's anonymity, potential ability to identify sender, and desire to identify sender are influenced by several factors—including whether the communication is more interpersonal or mass-mediated. We predict, for example, that anonymous sources in an interpersonal context (with more opportunities for interaction, greater interdependence, and few norms favoring anonymity) will be perceived as less anonymous, will result in greater desires to identify the source, and will facilitate greater perceived ability to identify the source as compared to an anonymous source encountered in a mass-mediated setting. By extension, an organization communicating anonymously in a more inter-personal context will be reacted to rather differently than will one commu-nicating anonymously via more mass-mediated means. In addition to noting relationships between perceived anonymity of the sender, potential ability to identify the sender, and desire to identify the sender, the model predicts the latter two elements must be sufficiently present for identification efforts to be made about an anonymous source. In the absence of ability and desire to identify an organization, positive organizational evaluations are likely to follow; however, if either ability or motivation (or both) exists to identify the organization, then the receiver's response to that collective may be more nega-tive. Although we scarcely had any hidden organizations in mind when mak-ing such predictions, the model still offers some useful ideas about how mes-sage receivers react to anonymous message sources. Ultimately the success of the secret organization in remaining that way depends in part on how able and motivated various audiences are to reveal the identity of the organization in question.

Although some of the more general work on anonymity can be linked to organizations, in general anonymity is not widely studied in this context (see review by Scott, Rains, and Haseki 2011). I and my colleagues (Scott and Rains 2005) have argued that we should pay greater attention to anonymity in organizations because of its relevance across a range of organizational activi-ties (e.g., whistleblowing and other anonymous reporting of wrongdoing, use of anonymous communication technologies, anonymous feedback systems). Consistent with this focus on anonymity for members, other work has also noted that organizations are often seeking to identify disgruntled employ-ees or others accused of anonymously smearing the company (Bronco 2004). More relevant to our goals here is the desire for organizations to sometimes be anonymous. Leaks to the media from unidentified organizational spokesper-sons/officials; use of certain names or changing of one's name to disconnect from certain actions; choosing certain media channels for interaction (e.g., anonymous corporate blog); and the absence of a physical address, online presence, and/or other key contact information can all be seen as providing a sense of organizational anonymity. Nevertheless, little work has framed orga-nizations as anonymous actors.

Not surprisingly, anonymity raises a number of important legal questions. Although a right to be anonymous is generally supported in the United States under the first amendment to the constitution (see Bronco 2004), attitudes and legal rights vary across countries and cultures. Even in the United States, it is not entirely clear if the right to speak anonymously that is part of an individual's free speech also extends to an organization's rights as a legal entity. Thus, it is informative to look at relevant law related to the function of naming. In many countries there is substantial freedom in choosing names for an organization—and even in changing names or providing services under more than one legal name—as long as the new name does not create substantial confusion or deception for the public. Legal scholar Laura Heymann (2011) notes that, despite the significance we attach to them, names are not our identity per se but more of an indicator of identity. In fact, historically they have served primarily as a reference system for others to distinguish one entity from another. Her analysis notes that similar principles apply whether discussing personal or more corporate names: "Courts hold that the fact that a person or entity holds different names at different times is not deceptive, so long as others can determine at any particular time a name's referent" (438). Overall, Heymann's work would suggest only limited applicability of naming law to most hidden organizations because most of the law only applies to commercial activity, and it actually does little to help publicly identify organizations that operate with a new name or under something other than their legal name. Closely related to this is law examining the use of pseudonyms, which are not "real" in relation to a legal name (Lucock and Yeo 2006). In Canada, for example, pseudonyms may be protected for privacy and other reasons but may at other times be prohibited or required to link to a legal name. Even determining what counts as a pseudonym (user IDs? email addresses? social insurance numbers?) and how it may differ from other alternative names (nicknames, aliases, etc.) is unclear. Although legal work in this area would seem relevant to organizations operating under various pseudonyms or aliases, those linkages have not been clarified. Though not illegal, organizations doing business under other names may effectively be using a pseudonym or alias as far as any public recognition is concerned.

Secrecy

Swedish-born ethicist and philosopher Sissela Bok defines secrecy as *intentional concealment*. What is concealed could be almost anything, including one's identity. She notes in her book *Secrets* (1982) that secrecy is morally neutral, though negative views about it are more common, which results in frequent calls to divulge secrets, reveal information, and become transparent. But, as Bok contends, "control over secrecy and openness preserve central aspects of identity" (1982, 21). Others have also noted the virtues and challenges linked to organizational secrecy, claiming "secrets and the safeguarding of secrets are necessary, if not essential, to organizational survival and competitiveness. Secrets are delicate, however, and the controlled and deliberate management of secrets poses serious leadership and organizational challenges" (Dufresne and Offstein 2008, 102).

As far as *organizational secrecy*, Bok finds it especially problematic— at least when it combines power with secrecy. Some of the work involving secrecy and organizations that Bok and others have examined has focused on protection of trade secrets, whistleblowing efforts when organizations try to keep wrongdoing a secret, leaks of secret information, selective disclosure, and other related aspects, which are not directly relevant here because the identity of the organization is not the secret. However, organizational cultures that foster secrets or are themselves generally secretive may also encourage the organization to conceal aspects of its identity from others. In other cases, identity issues are intentionally concealed. For example, Bok discusses investigative journalism that may involve disguising the identity of the journalist and his/her employer to key others; secret police who operate in very different ways from uniformed officers with openly recorded arrests and named units; and undercover law enforcement that may hide the identity of officers and organizations during an investigation. In all these cases, a legitimate and identifiable organization is behind these efforts, but that identity may be hidden to aid accomplishment of organizational goals. When it comes to secrecy and national security, keeping the identity of individuals (i.e., secret agents) and the organizations for whom they work hidden is so vital that it is usually a crime to identify covert operatives (see Sales 2007).

Rhetorical scholar Edwin Black (1988) provides a rich discussion of secrecy and disclosure as "rhetorical forms that are consciously and deliberately employed" (140). As he illustrates through common idioms, secrets are prized possessions for those who hold them and we may go to great lengths to keep them secure. We keep certain documents and certain property hidden from others. Black goes on to note that we as a society have a general dislike of secrecy but are not entirely comfortable with disclosure either. As a result, some publics respond favorably to ideas of privacy, individuality, and secrecy while others embrace values linked to disclosure, openness, and sharing.

Although he is not specifically addressing organizations, his arguments make sense at a collective level as well.

Previously we suggested that anonymity was defined in part by whether some other had knowledge of the organization (or person) communicating. Thus, organizations keep secrets in part by protecting certain forms of knowledge. Management scholar Julia Liebeskind (1997) identifies two key characteristics of knowledge: (1) it is costly to attain, so firms are motivated to acquire a rival's knowledge if doing so can reduce costs; and (2) knowledge is embodied in significant part in employees and can be moved from one organization to another by moving the members. Although she and other knowledge management scholars have not typically construed the identity of an organization as a key piece of knowledge to be kept secret, this would seem relevant to various secret organizations especially. Liebeskind notes that the type of knowledge influences how readily it might be appropriated and how easy it is to protect. Codified knowledge about an organization's identity might be easier to obtain than more tacit knowledge that would require one to be a member (or get a current member to disclose); identity knowledge that is diffused across members and/or having few individuals with full identity information can help protect such knowledge from leaking; and most legal protections (patents, copyrights, trade secret laws) generally apply to other forms of knowledge (though trademarks could apply to certain forms of identity knowledge). Liebeskind also notes that firms can use several other mechanisms to protect knowledge: rules (restricting transfer of specified information, limiting social interaction with certain others, monitoring, sanctioning), various forms of compensation (intrinsic rewards, money), and structural isolation (geographic separation, secure perimeters). Again, although the identity of the organization is not typically what such secrets are about, the challenges and solutions are relevant to organizations attempting to keep at least parts of their identity hidden.

Privacy, transparency, and disclosure

Bok (1982) and others (see Hollander 2001) have noted a close relationship between secrecy and privacy, which has gained increasing acceptance as a basic right of individuals in a number of countries. Our feelings and other personal information about us, our bodies, our property, our thoughts, and so forth are all considered to be private in that they belong to the individual (Hollander); because these are identity markers as described previously, keeping them private helps to hide who we are from others. Experts have considered several workplace privacy issues (surveillance with new technologies, protecting the privacy of individual information/data, and policies related to both), with efforts to secure employee/customer information so as to ensure individual privacy potentially being somewhat relevant to our arguments here about the revealing of member identity information. Far less scholarship has looked at organizational-level and multilevel aspects of privacy (Belanger and Crossler 2011). However, we do clearly talk about private clubs and exclusive membership organizations. We make distinctions between the public and private sectors—noting, for example, that accountability and transparency are both valued more highly in the public sector than in the private sector in a study of organizations in the Netherlands (Van der Wal, Graaf, and Lasthuizen 2008). We differentiate between privately and publicly held organizations, especially in terms of fewer requirements of the former group to communicate information publicly. Communication researcher Sandra Petronio (2002) developed Communication Privacy Management Theory, whose first principle is the tension between concealing and revealing private information (which is inaccessible to others unless a person chooses to disclose it). Although her ideas are mainly used to explain interpersonal interactions, Petronio contends the theory can be applied to group and organizational settings; indeed, it has been used to examine issues such as communication technology use and surveillance in the workplace (see Allen et al. 2007; Snyder and Cistulli 2011)—but it does not appear to have been used to talk about collective organizational decisions about disclosing identity information or decisions by organizational members to conceal/reveal information about their organizational affiliation. Thus, even though privacy research does not appear to have specifically examined how some organizations may keep information about themselves private, privacy theory and research do point to the importance of this issue for the workplace and other collectives.

Other research stands in contrast to an emphasis on anonymity, secrecy, and privacy. Two prime examples that have fairly recently become common in our everyday language are organizational transparency and disclosure. Transparency does not mean "invisibility" (because we see right through it) but refers to "the degree of openness in conveying information" (Ball 2009, 297). Don Tapscott and David Ticoll's widely acclaimed 2003 book *The Naked Corporation* argued that new information and communication technologies meant firms could no longer hide their secrets—forcing them to be more transparent (see also Rawlins 2009). Furthermore, this visibility is linked to corporate social responsibility and public relations standards requiring full information sharing. Yet, just giving out information (disclosure) is inadequate if it does not truthfully communicate information in a substantially complete way (Rawlins). Others have suggested the amount of disclosure (which is primarily about disclosing information on finances, governance, and corporate social responsibility efforts) may depend on the organization's visibility, which is partly a function of size (large organizations tend to be more visible; see Brammer and Pavelin 2004; Marquis and Toffel 2011). Again, organizations may be less visible by staying smaller in size. Needs for transparency and disclosure extend beyond the corporate realm to governments and other collectives. In addition to general policies that may promote transparency in government, in certain countries mechanisms are in place to request what could constitute identifying information from the government (e.g., the Freedom of Information Act, or FOIA); however, in the United States at least, a number of national security measures have significantly narrowed the scope of this act (allowing certain government entities to remain more hidden).

Transparency is sometimes seen as a solution to the mistrust we may feel for various organizations. Some experts report that widely held principles of corporate governance demand transparency (Bandsuch, Pate, and Thies 2008). Transparency here is perhaps different than just conveying an image to an audience; rather, there is an assumption that the organization opens itself and makes a wide range of accurate information about it accessible to relevant publics. But once again, the concerns about transparency are focused on already relatively transparent organizations when it comes to communicating about their identity—suggesting this work has not even begun to examine organizations that truly lack or have limited amounts of transparency. Bandsuch, Pate, and Thies do note that future research is needed on levels/degrees/stages of transparency since ideas such as this are clearly more continuous than dichotomous. One promising direction in this area is work on organizational self-disclosure. Corporate image experts Mary Jo Hatch and Majken Schultz introduce this concept, arguing, "At an organizational as well as a personal level, allowing yourself to be known is a risk with many rewards" (2010, 601). Even though their focus is on brand co-creation, organizational self-disclosures may include the communication of a wide range of information identifying the organization and/or its members.

Organizational Stakeholders and Publics

"There are many different audiences for an organization's identity efforts" (Cheney et al. 2004, 123). Whether discussing image management, reputation issues, brand creation, expression of identification, other anonymity, selective disclosure, or organizational secrecy, it is nearly impossible (and indeed largely pointless) to do so without considering the "other." It is always some set of others we have in mind as we create a brand and craft an image, and of course there has to be some audience who assesses our reputation, to whom we express identification and disclose information, and from whom we keep secrets and remain anonymous—all suggesting an interplay between the organization's efforts to communicate its identity(ies) and relevant stakeholders or publics. Although the terms used for these groups varies—"public," "audiences," "receivers," "relational partners"—we shall label them "stakeholders" here given the prevalence of that term in the relevant literature.

Stakeholders may be other individuals, groups, or organizations who the organization wishes to influence (and/or who influence the organization). The focus on stakeholders comes from a family of ideas referred to as *stakeholder theory* that is traced back to Freeman's (1984) book *Strategic Management: A Stakeholder Approach*. This theory contends in part that organizational decision makers allocate stakes to various stakeholder groups, interact with different groups in relatively distinct ways, and work to manage potential conflicts with and between stakeholders (see Lewis 2007). Discussions of stakeholders more generally have pointed to different types that are more and less important to organizations based on their power, urgency, and legitimacy (see Mitchell, Agle, and Wood 1997). Just considering research broadly related to identity concerns, we find discussions of several different internal and external stakeholders. For corporate businesses we see competitors, customers, suppliers, communities, employees, investors, shareholders/stockholders, trade associations, government, boards of directors, owners, managers, lawmakers, future employees, human resources, unions, police, the physical environment, and mass public opinion (see Carmeli, Gilat, and Weisberg 2006; Illia and Lurati 2006; Jaakson 2010; Miller 2010; Simmons 2008; Woodward, Edwards, and Birkin 1996); for other types of organizations we might find a slightly different list of relevant audiences. Of course, the lack of research on hidden organizations allows only for speculation, but one can imagine that some of these stakeholders would remain relevant while others might change (e.g., less emphasis on regulatory groups, more interest in other underground/secret organizations). To all but the organization so completely concealed from everyone that no one knows of its existence, stakeholders matter—and perhaps they matter even in those most hidden of organizations who take extreme care to ensure potential stakeholders do not uncover their existence.

Although work on stakeholders usually talks about specific others (sometimes unique to each organization, sometimes a priori types), one can also categorize these more broadly. For example, publics may be based on more encompassing environmental sectors: enabling (government, regulatory, and licensing agencies), functional (suppliers, employees, financial institutions), normative (trade associations, professional groups, competitors), and a diffused sector composed of community, media, and the general public (see Grunig and Hunt 1984). Distinctions have also been made between relevant and remote environments in the crisis management literature (see Egelhoff and Sen 1992). Corman, Trethewey, and Goodall's (2008) research with extremist organizations suggests that highly divided audience types are not realistic anyway when dealing with certain organizational types. This issue of audience breadth ties to observations that the size of the audience matters when dealing with secrets (Simmel 1906). Discussions of counterfeit goods have identified resistors and promoters as two broad stakeholder groups (Amine and Magnusson 2007).

It is useful to consider here some of the foundational work on publics in the public relations literature. Public relations scholars James Grunig and Todd Hunt (1984) note that there is a difference between the general public opinion of the masses (which is not really a public) and specific publics for an organization. Specific publics vary in their level of involvement, problem recognition, and constraint recognition—resulting in different types of publics that demand different levels of attention from the organization. For Grunig and Hunt, the combination of those variables results in four types of audiences: active publics, aware publics, latent publics, and none (nonpublics). Although they note that all publics are situational, we can also start to see that there is something of a continuum ranging from highly active publics that are of immediate relevance; to aware publics that may soon become active; to more latent publics who are less immediately relevant and harder to reach; and then to the diffuse nonpublics (the masses) that are harder to recognize and perhaps influence because of their separation.

In large part, multiple identities are needed to address multiple stake-holders (and multiple stakeholders may demand various identities). Identity scholars Susanne Scott and Vicki Lane (2000) note the important role of stakeholders in assessing and creating identity—suggesting for our purposes that the audience to whom one is visible (or anonymous) matters. To the extent that these identities are manageable, the organization can focus on certain key stakeholders in their efforts to make themselves more or less visible. Similarly, companies may hide certain images from certain audiences (Brown et al. 2006). We also know disclosure varies by stakeholder group (see Brammer and Pavelin 2004). In fact, some relatively hidden organizations may act as though they have few, if any, relevant stakeholders beyond a very small group from which they recruit and/or seek to effect change. Thus, organizations may hide their identity from others to various degrees based on the stakeholder. Stakeholder audience still matters to these hidden organizations in terms of who one is hiding from (and who benefits from that hidden identity) and who might be trying to identify the organization (or help ensure it remains hidden).

A Few Identifiable Observations

Although we have only touched on some of the relevant scholarly research related to these organizational identity issues, we can begin to see some repeated findings and other themes emerging here. As one might guess, most of this literature has looked at for-profit corporations. However, there has been some direct mention of the organizations we wish to draw attention to here. Though it is limited, the work on organizations doing dirty work and especially those organizations viewed as core-stigmatized are two key examples. The investigative and undercover operations where individuals may hide their identity and the identity of their employer would represent another example where identity research mentions more hidden organizations. There are several other important ideas across the literature reviewed in this chapter deserving brief additional comment.

It would be easy enough to dismiss the literature on branding, reputation, and image as simply irrelevant with more hidden organizations, but such a conclusion is likely short-sighted. These ideas are still very important for any organization concerned about identity issues—but the form of the branding and the nature of the reputation and image may be fundamentally different. Rather than seeking broad visibility, a more localized appeal seems key. Furthermore, the expression of one's image and the creation of a favorable reputation may actually depend on an image of effective concealment—and one's reputation can be enhanced by maintaining that concealment. Although organizational identification is perhaps more obviously relevant even to more hidden organizations, it too takes a different form. Rather than a focus on expressions of identification, one's attachment can sometimes be best practiced by remaining quiet about membership or other affiliation with their organization. In all these cases, the notions of silence and secrecy are present.

We should also pay attention to the likely relevance of the work on privacy, transparency, and disclosure. Even though work in this area has tended to focus more broadly on issues of governance, finances, and social responsibility, there is clear relevance to how private and public we are about other identifying information. Additionally, even though very little has looked at organizational-level privacy and organizational self-disclosures of identity information, frameworks from those literatures are likely useful for considering how organizations and their members manage these tensions.

The work in both the organizational identity and organizational identification literatures points to multiple aspects of each. The accepted notion that an organization can have multiple identities helps us understand those organizations that sometimes seem to be very hidden and in other situations clearly are not (or that have certain subunits of the organization that may be largely invisible while other elements are more visible). In fact, some organizations may manage different needs for transparency and secretiveness by essentially taking on multiple identities (some of which are hidden, others that are not). Similarly, the organizational identification literature notes that our attachments are also multiple and complex; for example, we may attach to more than one organizational identity or may experience schizo-identification when we both identify and disidentify with the same organization. Such possibilities may help us explain how members manage identifications with certain hidden organizations—especially when a member identifies with a hidden organization that is socially unacceptable or incompatible with other member identifications, or when a member identifies with one organizational identity but not another.

One of the key issues to emerge here is the importance of motivations for the organizations, organizational members, and relevant audiences involved. Individual members identify with an organization for different reasons. Although identification with a largely hidden organization may satisfy some needs, desires for self-enhancement that depend on public knowledge of one's affiliations are not well met. The work on anonymity also notes that individuals and organizations may have different motives for being anonymous, some of which are seen as socially acceptable and others which may be strongly questioned. The motives of various audiences to identify an anonymous communicator also factor into the success of efforts to uncover an organization's identity and assessments of that organization more generally. In short, the motive matters.

Gary Marx's (2004, 2006) identity work so often referenced in the anonymity literature provides some useful insights into aspects of organizational identity. It also provides an extensive list of what an organization might desire to conceal if it wishes to remain hidden. Although there is an obvious tendency to focus on names as the most revealing part of one's identity, other aspects can be very important as well when it comes to more hidden organizations: various addresses/locations, communication behaviors, pictures/images of leaders and various organizational objects, identifying characteristics, network and industry affiliations, and so forth. The more of these we can know and/or recognize, the less hidden the organization.

Across this work, we can also see that knowledge and awareness are important issues. Identity information is a type of knowledge to be protected, shared, negotiated, and even stolen. Knowledge issues are also crucial to defining one's anonymity and assessing reputation. Additionally, this literature reminds us that these identity issues are not present and absent, but rather they are matters of degree. It makes little sense to say an organization is or is not anonymous, a reputation is or is not strong, or a member is or is not identified with a secret group. Instead, all these ideas are best thought of as varying across a range of possibilities.

Finally, but not lastly, audiences matter. Especially in a communication-based view of organizations and organizing, one has to actively consider the role of various audiences in shaping identities. The relevant stakeholders and publics for some hidden organizations may be slightly different than the typical set relevant for many highly visible organizations—but there are still stakeholders that matter. Those stakeholders are either the ones assessing our reputation and trying to identify the organization or they are the ones from whom we are trying to keep a secret and maintain our anonymity (and of course, often they are doing both). The importance of relevant audiences is one of several key aspects of the framework we develop in the next chapter.

4 Unveiling a New Framework of Organizations and Organizational Regions

To this point, we have seen clear evidence of the existence of a range of somewhat hidden organizations in our society but very little research on them by organizational scholars, especially concerning their choices about keeping identities secret. Additionally, we see sizable bodies of scholarship examining issues such as identity, branding, image, reputation, identification, anonymity, secrecy, and transparency, but with almost no application of those ideas to organizations that do anything other than expend great efforts to actively promote their identities to relevant others. Consequently, it is not surprising that we have relatively few theories or classification schemes that consider organizations in a diverse sense beyond businesses and almost nothing that includes the various hidden organizations introduced in this book. As was argued in the opening chapter, given the growing importance of these hidden organizations we need frameworks and language that facilitate an expanded view of organizations and allow for comparisons across differing types of organizations. This chapter's main goal is to lay out the basics of that framework.

Even in the absence of such a framework, there are clearly calls for work that could usefully expand and compare these various organizations. Australian business scholar Kym Thorne has argued that "it is possible that a more useful and enduring alternative framework for organizations could focus on the visible and invisible aspects," suggesting "a new classification of organizations into visible and invisible organizations" (2005, 602). Others have specifically noted, with regard to secret societies, "Although it is acknowledged that research has been conducted into the evolution of individual secret societies, comparisons between these groups' evolutions is seldom considered" (Lydon 2004, 10). The strongest calls for renewed theoretical thinking along these lines comes from terrorism scholars. Abrahms (2008) says we need new, nonrational models to better understand terrorist organizations. Jones (2006) warns that organizational theory based largely on the private sector can only take us so far. Shapiro (2005) examines the design of covert organizations, noting social movement literature is not able to analyze organizational design decisions. Mishal and Rosenthal (2005) introduce a new typology of terrorist organizations to go beyond hierarchical and network structures. Noting that groups like al-Qaeda took on a global focus, while Hizballah and Hamas adhered to a more local mission, they introduce the idea of the "Dune" organization to describe al-Qaeda as a fast-moving entity that links and disconnects with local groups while creating a global effect. Yet their typology is traditionally based on specialization, chain of command/control, time definitions regarding planned implementations, and internal communication structure. "Still missing from this line of research, however, is an analysis of the topology of 'dark' networks hidden from view yet that could have devastating effects on our social order and economy" (Xu and Chen 2008, 58). As Mayntz (2004) notes, major dimensions of organization studies (including organizational identification of members) can indeed be applied to organized terrorism—leading him to conclude, "In sum, reflections on the organizational forms of terrorisms can not [sic] only direct the attention of organization scientists to a sector gravely neglected so far, but raise questions that would, if pursued, stimulate organization theory to become—again—more inclusive, and more comparative" (17).

Although we should be excited by the call for such theory, the goals of any single effort must be realistic. Consequently, we are not trying to offer the defining classification scheme for all organizations everywhere. We are not addressing a variety of issues that may be highly relevant for certain organizations and their stakeholders (e.g., profit, member satisfaction). The framework developed here is perhaps better thought of as supplemental or complementary to other established models and classification schemes. Nevertheless, it is an important reconceptualization that is potentially useful in two key ways. First, it allows for a much broader range of organizations than most other models that begin with an assumption of manufacturing/production or similar firms. As a result, it facilitates useful comparisons and contrasts across these varied collectives. Second, it brings to the forefront an issue fundamental to all organizations but not previously used to help classify them: communication of identity by the organization and its members to relevant audiences.

In this chapter, we shall develop a framework for organizations based on three key dimensions tied to the communication of identity. This effort will help us talk about types of organizations and regions in this framework where we find different organizations based on their identity efforts. At brief glance, the model offered here could be dismissed as little more than another 2 x 2 (x 2) typology of organizations. We trust that a closer read will make it clear that the relatively simplified graphic description provided is indeed only a model of something much more complex and important. After all, as we noted in the opening chapter, the need for classification and categorizing is fairly elemental and can be useful as a sensemaking framework regardless of one's metatheoretical assumptions.

Organizational sociologists Michael Hannan and colleagues provide some useful perspective and helpful language in efforts to build contemporary organizational theories—specifically noting the importance of fuzzy sets, partial membership, and even hybrids that cut across certain categories when it comes to describing organizations (Hannan, Polos, and Carroll 2007). We shall borrow a few of those ideas in developing a model that allows for partial and multiple membership rather than strict categorization. We shall also attempt to allow for greater fluidity and permeability than is found in more traditional forms of classification. Hannan and colleagues' ideas about schema development and the use of category membership criteria to group similar organizations is also useful, especially as a way of classifying other organizations not initially considered based on the relevant criteria. The framework we develop here is essentially a scheme, which they define as "a kind of model (simplification of reality) that explains for a cluster, type, or category which entities are in, which are out, and the variations between those extremes" (312). Although we do not begin with audience segments and the categories of organization they create, we will give audiences substantial attention and use some classification terminology suggested by popular discourse. Perhaps consistent with the spirit of Hannan, Polos, and Carroll's arguments, we shall not follow their logic completely in developing the theoretical framework advanced here, but we shall very loosely draw on their ideas of category, schema, types, identity, and grades of membership to move toward this expanded scheme of organizations.

Three Key Dimensions of the Framework

We can suggest here three key dimensions for analyzing sets of organizations based primarily on the existing literature reviewed in the previous chapter as it might apply to the sorts of organizations described in the chapter prior to that. We can label these three dimensions *organizational visibility, member identification,* and *relevant audience*—each existing along a continuum on which we can describe organizations as *relatively* closer to one end or the other. These dimensions begin to form the permeable boundaries that usefully create regions where we may find different organizations operating. Although the focus is on the creation of these organizational regions as defined by these three dimensions, it is often clearer to talk directly about organizations that are more or less visible, whose members are more or less identified, and whose relevant audience is more or less public. Table 2 highlights each dimension and prominent characteristics associated with the relative sides of each continuum. We turn next to an elaboration of these characteristics for each dimension.

Organizational visibility (OV)

The degree of organizational visibility concerns how recognizable or identifiable an organization's identity is. We can conceptualize this dimension as ranging from highly *recognizable* to highly *anonymous.* At its extremes, this captures those contexts that include organizations trying to be completely invisible to all others at all times and those striving to be fully visible to all others constantly. Along this dimension, it will be more appropriate to talk about organizations that are relatively more recognizable (more about the identity is revealed than concealed) and relatively more anonymous (more about the organization's identity is concealed than revealed). Google, BMW, LEGO, and others high on most reputation lists are relatively recognizable organizations; relatively anonymous collectives are those such as Navy SEAL Team 6, Skull and Bones, and the Continuity Irish Republican Army (each of which we will examine further later in the book).

Organizations that are visibly recognizable tend to disclose information about their identity or identities. They advertise, create logos and slogans, and otherwise promote their name and work (products, services, social

TABLE 2. Prominent Characteristics for Three Key Dimensions of Framework

Organizational Visibility

Relatively Anonymous	*Relatively Recognizable*
Conceal identity information	More disclosure about identity
Limited advertising or visual identity	Advertise, use logos and slogans
Little use of name; low name recognition	Promote name for high name recognition
Use of front names/pseudonyms	Advance mission/vision statements
Discreet locations with limited signage	Linked to known physical location
Lack contact information	Provide contact information
Conceal partner info, other demographics	Share links to partners and demographics
Limited use of identifying pictures/images	Pictures/names of leaders
Limited online information about identity	Established and revealing online presence
Use of channels that help conceal	Use of channels that make visible
Seek deniability for actions	Seek credit for actions
Smaller organization in size	Somewhat larger organization in size

Member Identification

Relatively Silent	*Relatively Expressed*
Fail to acknowledge membership	Proudly stating organizational membership
Little "talking up" or use of "we" language	"Talking up" and "we" statements
Do not talk about mission/vision	Know and can recite mission/vision
Avoid providing organization's name	Name organization easily/quickly
Limited sharing of website and contact info	Share website and other contact info
Keep quiet about organizational decisions	Express decisions in organization's favor
Neglect to defend organization	Defend organization when attacked
Lack of nonverbal displays (mugs, etc.)	Nonverbal displays (clothes with logo)
Lack of knowledge about identity	Knowledge of identity to share

Relevant Audience

Relatively Local/Limited	*Relatively Mass/Public*
Smaller, more immediate, better known	Sizable, more diffuse, less familiar
Local reputation matters more	General reputation matters more
Local media, interpersonal more utilized	Major mass media more utilized
Fewer resources given to public relations	More resources given to public relations
Activities relevant to a smaller stage	Activities played out on larger stage
Easier to promote identity but harder to hide it from these close others	Challenging to promote identity to all but easier to hide it from masses
Members interact mostly locally and organization operates mainly locally	Members travel more widely; organization operates in diverse locations
More definitive stakeholders	Less definitive stakeholders

actions, etc.) as part of their branding efforts. This is likely the result of a conscious effort by marketing and communication professionals tasked with responsibilities for managing the organization's identity and its related products/services. These organizations often have strong name recognition as a result. These visibly recognizable collectives may advance mission statements and other language that publicly states who they are and what they value. We would regard them as very transparent, at least about who they are and what they do. Typically, these visible organizations are linked to a known physical place or places, complete with mailing address and other contact information. Other identity markers we might expect to be clearly communicated could include industries and professions to which they are linked, demographics and other data about the organization (founding date, number of locations, number of members, sales figures, etc.), and pictures of the organization (key leaders, good/services, significant rituals, etc.). They also likely have an established website belonging to them that locates them online. They may use various other communication channels that easily tie the message to its source. This recognizability is also frequently correlated with greater size, which helps make the organization more visible because of the number of members/employees, active production of goods/services, and efforts to devote significant resources to identity management concerns. Furthermore, these relatively recognizable organizations are ones that seek credit for their actions and who presumably believe they benefit greatly from this visibility.

Conversely, more visibly anonymous organizations tend to conceal information about their identities. They fly under the radar or work behind the scenes, rendering them largely or completely unrecognizable. Here you are far less likely to see resources devoted to extensive advertising, creation of visual identity, or promotion of names and products as these organizations often lack marketing and public relations functions in a traditional sense. In some cases a name may be known or linked to an organization, but relatively little else is known about who the organization is or what it values. In other situations, a name may be a front or a pseudonym for the anonymous organization controlling the more recognizable one. In still other cases, no name may be readily known at all. In all these scenarios, name recognition for an anonymous organization is often relatively low. Here we may find other concealment strategies such as reduced signage and discreet locations. Indeed, these anonymous organizations are not easily linked to a physical address, may lack readily available contact information, and may include little or no online presence locating them on the Internet. These anonymous collectives are more likely to conceal the following: demographic data about the organization; pictures and images of organizational leaders, members, and significant events; partner organizations; and certain organizational activities they wish to keep private. Also, they may use communication channels that do not necessarily record or document information about the message source. These organizations may promote their valuing of secrecy; but, for a variety of potential reasons, they do not actively publicize most of their work or activities. They are more anonymous because they are typically smaller in size—which both attracts less attention and makes keeping secrets somewhat more possible. Furthermore, anonymous organizations avoid being linked to their actions and thus maintain deniability while minimizing accountability. They would lack much of the transparency about their identity that we see in more visibly recognizable organizations. In all likelihood, these organizations believe it is beneficial for them to be anonymous.

Within this dimension of organizational visibility, it is also necessary to discuss the motivations behind an organization's choice to communicate identity in ways that make it relatively recognizable or relatively anonymous. Motivations may vary in organizational efforts to be relatively recognizable—ranging from narcissistic obsessions about the organization's image to genuine goals to better serve others by being easily accessible—though we shall concentrate less on those here. In terms of drivers related to being more anonymous, the research literature suggests motivations based broadly around protecting one's identity so that views can be openly expressed without concern of retaliation versus hiding one's identity to avoid accountability for one's actions. Some organizations are relatively anonymous because they lack resources to communicate identity or otherwise do not know how to do so. These motivations suggest an organization that may wish to be more recognized but is unable to accomplish that (since this is not a strategic choice to be anonymous it is of less relevance to us here). In other cases, an organization may not have a clear identity to communicate. This could be a result of inadequate attention given to clarifying who the organization is (e.g., a startup organization that is still discovering itself or an emergent grassroots collective that has not settled on its core characteristics) or a strategically ambiguous effort to keep the organization's identity hidden by never clearly establishing what the identity is.

Other motivations are more straightforward. Some organizations may simply see little or no need to communicate identity to others because there is no value in doing so (e.g., an isolated business not linked to others in meaningful ways or one whose stakeholders do not care about its identity). Other organizations may be motivated to conceal their identity(ies) as a means of protecting themselves from harm or protecting those they serve from harm (e.g., a shelter for victims of domestic violence). Some organizations seek anonymity because they are embarrassed/ashamed of what they do (which may be seen as socially unacceptable activity) or in an effort to avoid accountability (e.g., organized crime avoiding law enforcement). As these examples suggest, it becomes easy to imagine several different motivations for not communicating one's identity—and such attributions matter because we may evaluate the organization quite differently based on this.

Additionally, it is important to remind ourselves that an organization may have more than one identity, so this sort of evaluation becomes relevant for each identity. For those organizations where recognizability is always key, we might expect all identities to be promoted and made visible; conversely, for those where the identities of the organization are all kept anonymous, you might see consistent efforts to conceal identity. The more interesting (and more difficult to classify) organizations are those where some identities are relatively recognizable whereas others are more anonymous (e.g., organizations with both legitimate aspects and criminal operations).

Another important issue here is to consider whether this visibility, and any determinations of recognizability or anonymity, are best thought of as goals of the organization or assessments by relevant audiences. The short answer is that both the organization and its audiences are critical to this, and we shall examine the audience in greater detail as a distinct third dimension in the framework being proposed. Having said that, for analytic purposes, we shall begin by talking about organizational visibility as the organization's strategic efforts to either reveal or conceal its identity to various degrees. This is a reasonable starting point because it is the organization that consciously makes choices about what to reveal and what to conceal, and we would be writing a rather different book here if the focus was primarily on those organizations where various audiences consider the organization to be recognizable or anonymous regardless of the organization's intentions. Before examining the audience in greater detail (and the obviously dynamic nature of organizational visibility), we turn to a second dimension where audience will also matter.

Member identification (MI)

This dimension is concerned with the extent to which organizational members actively express a sense of connection to, affiliation with, and/or oneness with the organization. As noted in the previous chapter, identification here refers to a perception of belonging where organizational members view themselves as one with their organization (Mael and Ashforth 1992). For identified members, their identities become highly congruent with one or more organizational identities. Although organizational identification has typically been examined as an individual-level construct, we can also talk about the general identification levels of an organization's members as a way of continuing to talk about the organization. This is not to discount some individual choices about how one identifies; but we regularly see similar levels of identification across organizational members, which allows us to talk about member identification at a higher level of analysis. This aggregated identification of members matters because it becomes another way in which the identity of the organization is revealed or concealed through talk and other behaviors of its members.

Important to the framework developed in this chapter, the emphasis here is on more communicative/behavioral forms of identification as opposed to cognitive ones. This is not to say that cognitive views of organizational identification are not important, but rather to emphasize that the key for helping distinguish hidden organizations from others has to be more concerned with expressions of that identification. Behavioral/expressed identification is often aligned with a cognitive sense of identification where members feel a sense of oneness and belonging. In many organizations, we would expect that as a typical representation of identification (I feel identified, so I communicatively indicate that to others); however, such alignment does not necessarily hold in certain hidden organizations, where expression of identification could actually represent disloyalty if one is not supposed to reveal membership in the collective to others. In other cases, one is silent about their identification even though they may actually feel the connection. In some hidden organizations (e.g., the Mafia), this silence may reflect an appropriate manifestation of identification. In other cases where the organization's reputation is questionable or the image is stigmatized, a member may not wish to actively display their belonging to the organization. Of course, sometimes a lack of expressed identification occurs because there is no cognitive identification either (what we might call *disidentification*) and it is possible to fake identification by expressing something that is not felt (which we could call *misidentification*);

however, we shall be somewhat less concerned with these latter two forms. Thus, the focus with this dimension is on the expression of or silencing of organizational members' identification (where both extremes of communicative/behavioral identification can actually reflect strong feelings of oneness or belonging).

We can conceptualize this dimension as ranging from very *expressed* to very *silent* identification. At its extremes, this captures those organizations whose members express full identification with the organization at all times as well as those organizations whose members remain completely silent about their level of organizational attachment to all others at all times. Of course, it will be more appropriate to talk about organizations whose members' identification is relatively expressed (more about organizational member attachment is revealed than concealed) and relatively silent (more about organizational member affiliation is concealed than revealed). Royal Dutch Shell, Scientology, and most small businesses (e.g., Jackie Evans) and nonprofits (e.g., Any Baby Can), each of which we examine in this book, represent organizations where members are relatively expressive of their identification. We will also examine the Ku Klux Klan, Earth First!, and a set of men's bathhouses as examples of organizations where members are usually more silent about their affiliations.

Expressed identification is characterized by members proudly stating and acknowledging their organizational membership. They may engage in "talking up" the organization, using "we" statements, and reciting the organization's mission/vision or other identity statements as an indicator of their oneness with the collective. They can and do name their organization easily; in fact, it may be one of the first things they mention when meeting someone new. Of course, it is not just the name of the organization that may be shared, but the members may readily know and share other identifying information: website and social media, physical address, phone number, and other contact information that might be found in an email signature block or organizational business card. Expressed identification may also be linked to efforts to verbally defend the organization when it is attacked or insulted by others. This expression of identification can also occur nonverbally as members communicate their attachment through wearing of company clothing, display of work-related photos, use of bumper stickers or coffee mugs with the organization's name/logo, and so forth. Furthermore, the ability to express identification assumes at least some knowledge of the organization—its identity, its goals, its values—so that members not only make assessments of alignment but also have concrete information to share as they talk about their organization.

Conversely, more silent forms of identification can be part of an effort to keep the organization and/or its members hidden from outsiders. For various reasons, members here fail to mention or acknowledge membership and may regularly avoid providing the organization's name. This could take the form of omission, denial, provision of false membership information, or even actual ignorance of the organization with which they are linked. Their public statements to others about what they do will focus on things other than particular organizational memberships or will provide relatively little information about the organization. We would not expect revelation of identifying information (organizational addresses or other contact information) and are less likely to even see anything like an email signature file or business card. We are also less likely to see any talking up of the organization, use of "we" statements to talk about the collective, verbal defense of the organization when attacked, or repeating of organizational mantras. These members may act in ways that do not overtly promote the organization or seem detached from it. This more silent expression would limit nonverbal indicators: little or no wearing of identifying clothing or visible body art usually associated with the organization, no mugs or bumper stickers or other items indicating one's membership to most others, and so forth. Finally, this silent identification may also be facilitated by a lack of full knowledge about the organization and its identity—making revelation of any secrets by members that much more difficult.

Just as organizations have multiple identities to which members may attach, so too do the organizational members have multiple organizational identities. Though that work on multiple identification targets (see Scott 1997; Scott, Corman, and Cheney 1998) has typically examined competition and compatibility between organizational versus other related targets (workgroup, profession, various social identities), we can also talk about members actively expressing identification with one organizational identity (e.g., the public face of some secret society) and remaining relatively silent about their identification with another identity of that same organization (e.g., the more backstage, private identity of that secret order). Schizo-identifications where we may both express identification and be silent about our attachment are also possible, though perhaps less likely except for those organizations with diverse identities. These cases where member identification is both expressed and silent are potentially most interesting and quite problematic.

The motives for this expression or silence surrounding members' identification may vary substantially, just as we saw with the organizational visibility dimension. As we discussed in the previous chapter, identification stems from needs for safety, affiliation, self-enhancement, and more transcendent goals (see Pratt 1998). Expressions of identification may further reinforce many of these same needs for an organization's members. Perhaps more relevant here is a focus on motivations for not expressing one's identification, or silencing of that attachment, especially considering the lack of prior attention to this issue. In some cases, we see this lack of expressed identification as a result of members who are not sure how to express their belonging or who lack resources and opportunities to do so. Although such examples do exist, especially for those who may be more socially awkward or who lack a network of others with whom to communicate, these explanations do not reflect a conscious choice to remain silent (and may actually be better described as situations where the members wish to express their belonging but lack the capacity to do so). Related to this, in some organizations members may not be sure how they feel and thus are silent because they are not yet clear if they wish to communicate their identification to others.

Other motivations reflect a more strategic choice on the part of the organizational members to keep silent (or express) their identifications. In some organizations, there may not be a felt need for members to express identification; consequently, a silencing exists because there is no value in stating that belonging. In what is likely a larger motivation, some organizations' members may silence their identification as a means of protecting either themselves or their organization. If we think we might be retaliated against or otherwise attacked for an affiliation, or if we think admission of membership could somehow damage our organization (perhaps by revealing it), then we will keep this information concealed. The opposite side of that same coin is the motivation to avoid accountability or embarrassment about being affiliated with an organization that is perhaps seen as doing something or being something illegal, immoral, or at least nonnormative. Silencing can actually help distance us from something we know or fear others will find unacceptable. Again, we see the tension between motivations to protect ourselves from unjust attacks versus motivations to avoid responsibility for our actions, both of which can be found in more silent forms of member identification.

Finally, just as we saw with the first dimension, it is difficult to talk about member identification without also discussing issues of strategy and audience. We do wish to view identification as a choice that the organizational members make, even if it is a collective one (or at least one that is very similar across organizational members). There may be some less strategic motivations that result in silent or expressed attachment, but the most relevant issues here are those decisions about how much or how little to express belonging, membership, affiliation, and attachment with the organization to others. But a decision to view member identification as a strategic choice here does not minimize the importance of the other, that is, the audience. We turn to this third dimension of the audience now.

Relevant audience (RA)

Our discussions of both organizational visibility and organizational member identification have already made it apparent that a consideration of relevant audience is vital. In thinking about identity construction as a communication process, we have to realize that an organization's identities are a function of both its own efforts (who it believes it is, how it wants to be seen, and the communication strategies then used to try and accomplish that goal) and the various stakeholder groups evaluating it (who are considered when constructing an image, who assess an organization's reputation, and whose feedback about the identity is critical to the organization). It is difficult to even discuss visibility without considering the audience as a huge part of the organization's efforts to be recognizable or anonymous. Questions of visibility, recognizability, and anonymity demand that we ask, "Visible to whom?" "Recognizable to what groups?" "Anonymous to which audiences?" and "Hidden from whose view?" That degree of organizational visibility may not be the same for all observers. This is because organizations may be more or less revealing based on the most relevant audiences. As the models of anonymity described in the previous chapter suggest (Anonymous 1998; Rains and Scott 2007), the message receivers are crucial to the success of one's attempts to even be anonymous or recognizable. We adjust our identity strategies, sometimes extensively, based on audience feedback about name recognition, reputation assessment, or ability to recognize us when we are trying to remain anonymous. Thus, a communicative process is implied here in the strategic considerations about relevant audiences.

Just as we saw with our first dimension, an organization's member identification decisions are also made with audiences in mind and are dynamically influenced by actions and reactions from relevant stakeholder audiences as well. As I have argued elsewhere (Scott, Corman, and Cheney 1998), our identification efforts are a dynamic process that partly involve what we are doing and with whom we are interacting. As we express identification, we express it to others. As we keep our attachment silenced, we avoid or limit expression to certain audiences. Later decisions about how much to reveal or conceal about our identification as organizational members is constantly being influenced by audience reactions, changing societal norms, and more immediate levels of attention and focus given to the organizations of which we are a part. Clearly, we may express our identification to an internal audience differently than we might to an external one. We know some organizations have cultures where members can talk about their work and the company to some groups (e.g., family) but not to others (e.g., media). Thus, member identification—even in its more silent forms—is a communicative process that has to consider the relevant audience(s).

While it is clear that audience is highly relevant to our discussion, it is equally apparent that this audience dimension is perhaps the most difficult to adequately define. If one were really going to talk about a complete analysis of relevant audiences for organizations, we would have to turn in greater detail to the relevant work from stakeholder theory, public relations, relevant environments, and other research that has examined those with whom an organization interacts. Doing that for hidden organizations would demand additional effort. The notion of audience is truly multidimensional and could be characterized in many different ways. However, given our focus here on providing a framework to compare and contrast different organizations in terms of how they and their members communicate identity to various audiences, we need a continuum that contributes to that goal by differentiating organizations broadly rather than one that attempts to provide a complete picture of relevant stakeholders/publics/audiences. Thus, we can define audience here as the set of message receivers who either assess organizational visibility or from whom the organization's identity is hidden, and to whom one either expresses their organizational identification or from whom one conceals that belonging and attachment.

Amid the many potential ways to characterize the audience continuum, it is most useful here to describe a dimension ranging from a more mass/public audience to a more local/limited one. *Mass/public*, or just *mass* as a term we can use here, refers to usually sizable audiences that are broader and more diffuse in nature (e.g., European consumers, citizens of an entire country, potential recruits from across the globe). This would include what we often refer to as the general public and public opinion. For organizations whose most relevant audiences are more public, general reputation really matters as something to be promoted or hidden. Consequently, these organizations must pay greater attention to the mass media, especially national and international media, as a way to control one's identity communication. They must also devote organizational resources—which could include communication professionals with such expertise, a sophisticated online operation, and so forth—to communicate or conceal who the organization is and what it values to a broader audience. The organization's activities and work play out on a larger stage when their most relevant audience is the broader society and the public at large. It is not that these organizations do not have or value other audiences, but the key is that they are also attempting to communicate (or conceal) identity to this larger audience—which in turn influences the organization's identity. Getting knowledge about an organization's identity to a mass audience—and making it resonate when one seeks to be known—can be a real challenge. But it is worth it to some organizations, because the more people in the audience who know about an organization the more recognizable it becomes. Conversely, hiding one's identity from such a large and diffuse public may be more easily accomplished given the difficulty of such an audience becoming familiar with an organization (especially one wishing to hide who it is).

Turning to member identification, members may express (or remain silent about) their belongingness and oneness with a more mass/public audience when they communicate with strangers in public, interact about the organization to the media, and talk about their affiliations and membership in the organization to a range of others outside their immediate family and friends. In cases where a member may travel widely, interact with the media regularly, or come into contact with a diverse range of others, the relatively more relevant audience for these organizational members is a mass/public one. A mass audience may become more relevant for organizations that operate in multiple and more diverse locations or when their members come from a wide range of locales. Finally, in many cases, these audiences are both difficult to reach and or to clearly place boundaries around, at least relative to more local or limited ones. Expressing identification with an organization to a mass audience is likely to be difficult, even though doing so helps make identity more widely known. This effort may benefit greatly from the use of communication technologies (e.g., social media) that afford organizational members an ability to widely convey their identification. Conversely, hiding one's identification from such a diffuse public may be more easily accomplished given the difficulty of such an audience becoming familiar with the attachments of organizational members (especially ones wishing to hide such information).

At the other end of this continuum are what we might label more local/ limited audiences. These audiences are often smaller and consist of more immediate others (e.g., members of a small industry, a town or community, friends and family). These organizations whose primary audience is a more local one may not have a public reputation to manage (only a local one)—which may be easier when it comes to establishing a reputation and getting known locally but harder in efforts to hide identity knowledge given the close proximity. Indeed, other work we have already discussed notes that motivated and skilled audiences, which we can speculate would be more local and immediate to the organization, are better able to identify anonymous messages (Rains and Scott 2007)—making it especially difficult to maintain anonymity amid that audience. When a more local audience is most relevant, only the more local media have to be managed when it comes to communicating identity, which may allow for fewer resources to be devoted to interaction with such audiences (limited public relations staff, limited online efforts, etc.). Furthermore, local/limited audiences likely allow for greater interpersonal/nonmediated interactions. The activities and work of these organizations matters most to the specific communities in which these organizations operate. It is not that these organizations dismiss a more mass/public audience, but their primary audience is simply a more proximate one. For the organization, this more local audience represents a different type of stakeholder than is found with the mass audience—potentially one that has greater power, urgency, and legitimacy in several situations (Mitchell, Agle, and Wood 1997).

Similarly, when this local audience is most relevant, members may express (or remain silent about) their organizational attachment relatively more to close family and friends, others in the organization, or to proximate community members. These members likely come into less contact with strangers/outsiders or national/global media. We would expect a more local audience to be most relevant for organizations that operate in one or very few places or who are structured in ways that isolate members or sub-units from others in the organization. Local audiences are typically more recognizable as distinct publics and may be more immediately relevant to the organization and its members. The communication channels used to express identification to local audiences are more likely to be more interpersonal and nonmediated.

As we have discussed previously, multiple identities and multiple identifications are often a strategy to reach different audiences or a response to the varied demands of those different publics. A single organization may have some identities or organizational units (subsidiary organizations, front organizations, covert forces), who primarily care about a relatively local audience, and other identities or aspects who manage communication about who they are to a relatively more mass group of others. Organizational members are similar in that some identities may get expressed to or withheld from a very local audience whereas other aspects of who they are get communicated to or concealed from a much more public set of others.

Although it is important to include the relevant audience here, we do not wish to hide the fact that this framework still privileges the strategic choices of the organization and its members over actual audience perceptions and reactions to the communication of identity. Even with the relevant audience as a dimension, the framework being advanced here is still focused on the organization's view (and the view of organizational members as a set) of which type of stakeholder is relatively more important in its communication efforts about identity. We are not examining the audience's actual assessments of reputation or the public's ability and motivation to identify a hidden organization. In several ways this restricts our ability to fully understand the processual nature of identity communication by organizations and their members to these various audiences, because we do not actively consider the audience as a co-communicator in what is ultimately a recursive process of identity construction. Terrorism scholar Philip Jenkins (2003) makes a convincing argument that terrorism and terrorist organizations are social constructions involving audiences as they interpret official reports, media coverage, and other rhetorical information about these organizations and their acts—and the essential role of consumers and other audiences for these messages is a clear reminder that social constructivist views are quite relevant in our efforts to understand hidden and more visible organizations. These are limitations to which we return in the final chapter.

Eight Regions and Four Categories of Organization

If we combine the three continua just described into a multidimensional space and look toward the ends of each, we can begin to describe eight organizational regions. These regions reflect differences in how organizations and their members communicate their identity to relevant audiences. We can also use them to describe different organizations that tend to regularly operate in certain regions. We shall use the term "region," which reflects more of a general space where similar organizations might be located, rather than "type," which connotes something more fixed and less permeable.

Figure 1 provides a graphic representation of this framework. Again, for organizational visibility (OV) this continuum is labeled as recognizable (R) or anonymous (A) at its endpoints. For member identification (MI), we have described expressed (E) and silent (S) forms at the ends of this continuum. Finally, for relevant audience (RA), a distinction is made between more mass/public (M) and more local/limited (L) message recipients. Halfway between each endpoint is a middle that helps depict the relative position of anything placed along that continuum (allowing us to talk about relatively recognizable or relatively anonymous, relatively expressed or relatively silent, and relatively mass or relatively local). At the approximate intersection of these relative positions along the three dimensions, we get eight unique regions that we shall describe with much greater detail in the following three chapters. For now, we simply label them as Regions 1 through 8 and indicate their relative positions along each of our three dimensions.

Although all three dimensions are clearly important, they are not equal in the degree to which they make an organization more or less hidden. We shall take the view here that organizational visibility is the most critical dimension, since this reflects the organization's strategic efforts to gain recognition or anonymity for itself. The goal-driven efforts of the organization and the allocation of resources to help reach those identity visibility goals make this dimension the most consequential of the three. Slightly less important are the expressions by the organization's members about their own belonging and membership. Although this communication about member identification

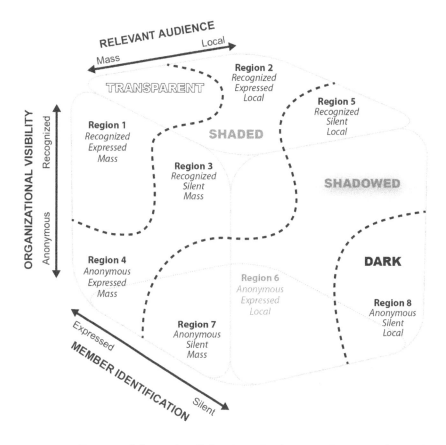

FIGURE 1. Framework for Regionalizing Organizations Based on How They and Their Members Communicate Identity to Relevant Audiences.

could come from multiple sources, even the collective voice here says less about how hidden or revealed the organization itself is as compared to the organization's visibility. Finally, we know audiences are vital to the communication of identity, but the distinctions between more mass/public and local/ limited audiences are less important than the other dimensions here. Consideration of a relevant audience by the organization and its members is of secondary importance to actual efforts to be recognizable and expressive or anonymous and silent about the identity itself. Based on the relative importance of the dimensions, we can number these regions in order from the least to the most hidden.

As an additional way to describe these regions and to compare them to one another, we shall examine four categories of regions (and of organizations fitting in them). In doing so, it is useful to consider these combinations in terms of a light absorption metaphor, which uses terms like "transparent," "translucent," and "opaque" to describe the amount of light that passes through or is not absorbed by an object. Such a metaphor helps to emphasize the extent to which we can *see* the organization and the extent to which its characteristics are reflected or revealed. In terms of the work here, this refers to identity-related communication being shared by the organization and its members to relevant audiences—is it open and apparent for all or is it hidden from relevant others? Is such core information visible and thus made widely available, or is it masked and kept shielded from key stakeholders? Building on others who have used this metaphor to describe organizations (see Carpenter and Stajkovic 2006; Kanter and Fine 2010), four categories are examined here: transparent, shaded, shadowed, and dark. They are distinguished in Figure 1 with the curved dashed line loosely encompassing certain regions in this framework.

Transparent suggests the organization and members are known substantially and widely. Transparency is already a familiar term in some of the research about organizations, secrecy, and disclosure. We use it in a slightly more specific sense here to describe regions and organizations where the identity is communicated openly to a large audience. In this extreme, organizations are recognizable, members actively express their identification with the organization, and all this is done for a mass/public audience. Region 1 is the only one we would categorize as transparent—though it is a sizable region in terms of number of organizations operating there and scholarly attention received.

Dark, at the other extreme, describes a region where organizations and their members are substantially or completely hidden from all. Dark is also a term found in popular and scholarly terms such as "dark networks." Here the organization remains anonymous, members keep silent about their affiliation with the organization, and all this is done even with a more local/limited audience that is much closer to the organization. Region 8 is where we find dark organizations. This region may be less populated (though knowing that with certainty is difficult), but it is very deserving of attention given how little we know about what may be very consequential collectives operating here. Chapter 5 will examine both of these extremes.

Shaded describes a category of regions distinguished by the existence of enough light to help make the organization and/or its members viewable or known, but with some identity elements remaining shielded and less visible. The terminology here is once again consistent with other usage that references shady operations or shady businesses that are not completely open. The shaded regions are similar to transparent regions along any two of the three dimensions in our proposed framework, but not all three. Regions 2, 3, and 4 are all shaded based on this categorization, which we will examine more closely in chapter 6.

Shadowed regions are characterized by much less visibility and familiarity. Here much is obscured from clear view—but certainly not all. This, too, is a term we see in popular and scholarly use (shadow economy, shadow workers). Shadowed regions share only one dimension in common with the transparent region and are similar to the dark region along the other two dimensions. Regions 5, 6, and 7 are categorized as shadowed. We will examine this category and regions and organizations within it more closely in chapter 7.

Exposing a Few Caveats

Before we start examining the various categories and regions and organizations primarily fitting in each, several important caveats are in order. First, Figure 1 likely implies more division and clarity than is often the case. Because each dimension is continuous, the edges of every region—and thus the borders of the various categories as well—are likely quite blurry. The extremes are distinct and clear, and we can say with reasonable confidence that each of the eight regions proposed here is generally distinguishable from other regions. However, we must also recognize that few organizations are located at the extremes of these dimensions. Determining a relative position along any of these continua may prove to be more an art than a science—a problem magnified when trying to assess relative position along all three continua simultaneously. Even though we have discussed several characteristics of relatively recognized/expressed/mass and anonymous/silent/local anchors, we have said much less about which characteristics are most important.

Taking the organizational visibility dimension as an example, we would often expect an organization that brands itself and seeks strong name recognition to be one that also widely shares contact information and publicizes its leaders and accomplishments. Those organizations are easy to place along this dimension. But some organizations may share contact information and post pictures of leaders but do little to actively brand themselves or seek high name recognition—or an organization's name may be readily recognizable but little else about its identity is known. These organizations are much more difficult to position, especially in the absence of relative importance of the various qualities that characterize recognizability versus anonymity. The provided descriptions offer guidance on positioning, but more sophisticated exploration will be needed to better understand which features most contribute to a sense of recognizability and which are most strongly linked to levels of anonymity (a topic we will examine in the concluding chapter).

Related to this concern is the variation even toward the extremes of each dimension. A public audience that is global may be substantially further down the continuum from a nationwide audience, even though both represent mass audiences. A relevant audience limited to a highly select group of potential customers in a small Japanese community may also be much more localized than a relevant audience that includes a multicity region in Central Italy, even though both are relatively local/limited. As another example with the member identification dimension, expressed identification includes those who shout and proclaim loudly as well as those who more subtly display their membership to others. On the other end of the spectrum we get identification that is never mentioned to anyone as well as instances where it is only whispered to a few. Again, the provided descriptions offer guides, but substantial variation exists along these dimensions. All this should further reinforce the understanding that these regions are fuzzy and best considered not in strict terms but relative to other regions.

Although it is useful to attempt to generally position organizations in various regions as displayed in our proposed framework, the fluid nature of organizations and their identities makes this goal even more difficult. We may be able to talk about a primary or dominant region in which an organization generally operates, but we must allow for several qualifications that shift how the organization and its members communicate identity to various audiences in various situations. In this sense, it makes sense to talk about organizations that float within and across regions, hybrid organizations found in more than one region, and boundaries on dimensions that subtly adjust themselves for various reasons. In keeping with our light metaphor, organizations are perhaps usefully viewed as chameleons that change their communicated identities to either blend in or stand out, as adjustable lights with dimmers that allow them to readily vary levels of darkness and brightness, or perhaps even as slow-flashing beacons that sometimes seem dark and at other times appear to be quite transparent.

We can talk about four situational variations common to organizational scholars that help illustrate this fluidity and movement. *Microsituational* variations occur as we interact with others and assess what best serves the goals of the organization and its stakeholders. In everyday interactions, certain organizational identities may become more or less relevant depending on what we are doing and to whom we are talking in that moment. We may have a dominant identity and primary audience, but when we are engaged in certain activities a different identity may be activated and a different sort of audience may be most relevant. These sorts of shifts can explain movement within and even across regions in terms of the degree to which organizations and their members communicate identity to relevant audiences.

Other shifts span much greater periods of time and can be thought of as more *historical*. These could represent passing trends and fads that last for only a few months or years, or this could be reflected in more sustained shifts that last generations and decades. We might find periods in which anonymity and secrecy are more accepted in the broader culture than in prior or later times, which can change how organizations and their members communicate identity as well. The Ku Klux Klan in the United States, for example, has worn and rejected the hood in various historical periods, depending in part on the acceptance of the Klan and its members.

Another variation that may help explain some of the fluidity of organizations within and across regions are *crises*. Scholars have paid notable attention to organizational crises and effective crisis communication (see Benoit 1997; Coombs 2012). These crises could be natural disasters, wars, information privacy leaks, scandals involving organizational leadership, and so on—some of which are viewed as accidents and some of which are attributed to mismanagement or other organizational wrongdoing. Regardless, a crisis is a significant punctuation in what may be a preferred or dominant way of communicating identity and can thus lead to definite alterations—an organization may withdraw into the shadows to avoid additional public scrutiny, members may disavow affiliations with a scandalous corporation, or the focal audience changes dramatically as the organization attempts to restore its image and reputation with certain stakeholders.

One final variation here is better explained by changes in the *life cycle* of an organization (or entire classes of organizations). This explanation suggests changes in how we communicate identity over the course of a collective's existence. For some organizations, identity may not be clear or clearly communicated during its formative stages but may become more widely shared as it acquires the resources and sees a need for more fully articulating who it is to relevant others. We might also speculate that anonymity and secrecy are difficult to maintain or are seen as less crucial to one's identity over time, so that some organizations become less dark or less shadowed at later stages of life. All sorts of combinations are possible. The point is that the maturity of the organization and the stage of organizational life in which it operates can influence how identity gets communicated.

It is also important to remind ourselves that we may position an organization within these regions or we may position each of several different organizational identities in these regions. While it is reasonable to expect some alignment between identities to avoid dissonance—thus helping us locate organizations as a whole into certain regions—we also know that organizations have multiple identities, and organizations wishing to hide some of those identities may be more likely to lack complete alignment of all identities. In these cases, it may be helpful to place some organizational identities in one region and other identities in another. In a similar vein, certain subsidiary organizations or fronts may be positioned differently than the organization behind them. Issues of alignment between identities in terms of how organizations and their members communicate those identities to various audiences demands renewed attention to understanding how we manage multiple identities (see Scott and Lane 2000).

Even with these caveats about situations and multiple identities, there is still substantial utility in this framework. It provides a relatively unique contribution in its focus on the communication of identity and its ability to thus incorporate a diverse array of organizations into the various regions and categories detailed here. In fact, it would seem that any organization or collective that is organizing could be located in this framework and then compared and contrasted with other organizations. Just as the examples and research are contemporary and historic, we should also be able to place organizations from different time periods into this framework. Additionally, an effort has been made to draw on research and examples that are global in nature and to consider dimensions that have widespread relevance. However, needs for recognition, views about expression, and emphasis on mass versus local are not universal and demand some refinement for cultural variations and broader sociopolitical forces working for and against transparency.

With these caveats and scope limitations in mind, the next three chapters examine each region, grouped by category (transparent, shaded, shadowed, or dark). Within each, we attempt to provide some additional details about the identity strategies we would expect to find, examine some representative organizations that reasonably fit into those regions, and then discuss a key communicative process that varies somewhat across regions (socialization). The choice of representative organizations is made on the basis of available scholarly and other credible information—including personal experience in a few cases. The scope of this book excludes any elaborate efforts to collect original empirical data on these representative organizations through direct contact with them or their members. However, that has not precluded the ability to analyze surface features of websites for those organizations who have them, observe the buildings and locations of certain collectives I had access to, and even draw on personal experience for a few organizations where I was previously a member, employee, or outside consultant. Hopefully that additional insight will help establish the legitimacy of the proposed model. As stated at the outset of this chapter, this framework is meant to supplement existing models and typologies, not replace them. Adding this model to the broader conversation will hopefully facilitate not only an expansion of how we view organizations but also a comparison and contrast of those varied collectives that compose the organizational landscape relevant to the twenty-first century.

5 Taking It to the Extremes

Transparent and Dark Organizations

aving put forth a framework to help us think about a wide range of organizations on the basis of how they and their members communicate identity to various audiences, we now turn to the important task of adding some flesh to that skeleton. As a way of more fully exploring this proposed model, we need details about each of the regions and organizational categories. For each of the next three chapters, we will specify characteristics of these regions and offer a couple of extensive examples of organizations that might be generally situated in each region. Providing that information will allow us to engage in some useful comparison and contrast across these regions and categories. For each we will also examine the important process of organizational socialization—which seems highly relevant regardless of the organization in question but might take different forms or emphasize different goals in these varied collectives.

We begin in this chapter with an examination of the two most extreme categories (transparent and dark organizations) and their fundamentally opposite regions. Doing so allows us to set up some useful points of comparison for the more nuanced chapters that follow examining more shaded and shadowed organizations. However, it is important to remember that even within the transparent and dark regions examined here, there is still variation in just how visible the organization is, how much members express identification, and how large the relevant audience may be; indeed some transparent organizations are far more transparent than others and some dark organizations are substantially darker than others. Figure 2 displays the relative

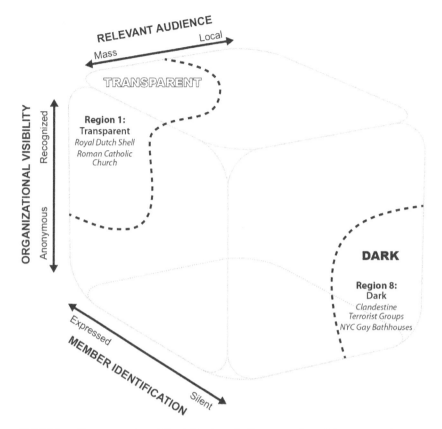

FIGURE 2. Transparent and Dark Regions in Framework and Representative Organizations for Each.

positions of the regions in the transparent and dark categories. It also lists two useful examples for each region—Royal Dutch Shell and the Roman Catholic Church (Vatican) for the transparent region and clandestine terrorist groups (such as the Continuity Irish Republican Army) and men's bathhouses (such as New York City's East Side Club) for the dark region—that we will later discuss in detail.

Transparent (Region 1): Recognized, Expressed, and Mass/Public

Given our emphasis up to now on various hidden organizations, it may seem odd to begin our specification of the model with the set of organizations that are generally *not* hidden. However, our broader goal is not to ignore or in any way discount the more visible collectives that are so prominent in the organizational landscape; instead, we need to be able to discuss them alongside and in comparison with other types. In fact, given that so much of our theorizing and research (including the work related to communication and identity) is based on these more transparent organizations, they represent a useful point of departure.

The transparent organizations in this region are characterized in three ways: (1) they make efforts to be visible as an organization, (2) their members express their belonging to the organization, and (3) the relevant audience is a relatively large or mass one. The combination of these three elements is what defines the transparent organization for our purposes; the organization and its members reveal their identity to a wide range of the public. Figure 2 positions this region based on its unique combination of attributes. This is very much in line with other scholars who have defined transparency as "a state in which the internal identity of the firm reflects positively the expectations of key stakeholders . . . A primary mechanism for achieving 'transparency' is expressive communication with stakeholders: expressive communications seek to represent the organization's identity" (Fombrun and Rindova 2000, 94).

First, these transparent organizations are relatively visible, meaning they do more to make their identity recognizable than to keep it anonymous. This is facilitated in part by the relatively large size of many of these organizations (which may also provide resources to promote identity). With these organizations we would expect substantial disclosure about their identity, which might include corporate/organizational branding efforts that promote name recognition. We might expect these organizations to advertise in ways that include the organization's name and other aspects of its core identity. Transparent organizations regularly have visual logos and perhaps even slogans that link to them. Additionally, these are the organizations who likely have mission and/or vision statements that are on display and widely available. Other organizational demographic data and information about partner organizations, all of which reveal more about the organization, are also made available. Another aspect of their organizational visibility is the clear link to a recognizable physical location, which may mean an address or even a building/structure linked to that organization. Other contact information (phone and fax numbers, web addresses, etc.) is also provided in various places. These transparent organizations may also offer pictures of their location, their leaders, and their members. All of this is accomplished through a wide range of channels—including online ones that allow for broad reach and where it is easy to attribute communication to the organization. Indeed, these groups generally seek credit for their actions and work hard on constructing an image to enhance their public reputation.

Second, the members of these organizations express their identification to the organization relatively more than they keep silent about it. In these organizations, we typically find employees and other members proudly stating organizational membership and noting their affiliation with the organization. The name of the organization is mentioned quickly and readily when they are asked about what they do or are describing themselves to others. Members typically use collective pronouns like "we" and "our" (not "they" and "their") and other positive language when talking about the organization and their role in it. They may even recite company missions, visions, or other phrases known to members. This expression of identification by members also involves defending the organization when it is criticized and a variety of nonverbal displays (wearing a hat or shirt with a company logo, having a bumper sticker with the organization's name prominently displayed, or proudly showing one's membership card to others). This expressed identification is also revealed in how knowledgeable organizational members are of the organization and what it represents. That knowledge includes being able to share basic identity information like the company's website and other contact information. Additionally, the decisions that these identified members make are ones that promote the organization's goals.

A final characteristic of these transparent organizations in this region is the relevance of a more mass/public audience as opposed to a highly localized one. These groups are generally trying to be recognizable and to express their belonging to a large audience that may even include the general public. For these organizations, a more general reputation matters greatly. To reach such a large and diffuse audience can be a challenge, so these organizations are more likely to use major mass media in their advertising, public relations, and other outreach efforts. They also have to devote more resources to their various communication functions. In most cases, these organizations are operating on a larger stage—national or global—as they provide products or services to a wider range of others. These organizations likely operate in more locales and more diverse locations and their members may travel more widely and interact with a relatively varied audience.

These transparent organizations would seem to describe a great many of the major corporations, most national government offices, and many large nonprofits and NGOs. Reflecting back to the opening pages of this book and the multitude of organizations visible in Times Square at any one time, we get some indication of who these more transparent organizations are. It is important to restate that "transparent" here does not mean that these organizations are completely open and disclose everything to the public; in fact, we know that these organizations also have trade secrets and sometimes have to be pushed to disclose information—especially when we are not talking about a publicly held company. We also do not mean "transparent" in the sense that we see right through the organization (and thus see nothing). Transparency, for us, refers to the communication of identity matters more specifically. When focusing on that, we can readily identify those collectives where the organization makes itself relatively recognizable and where member affiliation with the organization is more likely to be expressed to a mass audience than a localized one. Two examples from the research literature help illustrate the transparent organization. These are not necessarily the best examples nor the most extreme; indeed, examples do exist of what we might call "hyper-transparent organizations" that spend excessive energy on identity management (see Christensen and Cheney 2000 and their discussion of Eccolet). The examples offered here help illustrate two different organizations that attempt to be relatively transparent for somewhat different reasons.

Royal Dutch Shell (RDS)

This oil industry giant is the result of a 1907 merger between Royal Dutch Petroleum and the Shell Transport and Trading Company. The shell logo of the company traces back to 1897 (Grant 2005). Despite some recent divestments, this company still represents a complex joint venture organization with numerous subsidiaries under the parent RDS company (or companies as they are sometimes viewed). The corporate website at www.shell.com suggests 93,000 employees for this company headquartered primarily in The Hague, Netherlands. A 2000 estimate valued its brand at $2.8 billion, which is sixtieth in the world (Boele, Fabig, and Wheeler 2001).

As we can see, an organization does not have to have a stellar reputation to be relatively transparent, and sometimes crises can influence reputation and subsequent efforts to become more transparent. Indeed, RDS has been an organization with a very high profile for the past century, though it has not always enjoyed a positive reputation. Most notably, allegations that its subsidiary Shell Nigeria unfairly profited at the expense of certain native Nigerians—and was perhaps even indirectly involved with government executions of individuals protesting Shell's practices (Crowley 2009)—created a dark picture of the corporation and its policies. The Brent Spar controversy (involving the proposed sinking of an offshore drilling platform) and subsequent boycott of Shell products also damaged the organization's image and bottom line (Fombrun and Rindova 2000). As one Shell report stated, "we looked in the mirror and we neither recognized or liked some of what we saw" (Knight 1998, 2). Perhaps for outsiders, their frustration was the *faceless* institution they saw that seemed to show little caring for others (see Livesey and Kearins 2002). Others have noted Shell was a giant, silent phantom that did not tell its own story (de Geus 1997) and that it "lacked a sense of self, an identity, to project to the outside world. Lacking this, the firm appeared opaque" (Fombrun and Rindova 2000, 90).

These incidents brought about fundamental changes in how the organization attempted to interact with its stakeholders and promote sustainable development, though some have questioned how effective their efforts have truly been (Wheeler, Fabig, and Boele 2002). As communication scholar Sharon Livesey argues, these events were "shocks to Shell's image . . . that foregrounded questions of identity for the company" (2001, 59). These two crises in particular contributed to "a transformation of Shell's traditionally secretive and inward-focused culture and discursive practices [into] themes of transparency, more open and wider communication, and listening better to the concerns of outside stakeholders" (80). Shell's new policy was part of "the company's emerging eco-identity" (65). Livesey further contends that "Shell was also explicit about its plan to tell its own story better" (79). Shell's 1998 sustainability report described company core values and a personal credo that included honesty, integrity, and respect for others. As others have described it, the changes were ultimately about questioning Shell's "being"—which is fundamentally about management of the organization's identity and communicating it to relevant stakeholders (Fombrun and Rindova 2000).

Today, the organization's identity is relatively visible. The corporate website has specific sections on "who we are" with information about its values and beliefs. Shell's CEO is pictured online and a range of contact information (mailing address, phone number, email, Facebook, Twitter) is readily available. A variety of techniques have been used to solicit audience feedback (e.g., "Tell

Shell," Shell Dialogues, webchats, forums, etc.). The site states the organization's vision: "To reinforce our position as a leader in the oil and gas industry in order to provide a competitive shareholder return while helping to meet global energy demand in a responsible way." The website also claims, "Shell helps to meet the world's growing demand for energy in economically, environmentally and socially responsible ways." The Shell name and logo are widely recognized and the organization depends greatly on its reputation.

The extent to which members actively express identification is a bit harder to trace (and it can be especially difficult to separate identification with a more immediate Shell subsidiary versus the Shell corporation for many employees), but evidence suggests that affiliation is generally articulated. Michael Heller (2008) with the Center for Globalization Research at the University of London provides a useful historical account of some of Shell's practices (both corporate and in the United Kingdom specifically) during the 1920s and 1930s. During that era the company used a variety of magazines and other media to help "maintain worker loyalty, attract and retain key workers and establish an organizational culture . . . to motivate employees and meld them into the beliefs, practices and values of the organization" (13). Indeed, many of those who worked for RDS were "individuals who had life long careers at Shell and invested ontological and personal capital into the organization. Many of them had personal connections with the company . . . and would send their own children into it" (16). The internal media helped instill corporate values and visions into members. "Without a core workforce who held and imbued the values and association of the organization it is difficult to see how the brand could have functioned or been taken seriously in its external markets" (18). Some of that changed following the Nigerian and Brent Spar crises. As one Shell manger put it, "Previously if you went to your golf club or church and said, 'I work for Shell,' you'd get a warm glow. In some parts of the world that changed a bit" (see Grant 2005, n.p.). But, beginning with the 1998 sustainability report, the company's leader wanted Shell's members to "hold their heads high in their communities and among their families and friends" (Knight 1998, 48). In 2011, *Money* magazine's list of the world's most admired companies put RDS in sixth place internationally in terms of people management. Online reviews of the organization posted anonymously by its members suggest moderately satisfied employees with a rating of 3.5 on a five-point scale (Shell Oil 2011). Thus, it would seem that Shell members today are generally expressive of their belonging to the organization.

Shell's communication repeatedly mentions its global focus, making its most relevant audience a very mass/public one. The company operates in more than ninety countries and territories. The international incidents with which it has been involved indicate the relevance of a mass/public audience for this organization. It has been described as one of the world's three most international organizations (Grant 2005), along with the Roman Catholic Church to which we turn next.

Roman Catholic Church: The Vatican

I have always found the Church as an organization to be fascinating, having previously been a member for about thirty-five years, having graduated from a Catholic university, and having formally analyzed the Church's communication as a member of my college's competitive forensics team. Even though it is at times shrouded in mystery (and even associated with certain secret societies) and its own members have had to hide their membership to avoid persecution in certain historical periods, on the whole we would have to consider the Church a relatively transparent organization in terms of how it communicates its identity. The Catholic Church also provides a different type of transparent organization than we see with RDS in that its goals are not for profit but more about spreading the teachings of Christianity to members and nonmembers across the world.

This is the world's largest religious organization and oldest formal organization (Cheney 1991). Without question, it is a complex collective with multiple identities and numerous suborganizations, though we focus here on the parent identity of the Roman Catholic Church headquartered in the Vatican City (see www.vatican.va). As sociology professor Ivan Vallier (1971) explains, the Church has three central features: (1) division of the earth into territories (e.g., dioceses) governed usually by a bishop; (2) the Holy See, headed by the Pope in the Vatican, which serves as the bureaucratic and sacred center; and (3) a vertical line from priests to bishops to the Pope and his staff. It is from the Vatican that most official communication emanates in this relatively centralized organization, and so that becomes an appropriate focal point.

As an organization the Church presents a fairly consistent message about who it is and what it believes, with a name known across most of the globe. Its unique symbols (e.g., the Pope, the crucifix, Saint Peter's Square) are highly recognized as well. Though bureaucracy and hierarchy make direct interaction with the Vatican complicated, contact information is widely available through multiple channels. In fact, Vatican City and the Church headquarters are visited by millions annually. The Pope as organizational leader is highly visible and names of other key officials are also widely available. It is an organization that has not always been the most adept in its crisis management (e.g., sex abuse scandals) but has at other times helped coordinate extensive public relations efforts (e.g., against the release of anti-Catholic films). Though perhaps slower than some other religious organizations to fully utilize the media, the Vatican today has its own radio, television, and press offices and ensures extensive coverage of various events—many involving presentations by the Pope that reinforce the organization's mission (Gutwirth 1999). It has also been slow to adopt new media (Stohmeier 2009), though it has clearly enhanced its use of a wide range of social media in more recent years (Woodward 2011).

Membership in the organization is extensive, with over a billion members (approximately one-sixth of the global population). Official Church information also reveals hundreds of thousands of priests, sisters, deacons, bishops, and other religious leaders (see Center for Applied Research in the Apostolate 2011). These members tend to readily self-identify as Catholic and generally report high levels of identification. One study (Hall and Schneider 1972) of priests noted extremely strong identification levels with the Catholic Church. Another study (D'Antonio 1994) found that in 1987 73 percent of lay members said they would always be members; in 1993 70 percent still said they would never leave the Church. Although a majority do not attend Church services weekly, many still know all or parts of the basic "profession of faith" where they as organizational members state what they believe. Those attending Ash Wednesday services may proudly wear the ashes on their forehead, and others may display coffee mugs, pictures, or other items linked to the Pope and/or the Church.

The Church organization operates globally with members on all six populated continents through its diverse network of churches, all of whom are linked back to the Vatican and the Pope. Organizational identity scholar George Cheney (1991), in writing about how the Church manages its multiple identities, suggests the Church is perhaps the best example of an organization with global reach. Without question, the efforts of the Vatican and the Roman Catholic Church play out on a large international stage where global reputations matter. Its status as a recognized sovereignty further reinforces the relevance of this mass/public audience. The Church in the modern era is a "more integrated, international organization" than in the past (Valleher 1971, 497).

Socialization

As another way of comparing and contrasting the different regions we are examining here, it is useful to examine the communicative processes surrounding socialization into an organization. Organizational communication scholar Fred Jablin (2001) talks about socialization as primarily involving entry and assimilation into an organization. Thus, this is a process that concerns both the organization's strategic efforts to recruit and retain members as well as individual members' experience of learning about the organization's culture and their specific job/role within it. The identity of the organization plays a potentially substantial role in shaping this experience, and the identification of the members is often thought to be an important outcome of socialization efforts. Thus, this process seems especially relevant here—providing an opportunity to talk about anticipatory socialization into vocations, organizational recruitment/selection/retention procedures, formal and informal assimilation processes, and members' information seeking (see Jablin). Although existing work on socialization is extensive, it has rarely been examined in situations where the organization and/or its members conceal identity information from relevant others.

We actually know a fair amount about how this process generally works in relatively transparent organizations, because that is where most of the research has occurred. As Jablin (2001) explains in his broad review, anticipatory socialization begins in childhood as we get information about various vocations (from family, schools, peers, and the media) or even certain specific organizations. It continues with more specific pre-entry socialization by specific organizations based on organizational literature (printed and online) and interpersonal interactions with interviewers, current members, and various others. Jablin reports mixed evidence on whether formal or informal sources of recruitment are best for retention, but potential members often rely on multiple sources. We also know realistic job previews have been widely used to help marginal members opt out and others to better socialize once they become members—as long as accurate, salient, and ample information about the organization is received. Studies of the employment interview have also suggested that person-organization fit is crucial, though that can be difficult to assess in a competitive situation where images are carefully managed by both the organization and the potential member. Once a member enters the organization (which begins what is typically called the encounter phase), socialization primarily takes the form of processes designed to help the member adopt the values and beliefs of his/her new organization. Members may actively compare what they anticipated with the organizational reality they encounter and engage in efforts to reduce the uncertainty typically felt by newcomers to any organization. To help with all this, some organizations will offer formal orientation and training sessions (portions of which may cover the organization's history, mission, and philosophies) as well as formal and informal mentoring and/or buddy systems. The strategies used by organizations to socialize newcomers may be structured or unstructured and may recognize the individual (through personalization and building on one's past experiences) or take a more generalized approach (mass socialization and stripping away individual uniqueness). In general these efforts provide multiple benefits to the organization and its new members. Members also seek out organizational information through various tactics (observation, asking questions, disguised conversations, etc.). They may also give out information and seek relationships with peers and supervisors to reduce uncertainty and negotiate role expectations.

We would expect Royal Dutch Shell, the Catholic Church, and other relatively transparent organizations to generally follow much of what we have described here. For an organization that is visible to much of the public and whose members regularly talk about the organization, we would expect a fair amount of anticipatory socialization. We see Catholic Churches and likely know of members even if our immediate family is not Catholic. We likely see Shell gas stations and their advertisements and are exposed to various opinions about the oil and gas industry more generally. Shell knows its reputation plays a key role in its efforts to recruit potential employees who want to work for a prestigious organization.

When it comes to decisions to join a transparent organization, we generally think of these as voluntary choices for both the individual and the organization. Of course, some members may become part of the Roman Catholic Church as children and then later make choices "confirming" their desire to be a member; but others might join as adults based on efforts to grow Church membership. The process of joining may involve a commitment to support the Church through one's service, prayers, and financial offerings. The recruitment process for religious leaders is much more rigorous and lengthy—providing a realistic job preview well before one is completely socialized as a full member of the religious clergy. Shell, too, would make efforts to grow the company by adding employees as job needs arise. Its website is filled with information about careers and jobs with Shell geared toward professionals, students, and graduates. It provides relatively detailed information about jobs and the application process in regions all over the world. *Businessweek* magazine reports the corporation actively recruits on college campuses, provides formal orientation programs, and makes efforts to recruit diversity but that it does not have a formal mentoring program (2006 Best Places 2006). The interview processes might be different in these two examples, but the broader point is that anticipatory and encounter phase information about the organizations is widely available and decisions about membership have to be agreed upon by both individuals and the organization.

In transparent organizations, we may find a wide range of information-seeking strategies—as members are able to ask questions, observe behaviors, test limits, and engage in other tactics with both organizational insiders and outsiders to familiarize themselves with their jobs and the organizational culture. Retention is important in these organizations given the costs of finding and training new members, but turnover is to be expected and is not problematic unless it becomes so great that replacements are not available or core knowledge is leaving with members. In short, socialization in these transparent organizations helps them come to know the organization and its identity and to develop a sense of identification with the organization. When this is done effectively in these larger, often more global organizations, they may benefit greatly from the positive public image that often follows. As we shall see, socialization processes do not work this way with all organizations; thus we turn next to dark organizations to help illustrate that difference.

Dark (Region 8): Anonymous, Silent, and Local/Limited

At the opposite end of the spectrum from transparent organizations are those we might label "dark." This, or course, connotes an organization whose identity is kept hidden and obscured from the view of others. We cannot see what is kept dark and may not even be aware it exists. "Dark" does not necessarily refer to a lack of social acceptability or absence of moral values associated with organizational activities, though cover of darkness can afford such possibilities; in fact, a dark organization could be engaged in prosocial actions. It is useful to examine these dark organizations next because they represent such a complete contrast to the transparent region and the types of organizations found there. Additionally, having specified these extremes will help us talk about the various shaded and shadowed regions that fall between transparency and darkness in the next two chapters.

The organizations in the dark region can be described in three ways: they attempt to be relatively anonymous as an organization, members stay relatively silent about their belonging and affiliation with the organization, and the most relevant audience is a more limited/local one. Everything remains relatively hidden, even to those more local others potentially most interested in identifying the organization and its members. Thus, this extreme Region 8 is synonymous with dark organizations. Figure 2 positions this region based on its combination of qualities, which are again quite opposite from what we just discussed for Region 1 and transparent organizations. Let us elaborate on the features of these dark organizations.

First, dark organizations are relatively invisible, which means they attempt to make themselves more anonymous than recognized. They do not wish to be known to others or have a name that is highly familiar. Dark organizations typically have names so they can refer to themselves, but they may sometimes use a front name or pseudonym to help hide the identity of the actual organization involved (after all, naming a dark element is thought by some to take away its powers!). They do not typically promote that name in advertising or corporate branding efforts (and may do very little, if any, advertising or branding of any sort). Visual identity elements (logos, graphics) are much less likely and slogans known to outsiders are rare (though various codes may be used internally to signal one another). Signage is small and discreet to the extent it exists at any physical location of a dark organization, and those physical locations are likely to be off the beaten path or kept secret and shielded from view. This anonymity might also be facilitated in part by efforts to keep the organization smaller and perhaps relatively decentralized. Dark organizations may or may not have an online presence—but to the extent they do, less is revealed about the organization's identity. There is less contact information provided, relatively less mention of vision and mission statements, and less visibility of organizational leadership (in terms of naming leaders or posting pictures). We may also get much less in the way of demographic information about the organization and other organizations with which it partners. The dark organization may use channels that help it conceal identity from most others (encrypted CMC, interpersonal interactions with only trusted others, etc.). Although it may seek some credit for certain actions, it is more likely to avoid attention and stay off the radar of most audiences.

Second, the members of dark organizations are relatively more likely to keep that membership silent as opposed to expressing it to others. The organization is not truly dark if its members are open about their membership. In these organizations, members do not talk about who they work for or particular organizations with whom they are affiliated. Involvement with such organizations remains a secret from most outsiders. This might include people working "under cover" or those who demonstrate loyalty by remaining silent. Members are unlikely to mention the name of the organization when talking with others and they are unlikely to use language that suggests membership (e.g., "we," "our," or "us"). However, they may have some specialized language that can be used to identify other members and make themselves known to insiders as an organizational member. Members may know organizational mottos or secret codes, but they would not share those with outsiders. In some cases, member silence is promoted by a lack of knowledge about the organization's identity (one cannot reveal what one does not know). In other instances, the silent membership may be promoted by actual denials of membership or downplaying of the organization. Only rarely is the organization openly defended or promoted, though this may happen in efforts to recruit others. Silent members are far less likely to provide contact information that reveals their organizational membership—so we would not expect to see sharing of business cards or other membership documents with addresses and phone numbers, nor would we expect widespread distribution of an organization's website by members. Members reinforce their silence by not openly displaying clothing, body art, and other nonverbal symbols that would reveal their affiliation. In some cases, they may use masks or other disguises to protect their identity as members. At times, the actions of the member do not seem to promote or even be connected to the organization of which they are part (further hiding their membership).

Finally, the dark organizations in this region are more likely to have a more relevant local audience as opposed to a more mass/public one. It is less difficult to be anonymous and silent to the general public (where it can be hard to get noticed anyway) than to one's more immediate local audience (who may have a stronger interest in identifying the organization and its members). Thus, the darkest organizations are those where the organization and its members can conceal identity information even from very local audiences that are likely more immediate and relatively well known to the organization and its members. The dark organizations and their members are not interested in the mass media (who likely pay them relatively little or no attention); they are more interested in local media from whom they must actively conceal identity information. They likely do not have the sophisticated reputation-management resources found in more transparent organizations, but they do need formal and informal structures and personnel that work to conceal identity and keep a close reign on certain types of communication. Interpersonal relations are important in dealing with these local audiences, and dark organizations carefully monitor those so as to limit interaction that may be revealing. The organizations in this region are operating on a smaller stage (and in fewer and less diverse locales) where their actions are most relevant to a more definitive community of others. Organizational members also operate with relatively local others and tend to travel less broadly.

Given this depiction, what might qualify as a dark organization? On one hand it could include all organizations operating in our communities whose existence is unknown; however, that sort of vague notion suggests potentially large numbers of hidden organizations, making it relatively useless. On the other hand, we could dismiss dark organizations completely as little more than the fiction of conspiracy theories—making it a theoretically possible type but one that has no actual examples in practice. Both ideas miss the mark, because even amid the obvious difficulties of seeing into the dark, we can begin to identify organizations that generally fit in such a region. Highly covert military or intelligence organizations operating in a limited scope would seem to fit the criteria for a dark organization. Certain secret societies and hate groups—where the organization and its members remain hidden from the local/limited communities in which they operate—could be placed here as well. Quite possibly, hacker/hacktivist organizations with a limited agenda would fit here also. Localized criminal organizations and gangs where members and the organization remain hidden might also be positioned in this category. Furthermore, we could talk about certain highly stigmatized organizations—where the collective and member identities are hidden from a relevant local audience—as falling into this region as well. Although somewhat difficult to obtain information on these sorts of organizations given efforts by them and their members to remain hidden, a few more specific examples can help shed some light on these dark collectives. As with the transparent exemplars, the relatively dark organizations examined here are not ideal types or even the darkest organizations we might discuss; but they do illustrate the main features of such organizations. Additionally, the two examples highlighted here are seemingly quite different from one another and have different motives for their darkness despite other similarities.

Clandestine terrorist groups

Much of the attention to terrorism, at least in the Western world, has gone to more global and transnational organizations that pose a broad threat. Especially since the attacks of September 11, 2001, the greatest attention has been given to those with Muslim connections operating largely out of countries with sizable Muslim populations (e.g., al-Qaeda, Abu Nidal, Lashkar e-Tayyiba). Furthermore, even though all terrorist organizations seek at least some secrecy for themselves and their members, there is substantial variation in just how anonymous various organizations are; thus we tend to know more about some of these extremist organizations than others. For the representative organizations offered here, we examine ones that tend to focus their interests more locally but still conceal their own identity and that of their members. Additionally, we emphasize clandestine groups operating largely outside the Muslim world—both because they have often received less attention given our focus on other extremists (and thus are better hidden) and because they are a useful reminder that dark organizations can be found almost anywhere.

The National Socialist Underground (NSU) was uncovered so recently that it is not found in listings of terrorist organizations as of February 2012. It has been described as a far-right German neo-Nazi terrorist group, discovered in November 2011 after a botched bank robbery that ultimately led to the suicide of two members before they could be captured. Amazingly, the NSU is now believed to have been in existence for thirteen years prior to that. In a DVD that was never released by the organization itself, the previously unknown group claimed responsibility for nine killings of Turkish and Greek immigrants and two bombings dating back to 2000—with an unidentified voice at the start of the disturbing fifteen-minute video describing the NSU organization as a "network of comrades with the fundamental principle of 'deeds instead of words'" (Cote 2011, n.p.). The group is also believed to be behind over a dozen bank robberies.

This dark organization's communication (or lack thereof) clearly contributes to its relative anonymity and the relative silence of its members. One insightful author/blogger following this issue points to a key reason police had not determined a neo-Nazi terror organization was behind these crimes:

> The main reason seems to be that the group not only left behind no notes, but never even mentioned its own name. Unlike the RAF [Red Army Faction], which used its attacks as a publicity stunt to sell its mind-numbingly didactic manifestos, the NSU chose to remain completely anonymous—possibly in order to remain in action as long as possible. (Nothnagle 2011, paragraph 10)

Accounts from the arrest of one of the NSU's supporters and possible members reveals secret phone numbers, clandestine rendezvous, and withholding of information from all but those who really needed it. There were false identities and passports, fake driver's licenses, and various disguises. Video surveillance of bank robberies now known to be the work of the NSU show members in hooded jackets and masks but without identifying marks (see Cote 2011; Gude, Robel, and Stark 2012). In addition to the ultimate silencing by the two key members who committed suicide, another key member blew up an apartment where all three had been in hiding in an attempt to destroy identifying information, and she has so far refused to say anything about the organization to authorities. Furthermore, there appears to be no website, no headquarters, and apparently no clear leaders. The number of members is unclear as well. Legal authorities have indicated they suspect more supporters are behind this group (Petrou 2011) and more recent reports suggest over 100 extremists who may be part of a larger movement in which the NSU was only a part (More Than 100 2012); but it is also possible that the NSU does not go very far underground. Thus, as of the time this was written, experts simply do not know who its members and leaders are; however, concerns about future interactions remain after police discovered a list with names of eighty-eight people the NSU is targeting.

We do know that the NSU and its members have been linked to other extremist groups. Several key members of the organization earlier formed the Jena Comradeship, which was a cohesive group of neo-Nazis in the city of Jena, Germany. Several were also involved with the Thuringian Homeland Security, another terrorist group linked to the state of Thuringia in Germany.

At least one suspected member is a longtime official in the far-right National Democratic Party (Gude, Robel, and Stark 2012). The apartment recently blown up to destroy evidence was in Zwickau, Germany. All these ties heavily link the group to the same small region of Germany. Even though its terrorist and criminal actions were spread across much of that nation, this particular group seems largely restricted to a very local/limited arena—fulfilling our last criterion for being in a dark region.

As a different example of a clandestine terrorist organization, the Continuity Irish Republican Army (a.k.a. Continuity IRA or CIRA) is a terrorist organization with goals of uniting Ireland. "Continuity" refers to the group's belief that it is carrying on the original Irish Republican Army mission to drive Britain out of Ireland. Officially, the CIRA is an illegal organization in Ireland and listed as a terrorist organization in the United States and United Kingdom. By some accounts, the CIRA is the clandestine paramilitary wing of the political party Republican Sinn Féin, which split from Sinn Féin in 1986 (What Are the Main 2011). For years, the CIRA did not reveal its existence to anyone outside a few in Sinn Féin —no paramilitary activity, no public press statements, and virtually no communication about itself at all. The one known exception is a public statement and photo published in the Republican Sinn Féin newsletter *Saoirse Irish Freedom* saluting a fallen IRA leader (but even that cryptic note does not explicitly mention the CIRA and the photos show no faces; see Final Salute 1994). Irish police forces suspected the organization existed but knew little—ultimately labeling it the "Irish National Republican Army" (Kerr 1997). The CIRA remained a secret organization until the Provisional IRA declared a ceasefire in 1994 (Gardham 2009), after which it became more active but still relatively anonymous as an organization. The leadership of the Continuity IRA is believed to be based in the Ulster and Munster areas, though this is not confirmable nor shared by the CIRA. In general, leaders and their whereabouts are kept largely quiet; however, a 2012 court case did reveal the alleged current leader's name (Alleged Continuity IRA 2012).

Unlike the Provisional IRA (and the Real IRA in 1998), the CIRA has not announced a ceasefire or agreed to participate in weapons decommissioning—nor does that seem likely. "The organisation remains a very serious threat" the Independent Monitoring Commission concluded (Sturcke 2009). It is considered partly responsible for the growth in terrorist violence in Northern Island from 2006 to 2010 (McDonald 2011). The terrorist organization profile from the National Consortium for the Study of Terrorism and Responses to Terrorism describes the CIRA on its website (www.start.umd.edu) as "a small group of hard-core dissident Irish republicans . . . implicated in a number of attacks in the past decade. The group is best known for conducting small bombings, most of them non-lethal, such as tossed explosives and car bombs. In addition to bombings, CIRA attacks have included robberies, kidnappings, hijackings, and assassinations." According to that same consortium, the group has claimed responsibility for some acts, while others have not been confirmed. Despite some rather high-profile attacks, the organization itself remains relatively anonymous. The name "CIRA" is sometimes left in graffiti or with an Irish flag in places where the organization has acted, but otherwise the organization leaves no calling card. There is no website and thus none of the identity information so often found there (no information on leaders, missions, contact information, etc.). There are no obvious markings or logos clearly linked to the CIRA, and the organization has no publicized headquarters or physical address. There are very few official announcements—though some YouTube videos put out by the group exist alongside its warning to police of upcoming attacks and its contact with the media when taking credit for those attacks; in all those cases, little besides the name of the organization is revealed. The CIRA is also thought to have secret training camps (Tonge 2004).

Because there are no known membership lists, exact counts of the organization's size are difficult. Estimates from a range of sources suggest 50 to 200 members in recent years. What little we do know suggests they are relatively silent about what is likely a strong commitment to the CIRA. Part of that silence is driven by the somewhat unpopular views they take. A recent survey by the University of Liverpool shows that only 14 percent of the nationalist community have some "sympathy for the reasons" why groups like the CIRA continue to engage in violence (McDonald 2010); thus members are not widely supported and may feel the need to keep their involvement with the organization a secret from most. Also quite important is the fact that membership in the organization is punishable by a lengthy prison sentence under U.K. law. Thus, it is not surprising that images of CIRA members online show only masked members. This is true in propaganda videos and pictures as well as in YouTube speeches. There is little evidence of markings on clothing, identification cards, or public talking about the organization that suggest anything other than silence of members.

The final element of this dark organization is its local/limited audience. As the Center for Defense Information notes, the CIRA operates exclusively in small regions within Northern Ireland and the Republic of Ireland. Targets generally include British military and Northern Ireland security targets as well as Northern Ireland Loyalist paramilitary groups. However, the CIRA does not have the capability of launching attacks on the U.K. mainland

(Hellman and Huang n.d.). It gets almost no international press attention, but certainly interest from local media. Thus, this combination of a rather hidden organization operating in a relatively local/limited way with largely silent members creates an example of a collective operating in this dark region.

New York City men's bathhouses

In that extensive list of organizations currently visible in Times Square that we saw in chapter 1, you will not find obvious representatives of the sex industry. To find an adult arcade or bookstore, you need to walk at least a block west. To find an even more stigmatized business like a men's bathhouse, you would have to travel many blocks away to somewhat less busy parts of town where such an organization is essentially hidden from all but its patrons/members. An online search suggests the New York City area currently has three men's bathhouses. One of those is located in Queens and is known as "Northern Men's Sauna." There is no website at all for this bathhouse, but there is a phone number and a physical address on Farrington Street (which, at least by New York City standards, is well off the beaten path). The building corresponding to the address looks like a small brick warehouse with large garage doors on each side and barely any signage indicating the entrance to the sauna itself (except for the word "Northern" above a doorway); thus, it is well hidden.

The other two bathhouses are in Manhattan, but also well off the beaten path. They are seemingly owned by the same company and operate with the rather nondescript names "East Side Club" (on East Fifty-sixth Street) and "West Side Club" (on West Twentieth Street). Both are on relatively busy one-way streets with a fair amount of pedestrian traffic—but they are distant from the businesses of Times Square or Wall Street. The entrance to the former is marked only with a street address number next to a doorway. Inside the doorway is an elevator and small directory noting the name of the club on the sixth floor. From the street, the sixth-floor windows are opaque. The West Side Club's entrance is even more difficult to locate given the lack of signage, which includes only the words "Dezer Building" and the number "27" between an antique shop and a parking garage. A building directory on the street says nothing about the club, but one inside a lobby area lists a variety of businesses—including the West Side Club on the second floor. Again, from the street the second floor is marked by dirty, blackened windows. These two clubs have similar websites that list an address, phone number, and directions, though contact information provides only a generic email address. Other website information might leave the average person confused as to exactly what this "club" is. Perhaps to some it would look like a gym for men—though the images may suggest the sexual nature of the establishment to certain audiences. They exemplify what has been called an erotic oasis (Delph 1978), which is a physically bounded and guarded setting that uses various devices to remain separate from the conventional world.

There are no pictures or mentions of the organization's owners or members and no such member list would appear to be available. In fact, websites for other men's bathhouses suggest that such records are not kept. There are apparently cards members can carry, but the trashcan at the exit of one of those Manhattan clubs contained what appeared to be several membership cards for individuals apparently not wishing to carry such identifying information. It is impossible without more specific research to know if "members" and employees readily discuss their affiliation with the bathhouse, though the research we have examined on stigmatized businesses suggests most would not express such information. Furthermore, health communication researchers have found that even bathhouse patrons often have negative views of the baths and do not wish others to know they were there (Elwood, Greene, and Carter 2003). Those researchers describe this as a code of silence, where members say nothing about being there or having seen anyone they know. Others have noted the importance of secrecy and anonymity by members as well (Hammers 2009).

The bathhouses appear on a number of directories, but obviously they cater only to a small portion of the residents and visitors to New York City. Their advertising is highly targeted and seemingly limited to a few publications primarily serving the New York City gay community (e.g., *Next* magazine)—and clearly not in mainstream media. Unless you were looking specifically for this sort of organization, you almost certainly would not just stumble upon it. To the locals that do notice it online or in some other directory, it may simply appear to be a gym or sauna for men. By listing themselves that way and using certain language on their website (if they have one), the organization remains relatively hidden to even most locals. These bathhouses have been described as vital institutions as well as one of the "dirty secrets" of the gay community, who may treat them with everything from quiet support to visible disdain (see Tewksbury 2002, 76).

The bathhouses have at times attracted attention that threatened their relatively hidden nature, most notably during the height of the AIDS epidemic.

Some communities closed these bathhouses completely. In New York City, several legendary baths such as the Everard Turkish Baths were forced to close down. Others that survived found new restrictions on their activity, which likely encouraged these organizations to go relatively dark even as homosexuality has become more socially accepted and laws have changed to reflect that.

Socialization

The anticipatory socialization for relatively dark organizations may be generally quite limited. Given the small numbers in most dark organizations, relatively few young people may come into contact with someone who was actually a member of such a collective or who has active information about such organizations. Even in families involved with criminal organizations or other dark organizations, mention of such information may not be made to children or teens. There are media portrayals of various dark organizations that have provided both glamorous and startling depictions of gangs, organized crime groups, parts of the sex industry, and undercover intelligence units. However, the organizations themselves are not typically the ones providing much of this information—again suggesting limited anticipatory socialization.

Actual recruitment into such organizations likely differs from more transparent organizations as well. Clandestine terrorist organizations generally do not publicly solicit new members; instead, members are more likely sought through trusted networks or through other dark organizations. The men's bathhouses also do not appear to advertise broadly, limiting recruitment efforts to highly targeted media or even to help wanted signs posted in the organization's lobby. It is easy to imagine other dark organizations also focusing on internally vetted sources for new members and employees. When the goal is to remain hidden, one must carefully recruit members who will share that goal; thus, there is more at risk for dark organizations if they do not recruit the right types.

Clearly, there may be vast differences in the job training required of members. Our two example organizations would illustrate that clearly given the formal rigors and high demands of terrorist cells versus the relative ease and informality with which one can join or work for a typical bathhouse. What may be more similar across various dark organizations, though, is the emphasis on keeping secrets. It is not hard to imagine that a key part of the assessment in such organizations is determining if the person will maintain the appropriate silence and discretion (keeping membership information concealed, not bringing unwanted publicity to the organization, not talking to authorities about the organization's activities, etc.). The motives for that secrecy may vary and include avoiding embarrassment. protecting oneself and others, facilitating participation, and providing voice—but in each case we become socialized (based on the values of the organization and/or the broader community) about how to act as organizational members.

Information seeking as part of the socialization process becomes limited in dark organizations. Members may only be able to talk to organizational insiders, and even that may be restricted to more covert forms of observation and surveillance (as opposed to direct questions). Organizations characterized by concealment of identity information also foster cultures where other forms of information sharing are limited. This can lead to more uncertainty on the part of members about how to best handle their jobs and potential crises—including situations where identity information may be threatened. A final socialization issue of importance in dark organizations is retention. Arguably, this is perhaps less crucial for those organizations that are dark because they are stigmatized. Members may actually hide their membership by being only temporary or sporadic members or working at such organizations for short periods of time—but, even then, they are unlikely to be a threat to the organization after they leave given their likely silence. Retention is especially crucial for those organizations involved in more illegal or high-stakes terrorism and counterterrorism efforts where defections and departures could lead to unwanted disclosures when one is no longer surrounded by organizational members. Thus, it is understandable why many organized crime groups and gangs may not allow members to leave voluntarily (Bovenkerk 2011) and why terrorist organizations value socialization to "avoid the disastrous extremes of exit and voice by soliciting the loyalty of members" (Crenshaw 1988, 23).

Now You See Me, Now You Don't

In summary, transparent and dark organizations represent relative opposites when it comes to the communication of identity to various audiences. Whereas transparent organizations are relatively recognized and have members who tend to express their affiliation to a relatively mass/general audience, dark organizations are more anonymous than recognized and have members who keep their affiliation silenced to even the most local and immediate of audiences. Transparent organizations would seem to describe a great many of the major corporations, most government offices, and many large nonprofits and NGOs in our world. In other words, any organization in which it and its members attempt to communicate its identity to a general/mass audience is transparent. Conversely, dark organizations could include highly covert military or intelligence organizations operating in a limited scope, certain secret societies and hate groups, localized criminal organizations and gangs, and certain highly stigmatized organizations where the collective and member identities are hidden from a relevant local audience. Socialization processes for these two different types of organizations would seem to vary vastly. Yet, for all these differences, transparent and dark organizations share a common interest in and necessary attention to how identity gets communicated to various stakeholder audiences. We turn next to some of the possibilities between these extreme regions that may also be characterized in terms of how identity gets communicated to others.

6 Hiding Only a Little
Shaded Organizations

Although it is useful to begin our elaboration of these hidden organizations at the extremes, those far ends of the spectrum provide only limited insight. We know a great deal already about transparent organizations and their often extensive efforts to communicate identity to a wide-ranging audience. Conversely, few organizations may fit our criteria for truly dark collectives, and even fewer are at least visible enough that we can reasonably analyze them as examples. In practice, it is reasonable to suspect that most of the organizations we might describe as hidden are only partially, rather than completely, obscured.

In this chapter we consider three regions we can label as shaded. As we introduced back in chapter 4, *shaded* describes a category of regions distinguished by the existence of enough light to help make the organization and/or its members viewable or known but with some identity elements remaining shielded and less visible. The shaded regions are similar to the transparent region along any two of the three dimensions in our framework, but not all three. Thus, Regions 2, 3, and 4 are all part of the shaded category. For each, we will characterize how organizations operating in that region communicate identity and to whom, suggest some representative examples of collectives typically found in that region, and then describe how socialization might work there. Figure 3 positions the shaded regions relative to one another and highlights several example organizations we will discuss in this chapter.

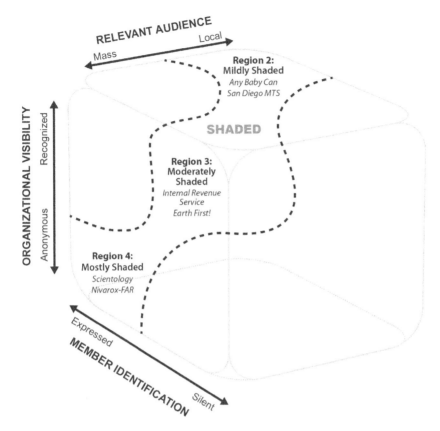

FIGURE 3. Shaded Regions in Framework and Representative Organizations for Each.

Before doing that, though, it is useful to remind ourselves that a shaded organization need not be a "shady" organization. These shaded regions may be home to organizations we see as good or bad. They or their members may hide who they are from certain audiences for a range of reasons. We will attempt to take all that into account as we explore these shaded regions and the organizations operating in those spaces.

Mildly Shaded (Region 2): Recognized, Expressed, and Local/Limited

The organizations in this region of our framework are only slightly hidden and have much in common with relatively transparent organizations. Like them, these mildly shaded organizations seek to make their identity highly visible and organizational members actively identify with the organization. However, these organizations and their members are not widely known or discussed given a more local/limited relevant audience. We will later discuss two organizations—Any Baby Can and the San Diego Metropolitan Transit System—that help illustrate this region.

First, like more transparent organizations, these mildly shaded collectives are relatively visible, meaning they work to make their identity recognizable rather than anonymous. Although they may often not be as large as more transparent organizations, they may still have some of the necessary resources to promote identity. With these mildly shaded organizations we would expect substantial identity disclosures, which might include various branding efforts that help make the organization's name highly visible and recognizable. Just like transparent organizations, we would expect these collectives to advertise in ways that include the organization's name and other aspects of its core identity. Mildly shaded organizations regularly have visual logos and slogans and they likely have mission and/or vision statements that are on display and widely available. Various demographic data and information about partner organizations, all of which serve to identify the organization, are also found. Another aspect increasing their relative organizational visibility is a recognizable physical location, which typically means a street address and a building/structure. Phone and fax numbers, a web address, and other contact information are also provided in various places. Like transparent organizations, these mildly shaded types may also offer pictures of their locations, their leaders, and their members. Even if they lack the full extent of channels found in more transparent organizations, the collectives in this region still have a sizable range of media options with messages clearly linked to the organization. These organizations tend to work hard on constructing an image that enhances their local reputation and they generally seek credit for their actions.

Second, members in mildly shaded organizations express their identification relatively more than they conceal it. This is consistent with what we saw for more transparent organizations, where we typically find employees and other members proudly stating organizational membership and noting their affiliation with the organization. The name of the organization is mentioned easily when members of mildly shaded organizations are asked about what they do or are describing themselves to others. Like people in more transparent organizations, these members utilize collective pronouns like "we" and "our" (not "they" and "their") and usually use positive language when talking about the organization and their role in it. They, too, may know and be able to recite company missions, visions, or other phrases known to members. This expression of identification by members also involves defending the organization when it is criticized and a variety of nonverbal displays (wearing company logo clothing, displaying a bumper sticker with the organization's name prominently displayed, etc.). This expressed identification can also be seen in how knowledgeable organizational members are of the organization and its identity, including being able to share the company's website and other contact information. Additionally, the decisions that these identified members in mildly shaded organizations make are ones that consider the organization's goals and interests.

But these organizations differ from transparent ones in one primary way when it comes to the communication of identity. They do not tend to have a relatively large mass/public audience. Instead, organizations in this region can be described as more local and not attempting to communicate identity matters to a broader audience. They do not need or want widespread attention or focus. In this sense, they are hidden from most people even though they may be quite well known in a more limited context. In general, organizations and their members in this region are less interested in the mass media—especially national/international media who likely pay them relatively little or no attention—but more interested in local media to promote identity to a more proximate community. Although they may lack the sophisticated reputation-management resources found in more transparent organizations, these organizations may still employ various formal/informal structures and personnel that work to promote the organization to the relevant audience. General reputations and public opinion may be relatively less important to these organizations, but a positive image with a more local/limited audience is quite valued. Interpersonal relations are vital in dealing with these local audiences, and mildly shaded organizations may use such channels to communicate identity locally. Clearly, the organizations in this region are operating on a smaller stage (and in fewer and less diverse locales) where their actions are most relevant to a limited/local and more definitive community of others. Members also interact with relatively local others and tend to travel less broadly in these organizations.

So, what sort of organizations do we find in this mildly shaded region? Predictably, they are similar to more transparent organizations, including a range of corporations, nonprofits, and government agencies. But they are not the major publicly traded international corporations, the highly visible national charities and nonprofits, or the major international and national government agencies; instead, these mildly shaded organizations are likely smaller corporations and small businesses that lack a global or even a national focus. They are the local nonprofits and the local government organizations that matter in the communities in which they operate but may be largely invisible to others beyond that. These are organizations that choose to communicate their identity to local rather than more dispersed audiences—usually voluntarily, though perhaps sometimes to stay in compliance with legal restrictions (e.g., a county government agency that is not expected to promote itself outside the county). Though some organizations may aspire to eventually communicate with a much larger audience, others actively avoid that public attention or may choose to focus on the local/limited audience given special connections to it (e.g., a "mom and pop" store dedicated to serving the community without a desire to expand beyond that). We would generally exclude organizations trying (but failing) to reach a broader audience (thus remaining only visible locally). Regardless of the motive for focusing on a relatively more local/limited audience, all the organizations in this region keep themselves hidden from a broader audience. Quite possibly, this region is filled with more organizations than any other given the number of small businesses and community organizations in the contemporary landscape. A couple of examples may help illustrate this region better.

Any Baby Can Child and Family Resource Center

A good example of this sort of organization is a relatively small nonprofit in Austin, Texas that I had an opportunity to get to know, and value, through two different projects during the time I lived in that community. This was an organization that always seemed happy to allow us to use its name—a sign of an organization that is more recognized than anonymous. The very first thing you see on the current version of Any Baby Can's (ABC) website (http://www. abcaus.org/)—after the name and logo—is "Who we are," which states, "Any Baby Can is a nonprofit in Austin, Texas that improves the lives of children by strengthening them and their families through education, therapy and family support services." There is an additional "About Us" section providing more identity information about this nonprofit, including information about the organization's history and initial director. The website provides a physical address, phone number, toll-free number, fax number, and email address. Additionally, every member of the leadership team is listed by name with full contact information—and most have pictures as well. They also list all members of the board of directors as well as other organizations who have donated to them or with whom they partner. At the physical address of the nonprofit, you will find a building with a large sign containing the organization's name and logo. There is staff dedicated to communication management, and the organization has recently begun using social media as well. This organization is—as a result of their communication efforts, community services, and fundraising events—a well-known "player" in the nonprofit community of Austin.

The nonprofit employs nearly one hundred staff members today. Both of our projects (conducted in the mid-2000s) involved assessing the identification levels of members, and employees were reasonably well identified with their organization even amid a major relocation to a new building space. A survey of the best places to work in Austin conducted by the local newspaper (Top Workplaces 2011) recently listed ABC as a top workplace, with numerous employees commenting positively about what they love about their job and why they want to stay with the organization. The organization was ranked thirty-ninth among small businesses in that poll, but it is one of the only nonprofits to appear on the list. That site also shows a picture of presumed organizational members wearing T-shirts with the company name. During those prior projects, leaders at ABC regularly gave us their business cards with all sorts of identifying information on it and often spoke with collective pronouns ("we," "us," "our," etc.).

The relevant audience for this organization is a very local/limited one. The website notes, "Each year, Any Baby Can brings help and hope to more than 6,000 of the youngest, sickest, and poorest children in our community and their families." Any Baby Can's list of supporters is all local and their events and money all go locally. The website and their print material include a number of stats and facts—mostly about babies/children in Austin and the county where it is located. Although there are two affiliated organizations in nearby cities that share best practices, ABC in Austin is independent; you will not find this exact nonprofit in other communities. The organization's mission, which began with state health funding dedicated to addressing special needs of children in the Austin area, has contributed to its limited/local focal audience. If you look at recent listings of the largest U.S. nonprofits (put out annually by *Forbes* magazine), you will find no mention of Any Baby Can, which again emphasizes their more local (rather than national) focus.

Thus, ABC and its members appear to actively communicate their identity to the local Austin community, resulting in a highly recognized brand name in the Texas capital city. But this organization remains hidden to almost all others beyond that community because of this narrower focus. This makes it mildly shaded in comparison to more transparent organizations that are more widely known.

San Diego Metropolitan Transit System

One of the best part-time jobs I ever had was working in public relations for San Diego's Metropolitan Transit Development Board (MTDB), which was later renamed the San Diego Metropolitan Transit System (SDMTS) and includes subsidiaries such as San Diego Trolley, Inc. and the San Diego Transit Company. Though this organization is a government agency with member cities throughout San Diego County, I always thought it had the feel of a small corporate business (and its web address is actually a dot-com). Working in the marketing and public relations area made me very aware of our efforts to communicate our identity—but to a very local/limited audience living in or visiting San Diego County.

The region's transit services have actually had a number of names dating back to the late 1800s. The San Diego Transit System name appears in the late 1940s, but MTDB and the San Diego Trolley did not emerge until the late 1970s and early 1980s—and today they are all combined as part of SDMTS. Regardless of the name and logo in use at the time, this organization has been active in pushing its brands, perhaps best illustrated by the San Diego Trolley car, throughout the region. Its extensive bus and trolley system display the company name(s) and logos on and in vehicles, in transit stations, and through various forms of signage at the highly visible downtown headquarters and other buildings around the county. The first tab on the organization's website (http://www.sdmts.com) is "About MTS," which contains general info on who the organization is, an organizational chart, a clickable listing of key departments, a listing of board members (with photos) and public board meeting dates, a message (and photo) from the CEO, and a historical timeline of the organization. Other tabs display various organizational publications (all of which prominently display the MTS name and logo) and provide contact information for the organization and key departments. There is a small staff dedicated to marketing and communications, which produces a variety of documents and promotional items publicizing the organization and its identity through various traditional and new media. As a result, the SDMTS, and especially its trolley subsidiary, are very well known in the area.

This agency, with its several thousand employees, does not typically make the list of top places to work in this huge metropolitan city. However, the positive reputation of the organization makes it generally easy for members to express to neighbors and others that they work for SDMTS. Full-time employees typically had business cards with the organization's name that they would give out when meeting with community members. When I worked there (nearly two decades ago and prior to it being SDMTS), it was not uncommon to see people wearing a T-shirt or pin or displaying a coffee cup or other items with the trolley/transit logo. We had several items like this available to employees on site and through the organization's transit store. I was one of those who proudly displayed that logo information, bought the company merchandise, and told others about my work there. I even used a project from my work as part of an educational design course I was taking at the time. As an indication of people's desire to stay with the organization, which is often an expression of identification, the current organizational chart still lists several names familiar to me from twenty years ago.

Although it is true that the trolley is a landmark known even beyond San Diego, and even though the SDMTS has won awards nationally for its operations (Grant 2009), the relevant audience for this organization is a very local/limited one. Its stated area of jurisdiction covers about 570 square miles of the urbanized areas of San Diego County as well as some rural parts of the county. The SDMTS board chairperson's remarks on the agency website note: "We are the agency responsible for moving 250,000 people in San Diego County to their different destinations every day. . . . We are a major partner in this community and want to continue contributing to its progress." All the organization's promotional material is restricted to the region of the county it serves. Going beyond that would be viewed by local taxpayers as inappropriate. It is likely that most hits to the website outside that region are by visitors planning to use the service when they are in the region. Organizational members do not typically travel outside the region as part of their work and thus their expressions of belonging remain very local as well. This combination of high organizational visibility and expressed organizational membership within the local community makes SDMTS an organization that is fairly well known locally but stays relatively hidden beyond that. It is in this sense that the organization is mildly shaded—resembling more transparent organizations except for its more limited/local audience.

Socialization

Given the similarities between mildly shaded organizations and more transparent ones, we should expect some similarities in their socialization as well. Indeed, decisions to join are largely voluntary ones for both the organization and prospective member. The selection process and formal application process are similar as well. For example, the SDMTS website lists jobs, discusses how to apply, and promotes MTS as a great place to work. Any Baby Can's careers section of their website also talks about open jobs, how to apply, and what the organization has to offer.

But there are some slight differences in how socialization may work in a mildly shaded organization. First, there is probably less anticipatory socialization about the organization directly. Fewer people have likely worked for any one of these organizations in particular or have direct knowledge about them. There may be information about the pros and cons of working for a smaller business or staying in the community but less specifically about the organization. Although the visibility of buses and trolleys may aid anticipatory efforts related to an organization like SDMTS, for most mildly shaded organizations there is very little knowledge and thus limited anticipatory socialization occurring.

A second difference is that mildly shaded organizations likely recruit less broadly and may emphasize local qualifications. They are not seeking members from across the globe or recruiting from universities outside their community. In fact, local citizens who know the community may be stronger fits. Locals who fit key demographics may be important also. The Any Baby Can website notes, "Any Baby Can places high importance on providing culturally appropriate services. Two thirds of staff are bilingual; 46% are Hispanic." Thus, employees fitting the demographics of the local community may be more heavily recruited into these organizations.

Like transparent organizations, a wide range of information-seeking strategies is possible as newcomers attempt to familiarize themselves with their job and organizational culture. However, for an often smaller organization operating in a more local community, there may be fewer outsiders from whom such information can be obtained (e.g., former members), making internal sources even more important. Additionally, retention in these mildly shaded organizations and their transparent counterparts is very important given the costs of training new people and the loss of organizational knowledge that accompanies personnel departures. But it may differ in that the slightly hidden organization provides somewhat less prestige for those members seeking wider recognition or broader opportunities; conversely, somewhat hidden organizations may be better suited for long-term retention of those members seeking to stay in one location without having to physically relocate to potentially advance in the sort of organization that has a much larger national or even international presence.

Moderately Shaded (Region 3): Recognized, Silent, and Mass/Public

The organizations in this region of our framework are only somewhat hidden and share much in common with relatively transparent organizations. Like their more mildly shaded counterparts, these moderately shaded organizations seek to make their identity highly visible. This slightly more hidden region may have a relatively more mass/public audience that is most relevant, but it is moderately well shaded because the organizational members do not generally express their belonging and membership with the organization. Figure 3 displays this region and highlights two different organizations we will describe in detail that may fit here: the U.S. Internal Revenue Service and Earth First!.

Like more transparent and even mildly shaded collectives, organizations in this region are relatively visible; that is, they work to make their identity recognizable rather than keep it anonymous. Doing so, especially to a mass audience, likely requires certain communicative resources and personnel even though these organizations are often not as large as more transparent organizations. Even these moderately shaded organizations still make substantial disclosures about their identity, which may include various branding and other promotional efforts that serve to increase organizational name recognition and visibility. These organizations also regularly have slogans and various visual logos associated with them as well as widely available mission and/or vision statements. Demographic data and information about partner organizations, all of which reveal parts of who the organization is, are also likely to be available. Like transparent and mildly shaded collectives, there is usually a recognizable physical location, which typically means an address or even a building/structure associated with organizations in this region. Phone and fax numbers, a web address, and other contact information are almost certainly available in various places. These moderately shaded types may also offer pictures of their locations, top leadership, and other core activities. They likely have a wide range of communication channels that are clearly tied to the organization. Like their transparent and less shaded counterparts, these organizations generally seek credit for their actions and tend to work hard on constructing an image that conveys their identity.

However, the moderately shaded region differs from the mildly shaded one in two important ways. Like transparent organizations, the most relevant audience is more of a mass/diffuse one as opposed to a highly localized one. The collectives in this region are generally trying to be recognizable to a large audience which may even include the general public. For these organizations, general reputation matters greatly. Reaching a large and diffuse audience creates certain demands on those in this region, including increased likelihood of using major mass media in various advertising, public relations, and other outreach efforts—often through various formal communication functions. In general, the organizations in this region are operating in a larger national or global arena as they provide products or services to a wider audience. These moderately shaded organizations likely operate in more locales and more diverse locations. This focus is clearly different from what we saw with the mildly shaded organizations and their more local/limited focus.

However, the key difference here that distinguishes this region from the more transparent and even more mildly shaded organizations is that the members in these organizations are relatively quiet about their organizational membership. They are more likely to display silence than clear expressions of belonging. For organizations in this region, members do not talk about their employer or particular organizations with whom they are affiliated. Involvement with such collectives often remains shielded from most outsiders. This might reflect a demonstration of loyalty by remaining silent but may also reflect some shame or embarrassment about the organization in which a member works/belongs. In this region, members are less likely to mention the name of the organization when talking with others and it is less common to use language that suggests membership (e.g., "we," "our," or "us"). Members of these moderately shaded organizations may know organizational mottos, goals, or secret codes, but they would not share those (or do so in very limited ways) with outsiders. For some members in these organizations, silence results from a lack of knowledge about the organization's identity; in other cases, knowledge about problematic identity may promote silence. For some members in these moderately shaded organizations, the silence could even take the form of denials of membership or downplaying of the organization. It is relatively less likely that the average member will defend or promote the organization to outsiders. In this region, members are less likely to provide contact information that reveals their organizational membership; thus, we would not expect to see widespread sharing of business cards or other membership documents that may exist. Depending on the motive for the silence, members may even use masks to conceal their identity. Members further avoid statements of affiliation by not wearing clothing or openly displaying other items with the organization's name/logo. Other actions of organizational members in this region do not reveal clear affiliation with the organization of which they are part (further hiding their membership).

Thus, moderately shaded organizations are like transparent ones in terms of the organization's recognizability to a larger mass/public audience; however, the actual members of the organization are more likely to conceal their affiliation than to express it. In many ways, this region is not one where we would hope or expect to find numerous organizations—in part because we know many people are in organizations they identify with and because we know people regularly wish to express their memberships. Nevertheless, we do find this type of hidden organization where members are relatively silent about their belonging. Organizations in this region could be large businesses or nonprofits or even major government agencies that perhaps have very poor reputations, which leads members to avoid the negative status associated with belonging to such groups. We might also find examples of major organizations engaged in what we described earlier as "dirty work," where members' activities have some sort of moral, social, or physical taint (Ashforth and Kreiner 1999). This region could also include visible national/international intelligence agencies using clandestine or undercover members. It is possible that even certain global criminal networks fit here when we know much about the organization generally but not about its members who protect the organization through their silence. We offer a couple of slightly more detailed examples of these somewhat unique moderately shaded organizations here.

U.S. Internal Revenue Service (IRS)

Even as a U.S. taxpayer who almost enjoys the annual spring ritual of preparing our family's tax return and as someone who always rather appreciated the inscription on the IRS building stating, "Taxes are what we pay for civilized society," I confess to still feeling like apparently many Americans do: The IRS scares me. That fear for most comes out of stories about unfriendly audits and the difficulty many face in trying to understand complicated tax law; but all this relates in part to the somewhat hidden nature of this organization. Because of the IRS's role as a tax collector and its bad reputation with the general public, even many of its own members hide their membership with the organization.

Having a reputation, good or bad, implies visibility; clearly, the IRS is a relatively well-known federal agency even though its culture is one that closely guards confidential and private records. According to their own familiar website (www.irs.gov), "The IRS is a bureau of the Department of the Treasury and one of the world's most efficient tax administrators." This bureau is highly visible in the United States, though the name "Internal Revenue Service" only dates back to the 1950s. The agency contains a section labeled "about the IRS" that includes organizational charts, strategic plans, mission statements, organizational history, and information about agency leadership. The mission is to "provide America's taxpayers top quality service by helping them understand and meet their tax responsibilities and enforce the law with integrity and fairness to all." The site also shows a picture of the current commissioner who heads the IRS and a bio about him. The home page even shows a picture of agency headquarters at 1111 Constitution Avenue, NW in Washington, D.C. Although numerous phone numbers are provided for tax-related questions and addresses are listed for mailing returns, there is only limited contact information to reach other organizational officials. The agency has a specific Communications and Liaison Office to "ensure that communications with customers, Congress and stakeholders are consistent and coordinated IRS-wide." That group also controls the IRS logos, specifically describing them as part of their branding efforts.

Clearly, the relevant audience for this federal agency is one of the largest nations in the world. The organization even lists its key stakeholders as including "national media" and "the American public." Information is available in six different languages to reach the larger audience of U.S. citizens of various cultural backgrounds. Local offices are found in every state as well as in Puerto Rico. According to the IRS website, the agency collects $2.4 trillion in tax revenue annually that funds most government and public services. As the current commissioner puts it: "The agency touches every facet of American society."

Unfortunately, many Americans have not liked the way the IRS has "touched" them. Historically, surveys have regularly rated the IRS at or near the bottom of customer satisfaction assessments (EHS Today Staff 1999). Tax collectors have been viewed negatively long before the IRS, but a number of scandals (including tax evasion for a former commissioner) and less than friendly tactics by collection agents have created a very negative reputation for the bureau that it has battled for decades. Under such circumstances, where the general public dislikes most things about the agency, employees of the agency may have a hard time publicly identifying with their employer. In fact they may very well hide their membership entirely. Few comments might kill a conversation faster than this response to a question about where one works: "I work for the IRS" (in comparison, the conversational dampener, "I am a communication professor," does not seem so bad). This lack of affiliation is further expressed in people leaving the organization entirely. Even today following efforts at reform, turnover is very high in the IRS. Recent reports suggest 16 percent of the 100,000-person staff leave each year (and only about one-fourth of those are retirements) and attrition rates of recent hires in critical positions is growing (Rankin 2008). Turnover has been linked to organizational identification in this organization and others. A study of IRS employees in 2002 revealed that a measure of job involvement and intrinsic motivation—which actually contained some items similar to organizational identification measures—was the strongest predictor of intention to leave the organization for these employees (Bertelli 2006). In that analysis, nearly 25 percent of respondents indicated they were considering leaving the organization.

One of the most informative looks inside this organization comes from an agency historian turned whistleblower. Shelley Davis's (1997) book *Unbridled Power: Inside the Secret Culture of the IRS* describes the agency as one with little pride—and even some shame—among many members. She recounts her orientation session where several speakers told the newcomers it can be "a social embarrassment to work here" where the basic message was "one of shame and discomfort about working for the IRS" (19). As one presenter told them, "You'll have an easier time of it if you tell people you work for the Treasury Department" (20). Davis claims this silence or even deception about who they worked for also led to members being silent about misconduct—contributing to a culture that made such actions possible. While she suggests there was some effort to promote member silence by keeping them in the dark, and that some members were silent out of a deep loyalty to the organization, embarrassment about the troubled bureaucratic agency seems to best explain members' own choice to be silent. Davis also notes that unlike many other agencies, the IRS did not have souvenirs and promotional items for members and customers; indeed, you are unlikely to find employees sporting their "IRS employee" T-shirt or driving around in a vehicle with an agency bumper sticker. Because of this employee silence in terms of their own affiliation with the organization, we can describe the IRS as a moderately shaded organization whose identity is not generally communicated by its members.

Earth First!

Another moderately shaded organization goes by the name Earth First! (EF!). EF! may have a radical identity, which has contributed in part to its relative recognizability (see Balser 1997). The organization's website notes EF! emerged around 1980,

> in response to a lethargic, compromising, and increasingly corporate environmental community. Earth First! takes a decidedly different tack towards environmental issues. We believe in using all the tools in the tool box, ranging from grassroots organizing and involvement in the legal process to civil disobedience and monkeywrenching.

Their online site goes on to describe the organization as "an international movement composed of small, bioregionally-based groups. . . . We apply 'direct pressure' to stop the bleeding, with a combination of education, litigation, and creative civil disobedience." Although some industry and law enforcement groups have called this organization a "radical environmental advocacy group" and even an "ecoterrorism organization," EF! describes itself as more of a social movement. They avoid the label "organization" because they see it as similar to "corporate" and being at odds with their desires for a decentralized, leaderless collective. However, management scholars Kimberly Elsbach and Robert Sutton (1992) persuasively argue that EF! is a social movement *organization* because it has the characteristics of such collectives (fundraising, media, a structure with local chapters that operate under the EF! banner, etc.). They further note that organizations like Earth First! have to present themselves to the media in ways that help to create more visibility for them.

The website itself (www.earthfirst.org/) does illustrate the organization's logo (a clenched fist with a circular, globe-like background) and its credo: "No compromise in the defense of Mother Earth!" It does not provide clear contact information for the organization or its leadership (only an email address to reach the webmaster). However, as communication scholar Kevin DeLuca (1999) explains, it is not that the organization hides its headquarters and leadership staff—it is that they are an organization that consciously chooses not to have either. The organization does have spokespersons, and for a while that role was filled primarily by founder Dave Foreman. DeLuca goes on to note that activist groups like Earth First! "practice an alternative image politics, performing image events for mass media dissemination" (10). More so than the website, the Earth First! journal is the voice of the organization and the radical environmental movement. It has a phone number, post office box/ city, and email address, and was originally edited by founder Foreman. The journal notes about the organization, "Our structure is non-hierarchical, and we reject highly paid 'professional staff' and formal leadership." This site does offer a directory of local chapters—with email addresses and some phone numbers and street addresses provided as well.

Although the organization is relatively visible, the members overall appear at least somewhat more silent than expressive about their belonging to this organization. Interestingly, the main organization claims to have no members (only Earth First!er activists) and the email lists to contact these members/activists are not shared. To be clear, EF! members are generally committed while they are members (their own website describes them as "the most diverse, passionate, committed, and uncompromising group of environmental activists") and some do actively express themselves as EF! members when they engage in activities like tree sitting or blocking roads with their bodies. Yet, critics in the organization have noted the rapid turnover of members from year to year (Rodin 2008). The organization does sell bumper stickers and T-shirts (though relatively few of these actually mention Earth First! by name and it is not clear if these are widely purchased and used by members). However, other activities (known as "monkeywrenching") are done very discreetly (e.g., tree spiking, sabotaging equipment) so that members can keep silent and let the organization take responsibility. Practices of civil disobedience and especially monkeywrenching (sometimes called *ecotage*) put members at odds with law enforcement and sometimes public opinion; consequently, specific members will avoid claiming responsibility for actions and will keep silent about their work on behalf of EF! to avoid being caught by law enforcement. Others add that because EF! is depicted by the media as violent and terroristic (DeLuca 1999), some members will be reluctant to reveal themselves to outsiders.

The EF! Journal website reveals the more silent nature of many Earth First!ers in that it offers multiple ways for members to communicate privately and even anonymously—including hushmail accounts and encrypted messages. It even directs members to an affiliated site called "Bite Back," which provides news about frontline attacks by EF! and other groups (but almost always posted anonymously with no mention of specific members involved). The main EF! website offers advice on not getting caught (avoiding jail time). Members have also been advised to engage in monkeywrenching alone or with only a trusted colleague to avoid arrest (Balser 1997). Additionally, founder Dave Foreman's (1985) book *Ecodefense: A Field Guide to Monkeywrenching* advised people on how to engage in ecotage and get away without detection.

Management scholars Elsbach and Sutton (1992) could not even get some Earth First!ers to talk to them about their work with the organization—and those that did were not as willing to disclose information about illegitimate actions as were members of other activist groups. More importantly, they argue that there is a communicatively important difference between the organization's official actions and the behaviors of its members. The organization can retain legitimacy by appearing rational and/or having safeguards in place. "The ability of these organizations to decouple illegitimate actions from legitimate structures and still maintain their identities as organizations was due partly to the loose coupling within and between the local chapters" (715–716) where members were. Thus, organizations could be visible and avoid negativity through this decoupling while individual members of more local chapters might avoid consequences by remaining shielded. Elsbach and Sutton go on to note EF! has even claimed historically that acts were carried out by *anonymous* individuals.

EF! has what they describe as their worldwide organization and website. But, they also have specific chapters and branches that operate in numerous countries across the globe (e.g., Australia, Croatia, Czech Republic, England, Italy, and the Netherlands) and throughout much of the United States. The organization's primary actions are in response to what they perceive as a planetary environmental crisis and have occurred at various locales across the United States (with a few in other countries also). As an organization, they seek out media attention (and have often received it) from mainstream news and have made efforts to influence national laws and public opinion. Their members may specifically hide from the same media and do not seek to express their membership to them. Thus, EF! is a moderately shaded organization in that the organization's identity is relatively recognizable to a mass/public audience, but individual members generally have to take steps to conceal their affiliation with EF!.

Socialization

For moderately shaded organizations where members are not generally expressive of their affiliation, effective socialization can be problematic. This is not to say that such organizations do not care about recruiting and socializing new members. We know that they have to bring in new members regularly, and when the organization itself is relatively visible it can do that in somewhat traditional ways. At first glance, however, recruitment may look very different from organization to organization in this region. For example, the IRS's online career section is fairly extensive and resembles what one might see on more transparent corporate sites, while EF! has relatively little beyond a suggestion that each chapter establish a website for potential members (and some chapters have links to "take action" and/or an orientation guidebook for new members); the IRS does this in a fairly centralized fashion whereas membership is largely based in the local chapters for EF!; the IRS has a more extensive process for actually selecting and hiring members whereas a group like EF! is more likely to take almost anyone who wishes to join; and the IRS may not seek certain types that do not fit easily into the existing culture whereas one of the EF! chapter orientation guides suggests it really needs people who have new ideas and will get things done even as new members.

What is somewhat unique about socialization in this moderately shaded region is that efforts must be made to overcome the negative reputations often associated with these organizations. In such cases, anticipatory socialization about specific organizations or the industries of which they are part may set negative expectations that deter many potential members. Current members who do not talk about their organizational membership (or do not talk positively about it) are not good sources of anticipatory socialization information at least from the organization's perspective. We do not typically see guidance counselors or popular media promoting these organizations as good places to work or important organizations of which to be part. Thus, organizations have had to seek out members on a different basis (e.g., improving America by working at the IRS or fighting Corporate America by becoming part of EF!).

For those that do decide to join, getting them completely socialized—reaching metamorphosis in Jablin's (2001) terms—is still difficult. The individual may join, but not fully value what the organization stands for; they may remain only loosely attached because the criminal or questionable nature of the work requires them to be able to separate if need be; they may be embarrassed about who they are and what their organization does, limiting full socialization into the organization's culture; and/or they may be well socialized but have to pretend that they are not full-fledged members (or perhaps not affiliated at all) for their own physical/legal safety/protection. The limited socialization may also occur when one cannot easily trust other members as they seek out information about the organization. When others are not necessarily well socialized either, when they are suspicious of newcomers and their motives, when they have seen others come and go readily, or when existing members are generally reluctant to talk about their organization and their work, they are poor information sources. Members cannot go outside the organization for such information either, so the socialization process may reinforce the modest and/or short-term identification levels by all but the most dedicated of members.

This lack of full socialization and identification directly contributes to turnover in these organizations. We have already noted that turnover in EF! and the IRS is quite high. People also tend to leave various forms of dirty work more quickly. Even certain criminal activities and undercover work come with stresses and dangers that likely limit retention. When turnover is high, new members must be sought more often, further emphasizing the socialization problems in these moderately shaded organizations.

Mostly Shaded (Region 4): Anonymous, Expressed, and Mass/Public

The last of our shaded regions is the most shaded of all. Though it still shares more in common with transparent organizations than dark ones (i.e., members express affiliation and the relevant audience is a large mass/public one), the organizations here are relatively more anonymous than recognizable when it comes to communicating identity. Again, Figure 3 positions this region relative to the rest of the framework and highlights two rather different organizations operating here that we will examine further: Scientology and Nivarox-FAR.

Like transparent organizations and even mildly shaded ones, the individual members of these mostly shaded organizations generally express their membership and belonging to others (rather than keep silent about it). In these organizations, we would expect to discover various members stating their affiliation with the organization. The name of the organization is spoken with relative ease when members are describing themselves and what they do to others. Typically, members even in these mostly shaded organizations use collective pronouns like "we" and "our" (not "they" and "their") and other positive language when talking about the organization and their role in it. Employees and other members may know and recite company missions, visions, or other similar phrases. This expression of identification could include defending the organization when it is criticized and a variety of nonverbal displays (wearing a jacket with a company logo, using a deskset with the organization's name prominently displayed, or proudly showing one's membership card to others) that reveal affiliation. This expressed identification can also be seen in the knowledge members have about the organization and what it represents (e.g., basic identity information like being able to share the company's website and other contact information). Additionally, the decisions that these identified members make in these mostly shaded collectives are ones that promote the organization's goals and interests.

What makes this region the most shaded is that the organizations found here are relatively invisible, which means they make themselves more anonymous than recognized. Organizations in this region generally do not wish to be known to most others nor have a name that is highly recognized. Of course, organizations in this region have names so they can refer to themselves, but they may use a front name or pseudonym to help hide the identity of the actual organization involved. They do not typically promote that name itself in advertising or corporate branding efforts (and may do relatively little, if any, advertising or branding of this type). Visual identity elements (logos, graphics) are less likely and slogans known to outsiders are less common (though symbols may be used internally to signal one another). Usually, signage is small and discreet to the extent it exists at physical locations, which are often themselves in less visible places. These mostly shaded organizations may still have an online presence, but less is revealed about the organization's identity compared to other shaded collectives: generally less contact information is provided, there is relatively less mention of vision and mission statements, and we find less visibility of organizational leadership (in terms of naming them or posting pictures). In this region, we might expect little in the way of demographic information about the organization and others with which it partners. The mostly shaded organization may even utilize channels that help it conceal parts of its identity from most others (e.g., interpersonal interactions with only trusted others, private or restricted mailing lists and intranets, etc.). Although organizations in this region may seek some credit for certain actions, they will regularly avoid the attention of most audiences. This relative anonymity might also be facilitated via efforts to keep the organization somewhat small and/or relatively decentralized.

What is perhaps a bit counterintuitive about this region is that the relevant audience is a more mass/diffuse (as opposed to highly localized) one. This is true in a general sense for the organization in terms of the relevant audience for its services. In most cases, these organizations are operating on a larger stage—perhaps one that is again more national or global—as they provide products or services to a wider range of others. These mostly shaded organizations likely operate in multiple, diverse locales and their members may travel more widely and interact with a relatively varied audience. More importantly here, the mass/public audience is very relevant for the members as they communicate their belonging/affiliation with the organization somewhat widely. But, when it comes to keeping the organization's identity more anonymous than recognizable, the goal is to do that in a way that conceals identity information from the mass/public audience primarily. Concealing it more locally is not the primary goal since that is not the primary audience. The organizations in this region do not want the broader public to necessarily know who they truly are—which may be accomplished by some active efforts to conceal information from that audience. It is that broader audience that is in mind when efforts are made to keep a low organizational profile. As we noted earlier, it may be less difficult to be anonymous and silent to the general public than to one's more immediate local audience, who may have a stronger interest in identifying the organization and its members—thus the focus on a mass/public audience rather than the more local/limited one is part of what separates this mostly shaded organization from the more shadowed ones to follow.

This particular combination of relatively expressive members in a relatively anonymous organization whose most relevant audience is still a mass/public one means that we may not find large numbers of organizations operating here. Mostly shaded organizations could include international secret societies where the organization is secret but membership is public; firms that operate on more than a local scale but still keep a low profile to avoid unwanted attention (that could make doing business more costly); far-reaching new religious movements or cults where the organization's identity remains largely hidden even as it and its members seek out a more public/mass membership; and larger organizations that hide their identity behind the use of various front organizations. In an attempt to better understand this region, we look at a couple of organizations that appear to operate primarily here. However, we do so with two qualifications. First, these organizations may only barely be located here (being very much on the fringe with other regions too). Second, the motivations of the organization for keeping its own identity hidden can vary vastly here. As we will see in our example organizations, one reason for being mostly shaded may have to do with hiding certain questionable identities of the organization. However other motivations may include a goal to maintain privacy, a lack of need for widespread recognition (or the resources required to attain it), and/or a desire to avoid attention that might expose certain secrets.

Scientology

This organization is a fascinating one in many respects. While it is not a perfect example of an organization in this region and may even be somewhat unique, it would seem to fit here better than elsewhere. In some ways this organization's identity (or at least one of them) is relatively recognizable (clearly it is known publicly thanks to media coverage and investigations into the organization's practices). Its own website (www.scientology.org), which is filled with videos and textual information, describes what Scientology is as a religious philosophy and offers information about how the organization is structured. There are creeds and codes about what members believe. There is information on the founder as well as the current chairman and ecclesiastical leader of the organization (including his picture). There is a media relations staff and spokespersons listed and depicted (though their job may involve as much concealing of certain information as promoting other parts of the organization's identity); however, those are the only members of organizational leadership mentioned. The headquarters is mentioned as being in Los Angeles, but contact information is difficult to locate (provided only in the "newsroom" link). Some other cities with churches are listed, but again, no specific contact information is provided in that text (there is a church locator feature that does provide addresses and phone numbers, but it takes several steps to access that identity information). The obscure link for "contact" only offers a space to provide one's own contact information and ask questions. There are physical buildings for the headquarters and the churches, some with sizable signage and others with somewhat less noticeable signs. The organization has even sponsored a Formula 1 race car, but it used the Dianetics book brand rather than the actual name of the organization. Numerous questions are answered online, though some responses about reasons for the organization's confidentiality and secrecy may not be very satisfying to most audiences. Religious media scholar Mara Einstein (2011) also notes that Scientology recently launched an expensive advertising campaign purportedly to explain, "What is Scientology?" (However, she concludes that it was really a religious branding effort to overcome negative publicity and drive sales.)

Despite all that, other evidence suggests Scientology as an organization—or at least certain identities it has—seems slightly more anonymous than recognizable. Religious studies professor Hugh Urban notes, "From its origins, the Church of Scientology and its founder have been shrouded in complex layers of secrecy . . . the more scrutiny the movement has faced from the government, anticult groups, and the media, the more intense its strategies of self-concealment have become" (2006, 358). Urban argues its tactics of secrecy and concealment mirror the FBI's and are expressions coming out of basic Cold War concerns felt by many Americans in the 1950s when the church was founded. He goes on to say that organizations "who face political persecution often adopt even more complex strategies of concealment as a basic means of survival. Scientology, however, would go further still, using the cloak of secrecy not only to protect itself but also to carry out aggressive acts against its enemies" (375), including lawsuits against anyone attempting to reveal its secrets. Professor Urban makes the case that Scientology's concerns with secrecy have actually grown more intense over the past three decades.

Part of that secrecy centers around fundamental confusion over exactly what kind of organization Scientology is. Debates rage about whether this is a self-help business or a religion—and it is possible that both identities can be found. It may even be seen as a criminal organization; in fact, *Time* magazine described the organization as "a hugely profitable global racket that survives by intimidating members and critics in a Mafia-like manner" (Behar 1991, 52). Others have suggested it is a social movement (Peckham 1998), similar to a secret society (Urban), or claimed it only pretends to be a religion—seeing the "masquerading strategy as merely a matter of marketing, a facade, behind which hides the true essence of the organization" (Beit-Hallahmi 2003, 48). Some have called it a quasi-religion or even a cult, where ambiguity about the group's core beliefs are actually used to gain affiliation and commitment. Scientology presents itself as a religious organization to get tax concessions and is classified in the United States as a nonprofit—though even that took decades to achieve and not all other countries view it similarly. Others who have critically looked at the organization's identity have described it as a deviant business that must borrow from science and remain a religion (Passas and Castillo 1992). The use of numerous front organizations (e.g., "The Way to Happiness Foundation") have also helped to hide the actual organization from others (Beit-Hallahmi). Add to all that a founder and initial leader described by one Los Angeles superior court judge as schizophrenic—and who was regularly hiding from others or creating new identities and disguises for himself and his organization (see Beit-Hallahmi)—and it starts to become clear that at least the very central identity of Scientology as a "business" is kept relatively hidden.

Additional insights into this organization are provided by two key book authors. Sociologist Roy Wallis wrote in his book *The Road to Total Freedom* (1977) that Scientology is more like a multinational business than it is like a church, describing it as a complex bureaucracy with multiple possible faces. Additionally, Wallis notes that the headquarters moved locations regularly and that the location of its founder (L. Ron Hubbard) was often kept secret. More recently, journalist Janet Reitman's *Inside Scientology: The Story of American's Most Secretive Religion* (2011) has provided a more comprehensive history of what she labels a "shape-shifting organization." In this work, she notes that "Hubbard summed up his philosophy: 'MAKE MONEY. MAKE MORE MONEY. MAKE OTHERS PRODUCE AS TO MAKE MONEY'" (emphasis in original, 96). A number of ex-Scientologists reinforce this claim that the organization was primarily about making money; furthermore, the payment of sizable fees to the organization by members/customers in order to learn otherwise secret core beliefs is highly irregular for an actual religious entity. Reitman's work also suggests that the same unit of Scientology (the Office of Special Affairs) that handles the public relations also handled its most secretive undertakings. She describes an organization with several fronts and brands that could be used to promote Scientology without ever having to say "Scientology." Additionally, Reitman notes that the top leaders of the organization have historically been hard to geographically pinpoint— at first aboard a ship whose locations were kept secret and later using secret summer and winter headquarters for Hubbard and a few other key personnel. Taken together, these books and other evidence do point to an organization whose core identity is more anonymous than recognizable.

Although details about specific members is not widely available (and the number of Scientologists is debated, though reported to be in the millions), members of this organization appear more likely to express their affiliation than remain silent about it. The website has profiles of multiple members from all walks of life where they state their name and say, "I'm a Scientologist." Members who are celebrities (e.g., Tom Cruise, John Travolta) have talked extensively about their belonging to the church and have advanced its cause. In general, members are encouraged and expected to go out and say positive things about the organization. Members are instructed not to go online and look at information critical of the church (Reitman 2011), which may make it easier to express identification. Others who experience attacks against their church become more loyal in their efforts to defend it (and occasionally even to correct it). "Most of the loyal members of the organization, those who are willing to identify themselves in public as 'Scientologists,' are actually employees or entrepreneurs working with and for the organization" (Beit-Hallahmi 2003, 19). Those expressions are not radical and extreme but would come from a "safe pointing" policy that urges followers to present themselves as rational, stable experts (Reitman). Additionally, to some extent, clothing helps identify members and employees of Scientology: counselors began wearing clerical collars to reinforce the religious nature of the organization; volunteer ministers in very recognizable yellow Scientology shirts can often be found helping after natural disasters; and uniformed members run the organization. Perhaps the largest expression of commitment is the significant amount of money members pay to the church. Another expression of affiliation is what the organization's website describes as the billion-year contract some employees sign to symbolize their eternal commitment to the organization. In general, the organization demands and attains strong loyalty (Reitman 2011); even though there have certainly been defectors who have publicly attacked the church, they have often remained faithful to Scientology while criticizing its leadership.

Clearly, the relevant audience here is a more mass/global one. Scientology boasts having members on every populated continent. It is regularly referred to as a global enterprise (Reitman 2011), with offices/churches in multiple countries. The website is available in a dozen different languages and talks about bringing Scientology to the world. Of course, it is also this somewhat broader audience from which the organization has had to conceal itself—especially as it deals with probes from mainstream media, various international governments, the IRS, the FBI, and others on a somewhat massive scale.

Nivarox-FAR

A very different, but *timely* example comes from the Swiss watchmaking industry. Described by some as the most important company you have never heard of, this organization makes tiny components, including the planet's smallest screws (Top Component Maker 2007) central to many of the world's mechanical watches. Although it has a clear physical presence in the Jura Mountains of Switzerland and a website (www.nivarox.com/fr) with basic contact information, the organization itself is almost as hidden as the tiny internal watch components it produces. This anonymity takes several forms. Being a company within the Swatch Group allows it to keep a low profile, which is important given the highly competitive and somewhat secretive nature of the watchmaking industry. Yet, it retains a sense of independence from Swatch that allows it to be its own company. Its location is relatively isolated, with headquarters in one of Switzerland's smallest actual cities (Le Locle). Nivarox-FAR's four manufacturing plants and nearly one thousand employees are all located in the same region, further helping it limit its exposure. It is a good-sized firm by Swiss watchmaking standards; yet few people outside the local community and the world watch industry know about it. The plants are closed to all but approved Swatch Group employees; even tours and interviews for journalists are rare. Its website is only in French. It neither lists nor depicts leaders/management, contains no vision/mission statements, and overall provides very limited information.

The organization does not sell directly to the public but has a well-established market with the Swatch Group and other independent watchmakers. In this sense, it rarely needs to promote itself. As Hermann Simon (2009) points out in his new edition of *Hidden Champions*, Nivarox-FAR controls 90 percent of the market for its products already. Others have described that position as nearly monopolistic (Top Component Maker 2007). Simon notes that hidden champions like Nivarox-FAR "operate in the 'hinterland' of the value chain, supplying machinery, components, or processes that are no longer discernable in the final product or service" (13). Simon's observations about other hidden champions seem to apply to Nivarox-FAR: they do not worry about image and focus on business.

Direct information on how members express identification is very limited. However, there is no reason to think employees are not proud of their employer and they may be generally willing to express their belonging to this organization. Although the secretive nature of the industry may limit how much members can say about what they do precisely, they are likely still relatively more expressive about their belonging to the organization than silent about it. Simon (2009) suggests that in hidden champions like Nivarox-FAR, who have worked hard to be the world leader in their market, it is easy to identify with such a proven winner. His research suggests that employee loyalty is one of the greatest strengths of any hidden champion—and that they typically have much lower turnover (which is a clear expression of belonging to the organization). We also can infer a little based on what we know about the larger Swatch Group that owns Nivarox-FAR. In 2011 the parent Swatch Group was named as the fourth-best company to work for in all of Switzerland (Best Places 2011). Additionally, the Swatch Group website says their strength is employees who have a loyalty to their brand, their factory, and to the Swatch Group overall.

The relevant audience for the company is more mass/public than local/limited. Although it is part of the Swatch Group, Nivarox-FAR sells its vital products to watchmakers around the globe and for a global market. Indeed, the entire industry has only one market: the world. It is also this global market and a global media from which Nivarox-FAR seeks to retain some of its anonymity. It benefits from other global competitors not knowing too much about it and from limiting media access to its core.

Socialization

The process of socialization is of substantial importance even in these mostly shaded organizations, as they still rely heavily on recruiting and retaining quality members and employees. For the most part, decisions to join these organizations are voluntary; but, as we see with both our example organizations, recruitment is also based in part on bringing in family members and subsequent generations of current members. Scientology specifically seeks out the children and friends of current members. Nivarox-FAR also has a history of multiple generations working for them. Friends and family are a more recruitable resource as well, because they may be some of the only ones that have much information (or, in some cases, at least much positive information) about these organizations. Very little specific anticipatory socialization would seem to exist for mostly shaded organizations unless one already knows a friend or family member who belongs. When one does know such individuals, who are often willing to talk quite openly about their organization, then a fair amount of favorable anticipatory socialization may occur.

However, mostly shaded organizations will still make active attempts to gain new recruits beyond friends and family of current members (whose numbers alone would often be insufficient for sustaining the organization). Because these mostly shaded organizations are largely anonymous to much of the public—based on their secretive nature, isolated locations, or other reasons—they cannot just expect most people to stumble on them and seek them out directly. We see that with Scientology or other organizations who actively recruit (i.e., "sell") potential members on the organization through both personal contact and information available online. Other organizations, like Nivarox-FAR, may use traditional job postings to attract members in ways that comply with laws and industry norms—but also seek out new employees more informally in the communities where they operate. In both cases, efforts to recruit end up being fairly localized to recruit members into a specific branch/church or because of the geographically restricted nature of what may be a relatively small or medium-sized organization. Recruitment is not as easy here as it may be for more transparent organizations. These mostly shaded organizations may either lack a high profile or not necessarily have a well understood or even positive profile; thus, recruits may look elsewhere first or need special convincing to join a mostly shaded organization.

These organizations may also be relatively selective in their recruitment. They may target people with specific skills when the organization is a highly specialized one; they may target someone with required resources (e.g., money) if the organization operates as a quasi-business selling services to its own members. Or, they may seek those who appear best suited to a less visible or more secretive organization (someone who does not need a high-profile employer or organization with a strong public reputation in order to be a loyal member). Scientology is known to use personality tests to lure people in, though it is not known how widely such tools might be used by mostly shaded organizations to assess the fit of potential members. Part of the goal here is to recruit members and employees who will be loyal. Despite some defections and turnover, both Scientology and Nivarox-FAR (as a hidden champion) demonstrate strong employee loyalty. In these mostly shaded organizations where the members express themselves but the organization is kept hidden, loyalty and low turnover may be especially important to protect the organization's hidden identity. How that loyalty is maintained may vary, but the key is the organization must take strong steps to keep turnover low.

The information-seeking aspect of socialization into a mostly shaded organization suggests somewhat heavier reliance on official organizational sources. These of course might include official documents and policies as well as information from peers and more senior members of the organization. Members can talk about their belonging and affiliation to outsiders, but outsiders are not likely to provide much information relevant to these more anonymous organizations. The nature of these organizations provides insiders with opportunities to gather information both directly and indirectly. However, all the relevant information may not be revealed immediately. Because of the somewhat secretive nature of these organizations, some aspects of who the organization is may be kept even from members for at least certain periods of time. Scientology would seem to demonstrate that practice to an extreme in that its secrets are revealed in stages as members become better prepared to receive them.

Closing the Shades

In closing, this chapter has considered three variations of shaded regions where we might find organizations. In terms of how the organization and its members communicate identity to various audiences, they share much in common with more transparent regions; but each has one characteristic that makes it at least somewhat shaded. In the mildly shaded region, identities are only known to a local audience—hiding the organization from the broader public. Organizations here are similar to the more transparent ones described previously: corporations, nonprofits, and various government agencies; however, these are not the major high-visibility collectives whose names are generally recognizable. These mildly shaded organizations are more likely to be smaller businesses and corporations that choose a more limited market focus as well as local nonprofits and the local government organizations that matter in the communities in which they operate but may be invisible to others beyond that. This region may have more organizations in it than any other. The moderately shaded region is distinguished by members who conceal their belonging to the organization for various reasons. Organizations in this region could be large businesses, government agencies, or even nonprofits that have reputation or legitimacy problems—leading members to at least somewhat dissociate with them. Here we might also find examples of major organizations engaged in morally, socially, or physically tainted "dirty work." This region could also include visible national/international intelligence agencies using clandestine or undercover members and even certain global criminal networks where we know much about the organization generally but not about members who protect the organization through their silence. Finally, the mostly shaded region is characterized by relatively anonymous organizations (but with members who express their affiliation and a mass/public relevant audience). This unique combination of characteristics suggests there may not be that many organizations operating in this region. These could include international secret societies where the organization is anonymous but membership is publicly expressed; firms (e.g., hidden champions) that operate on a larger stage but still keep a low profile to avoid undesired attention that might hurt business; new religious movements where the organization's identity remains largely hidden even as it and its members seek out a more public/mass membership; and larger organizations that hide their identity behind the use of various front organizations.

Although each shares some commonalities with one another, their distinctions are important. The type and degree of shading matters here, and the specific organizations we have examined help to illustrate that point. Clearly, there are variations within each region (sometimes pertaining to the motives behind the efforts to hide identity), but differences across regions are likely even more important. Our examination of differences in socialization help to illustrate some of the challenges and opportunities an organization faces depending on which aspects of it are at least somewhat shaded. These challenges become even more interesting as we move toward the increasingly dark organizations described as "shadowed" in the next chapter.

7 Under the Radar and Out of the Spotlight

Shadowed Organizations

U p until now we have mostly considered regions and organizations that are not extremely hidden overall. Even the mostly shaded organizations from the previous chapter have more in common with transparent organizations than dark ones. In this chapter, we take a turn toward the dark side. Each of the shadowed regions considered here has more in common with dark organizations than transparent ones. These shadowed organizations may be only partially hidden, but the shadow regions are clearly more concealed than not.

As first described back in chapter 4, shadowed regions are characterized by limited visibility and familiarity where much is obscured. The organizations operating here do so largely in the dark, but there is still enough light operating to cast some shadows and thus we can catch glimpses of the organizations and their members as they step out from the darkness. Anything shadowed may imply it is also sinister—and a number of organizations found here may indeed have questionable aspects. However, there is nothing inherently evil about operating in the shadows. As we will see, some organizations are shadowed as part of efforts to shield members, to safeguard clients or customers, and to protect what certain audiences may judge to be problematic organizational practices.

Given the challenges of being completely dark, these shadowed regions contain many of the most interesting and consequential hidden organizations found in both historical and contemporary organizational eras. Regions 5,

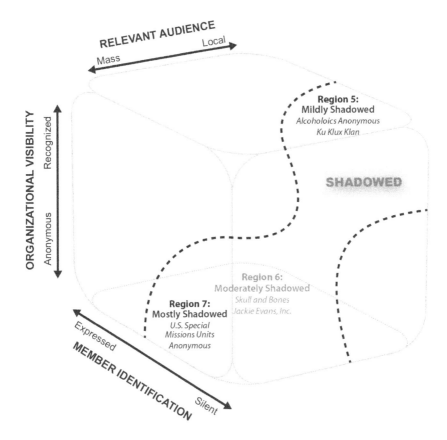

FIGURE 4. Shadowed Regions in Framework and Representative Organizations for Each.

6, and 7 are all shadowed based on the model we have presented here. Figure 4 displays these shadowed regions in relation to one another and offers representative organizations for each. Just as we have done for the regions in the previous two chapters, we will characterize how organizations and their members in each of these regions communicate identity and to whom, suggest some possible examples of collectives typically found in each of these areas, and then discuss how socialization processes might play out in each of these shadowed regions.

Mildly Shadowed (Region 5):
Recognized, Silent, and Local/Limited

The organizations found here are the least shadowed because they share one very important characteristic with transparent entities: the organization itself is relatively recognized. However, this region is kept in the shadows because members are generally silent about their belonging and the relevant audience remains a rather local/limited one. Two different but representative examples we can describe as operating mainly in this region are Alcoholics Anonymous and the Ku Klux Klan.

Like their more transparent counterparts, these mildly shadowed organizations are still relatively visible, meaning they work to make their identity recognizable (more so than anonymous). Although organizations in this region are typically not as large or complex as what we often find in the more transparent region, they may still possess some resources to promote their identity. Even in these mildly shadowed organizations, we will regularly find the organization doing at least some promotion of its core beliefs and other aspects of its identity so as to promote name recognition and visibility through certain branding, advertising, or public relations activities. These mildly shadowed organizations may also utilize slogans, logos, and other visual identity elements and even have mission and/or vision statements that are widely available. Image and reputation still matter to these organizations. Demographic information and data about partner organizations also tends to be made visible in these organizations. Of course, another aspect of their relative organizational visibility is the clear link to a recognizable physical location, which typically means an address or even a building/structure associated with these mildly shadowed organizations. Phone and fax numbers, web addresses, and other contact information are also provided in various places by the organization. Like their transparent counterparts, organizations in this region may reveal pictures of their leaders and locations. Additionally, we would expect them to use a range of communication channels that help promote them to relevant others.

Yet part of what makes this a shadowed region is that the members in these organizations are more likely to be silent about their organizational affiliation than to express it openly. For the collectives found in this region, members generally do not talk about their employer or the club/group of which they are a part. For a variety of reasons—including protection of one's self and loyalty to the organization—a member's involvement with these organizations is generally kept concealed from most others. For organizational members in this shadowed region, there is clearly less use of language indicating belonging (e.g., "us," "our," "we") and few, if any, mentions of the name of the organization when talking with others. Although members of these mildly shadowed organizations may know organizational mottos, visions, missions, and even secret codes/gestures, they are less likely to share those (or do so in very limited ways) with outsiders. In some instances this silence can be a product of limited knowledge about the organization's identity; in other cases, knowledge about the organization's identity (especially if it is somehow tarnished or questionable) may promote silence; in other instances, the silence could even take the form of denials of membership or downplaying of the organization. In this mildly shadowed region, organizational members are less likely to defend or promote the organization to outsiders. We would also expect them to usually avoid providing contact information that reveals their affiliation with the organization; in other words, sharing of business cards or other membership documents (if those exist, which they may not) is unlikely. Members of organizations in this least shadowed region also avoid statements of affiliation by not wearing clothing or openly displaying other items with the organization's name/logo. In some cases, masks or other disguises may be used to conceal members' identity. In general, organizational members in this region hide their membership in the organization of which they are a part through their restricted and strategic communicative behaviors and through other actions that conceal affiliation.

The final element that characterizes this mildly shadowed region is the relatively local/limited audience. Rather than promote themselves to a large mass/public audience, organizations in this region typically operate on a more local scale and are not attempting to communicate identity matters to a relatively broad audience. In this region, organizations may want local attention but not a more general public recognition. As a result, such collectives may be hidden from most others even though they may be better known in a more local setting. In general, organizations (and their members) in this region are less interested in the mass media (e.g., national/international media who may not be interested in them anyway) and more focused on local media to promote identity in the communities in which they operate. As noted previously, these mildly shadowed organizations may lack some of the resources used to manage reputations that we find in more transparent organizations; however, these collectives often have some capability to promote the organization to the relevant audience. Public opinion may matter less to these organizations than local reputations. Interpersonal channels are vital in these mildly shadowed collectives as they use those means to communicate identity locally. In general, the organizations in this region are operating on a relatively smaller stage and in fewer and less diverse locales. Members also interact with relatively local others and tend to travel less broadly in these organizations—though keeping their affiliations silent even among the local community can be especially challenging (but often still essential).

Who are the organizations in these mildly shadowed regions? Here we might find various locally operated offline support groups where the organization is known but the nature of the problem leads members to conceal their belonging. These would include various anonymous twelve-step groups (such as Alcoholics Anonymous, highlighted below) but also others involving stigmatized conditions. Even certain online support groups that are restricted in the scope of their efforts may fit here. Similarly, various hate groups—both online and offline—that target a more limited audience or operate in a restricted region may also be located here, especially if the organization makes itself known but the identity of members is kept concealed to protect them. We describe in some detail here the Ku Klux Klan as such an organization. Others have even compared the Klan to religious supremacist and terrorist groups that may promote their own identity locally but whose members remain largely hidden (see Ward 2011). A local street gang whose members remain hidden even as the organization is open about its identity could belong in this region. Additionally, certain forms of dirty work fit here where organizations engaged in tainted work must still promote their organization to a local audience, but where members may conceal their affiliation with the collective (e.g., a local garbage company or an independent adult video store). Possibly even some fraternal orders or secret societies that operate locally could fit here as long as the organization's identity is relatively visible while it is the identity of members that is kept hidden. A couple of specific examples may help cast a bit more light on this mildly shadowed region and the organizations found there.

Alcoholics Anonymous (AA)
On one hand, it may seem surprising to talk about such a well-known organization like AA as operating in a shadowed region. Most people will recognize the name AA and many have had direct or indirect experience with it or one of the

many twelve-step support groups modeled in its image. Indeed, the organization itself is relatively visible. It has created a sizable amount of attention and has been researched extensively (Rudy and Greil 1988). The general AA website (http://aa.org) explains, "Alcoholics Anonymous is a fellowship of men and women who share their experience, strength and hope with each other that they may solve their common problem and help others to recover from alcoholism." Information on AA is the first tab on that general website, which lists a substantial amount about the organization and its mission. Included for all to see is the history of the organization, information about its founders, contact information, and a physical address. Contact information for local offices is available and that is where one finds information on the numerous local meetings that take place. Many localities have their own websites that explain what AA is and provide local contact information.

From the beginning of AA in 1935, its members have recognized that word-of-mouth is not sufficient by itself to carry the program's message to the many people still suffering from alcoholism. Thus the organization has been very specific about making itself visible as an organization. It has a rather singular identity focused on alcoholism and is thus able to communicate that clearly. The national service arm of the organization produces a newsletter that is widely available. Although there is currently not a symbol for AA (the former triangle within the circle is sometimes still found on local sites even though it has been discontinued at the national level), the name, abbreviated name, and some key terms/phrases clearly signify the organization and have strong recognition.

The "anonymous" part of AA is not the organization as much as it is the members of the organization. In an open letter to the mass media, AA explains on its website:

> The principle of anonymity is a basic tenet of our fellowship. Those who are reluctant to seek our help may overcome their fear if they are confident that their anonymity will be respected. In addition, and perhaps less understood, our tradition of anonymity acts as a restraint on A.A. members, reminding us that we are a program of principles, not personalities, and that no individual A.A. member may presume to act as a spokesman or leader of our fellowship. If an A.A member is identified in the media, we ask that you please use first names only (e.g., Bob S. or Alice F.) and that you not use photographs or electronic images in which members' faces may be recognized.

As we noted in the opening chapter, the last two of the twelve traditions specifically discuss the importance of anonymity. Tradition 11 says, "Our public relations policy is based on attraction rather than promotion; we need always maintain personal anonymity at the level of press, radio and films." As the book *Twelve Steps and Twelve Traditions* (Alcoholics Anonymous 1952) explains, many organizations promote their organizational leaders as a way to promote the organization; however, AA has strategically avoided this as a way to publicize the organization and claims its reputation has benefited because third parties have promoted it instead. The organization promotes who it is through its work, but does not promote its members. Tradition 12 notes, "Anonymity is the spiritual foundation of all our traditions, ever reminding us to place principles before personalities." The organization's website reinforces that, noting repeatedly that the goal is to make known the program but not the individual participants: "Our anonymity, like our sobriety, is a treasured possession." Consequently, names are not collected at meetings nor is there any roll call or attendance record (Messer 1994). There are closed meetings restricted only to members, last names are almost never used, photos are not allowed, and members typically do not out others as members if encountered outside AA—all of which suggests members are relatively silent about their belonging to this collective.

Interestingly, AA claims it was originally something of a secret society. It is important to remember that when the organization was founded drinking was considered a moral failing and public drunkenness was a crime (Borkman 2006). While that moral taint is perhaps less strong today, joining such an organization is still viewed by many as a desperate, last-ditch effort to save oneself from alcoholism (Messer 1994). Thus, anonymity for members matters and individuals do not typically go around expressing their membership in AA to employers, neighbors, and others. Anonymity is a tradition, not a regulation; members are not forbidden from talking to others. Thus, members are the ones who choose to maintain the anonymity and not talk about AA or their membership in it. It can be humbling not to take credit for one's accomplishments in the organization and frustrating not to promote an organization one may appreciate, but the anonymity provides important safeguards for the organization and its members.

Communication scholar Diane Witmer (1997) notes that communication is a big part of meetings internally as members share stories and discuss recovery; however, that communication is primarily restricted to internal meetings and many accounts are based on open/public meetings. There is some celebrating of the group, but still maintenance of personal anonymity, in Witmer's study of one specific AA entity known as the "Friendship

Group." It is easy to imagine that some of the internal language is "we" and collectively oriented, but we would not expect to see that language used by individuals externally given the norm of anonymity. Witmer points out that many members jealously guard their own anonymity, even though that is not a focus of her study. Other scholars have pointed to anonymity as an affiliation strategy that "facilitates individual construction by avoiding ready-made constructions associated with names and faces. Anonymity fosters universality" (Young 2011, 716).

The anonymity of members also emerges as an issue related to AA's use of new technology. Some AA groups meet in Second Life and other online environments, where member anonymity may extend between members—further enhancing "deeper discussion of issues in a more open atmosphere" (Green-Hamann, Eichhorn, and Sherblom 2011, 474). The use of other social media can also be found, with Facebook pages and groups related to AA—although this has been done cautiously amid efforts to protect the identity of members. Combined, all this suggests an organization where members do not express their identification as much as they actively conceal it through organizationally encouraged silence.

The third aspect of AA that makes it mildly shadowed is that its primary relevant audience is a more local/limited one. Again, that may at first seem odd given that AA's website boasts approximately 116,000 groups and over two million members in over 180 countries (though again, that is just an estimate since there are no membership lists). This is in some ways a worldwide organization with a national/international headquarters, staff, and online presence. Yet both AA and numerous scholars make a convincing case that the organization is primarily about the local community meetings held daily. The AA Fact File (Alcoholics Anonymous 2012) notes AA is not organized in the usual sense: no governing officers, no dues, and no formal regulations. There is a general service office, but it is to serve the thousands of local groups and their meetings. Alcoholics Anonymous describes its national operations as more about service than authority (Seabright and Delacroix 1996). "The AA literature repeatedly emphasizes this bottom-up or 'upside-down' approach to organization. Instead of a traditional hierarchical organizational chart, AA describes itself as an inverted pyramid with the thousands of local groups positioned on top of the other governance bodies" (Zohar and Borkman 1997, 538). There is an organization-wide website, but their own promotional literature encourages prospective members to find them in the local phone book or newspaper. Customs emerge from local groups (like how members might introduce themselves at meetings with a phrase such as "My name is Bob, and I am an alcoholic") and then get shared; they are not imposed from the top. With AA, the emphasis seems to clearly be at the local group meeting level, because that is where its work is done in this decentralized organization. One belongs to a local AA group and money goes primarily to support that group. This decentralized nature may also help maintain anonymity for members.

Scholars have noted the relevance of the local audience and the local community meetings. "Our data drew heavily on meetings since they are the arena for A.A.'s basic formal activity" (Rudy and Greil 1988, 42). A number of scholars have taken note of AA's form as well, describing it as a minimalist organization (Seabright and Delacroix 1996) and an emergent, grassroots voluntary association, lacking a governing hierarchy or capital assets (Messer 1994). Perhaps the most extensive insights here come from sociologist and nonprofit specialist Thomasina Borkman. As she notes, AA has avoided bureaucratic form and oligarchic leadership. "From its beginning, AA developed an egalitarian and nonhierarchical alternative form of organization due to the cofounders' self-aware and deliberate work" (Borkman 2006, 148). The decentralized nature is just part of what keeps AA very locally focused. From the outset each local group was also different in its members and customs. It has also avoided accumulation of money. "The legally incorporated nonprofit entities at the national level were set up as services, not as governing bodies dictating to local groups, district committees, or regional bodies" (155). Borkman claims it is the thousands of local groups that direct the service organizations at the national level. "The basic organizational unit of AA is the local group, which is unincorporated and relatively autonomous from other groups as well as from the national-level service structure" (157). Thus, we have what is ultimately a locally focused organization that does not seek out a broader audience—helping place it in this mildly shadowed region.

Ku Klux Klan organizations

American history professor David Chalmers (1987) notes in his book *Hooded Americanism* the Ku Klux Klan was born shortly after the Civil War in the South of the United States during a time of tremendous social confusion. At the time it was called a "secret, nocturnal organization" (2) because of its clandestine meetings, masked vigilantes, and night raids. Yet by about 1870 the Klan was officially disbanded (though local groups still existed). In the 1920s, amid restlessness and postwar immigration following World War I, the

Klan resurfaced stronger than ever, with some estimating nearly five million members by the middle of that decade. Chalmers notes that the Klan became a considerable factor in communal and public life across many states. But this was again short-lived, and by the start of the depression the KKK's power had significantly diminished due in part to its extreme practices and immoral leadership. Ties to Nazis and an IRS tax lien in the 1940s that basically dissolved the organization—along with a decree from Klan leadership that the Klan would be organized in independent groups without a national organization (*Ku Klux Klan* 2012)—led the organization to splinter into numerous independent groups. These Klan organizations began gaining members again in the 1970s (Allen 1991). Although the Klan today is nowhere near its former size and lacks a central organization, an estimated forty different Klan groups are now operating in the United States—with a spike linked to the election of President Barack Obama in 2008 (Mangus 2009). The KKK is still considered the largest category of hate groups in the United States today (Bostdorff 2004), making it a very relevant organization to examine even now. Furthermore, understanding the KKK's organizations of today requires an appreciation of its roots.

Though sometimes referred to as the "Invisible Empire," the KKK as an organization is more recognized than it is anonymous. Even in 1865 it was a very "apparent" organization whose violence made it quite recognizable (Chalmers 1987, 10). The KKK in the years around 1920 is also unique in that it actually hired publicists to promote the organization; that, along with congressional investigations following an exposé in *New York World*, increased membership from a few thousand to about a million in just a few years. Chalmers notes that the organization has used public relations campaigns at various times to promote the organization and its image. The organization has also revealed itself through public scandals and an involvement in politics; furthermore, it regularly settled disputes in the courts, which revealed much about the organization—and did little to help its reputation (Chalmers). The KuKluxKlan.bz website specifically claims that the KKK is not a secret organization, because of their online presence, their mailing address and phone number, and their publishing of several articles, books, and newsletters. Indeed, many of the more prominent KKK organizations in the United States today are fairly revealing about who they are and what they believe. Leaders are typically named on the site, which may include logos and basic contact information (emails, phone numbers, etc.)—though a post office box is usually used in lieu of a physical address. Sections on the sites lay out "our beliefs," "our goals," and "about us" amid other information about the core mission of these groups. Most have newsletters, news releases, flyers, and/or various articles talking about the organization and issues central to it. Several groups are even legally incorporated as formal organizations. Additionally, the letters "KKK" are sometimes left at the sites where the Klan has performed various activities. As another sign of their recognition, they continue to use the KKK name because of the attention it brings them. At least one KKK organization won a case heard by the U.S. Supreme Court, which allowed it to post its name on a sign along the portion of an interstate highway it adopted in Missouri; more recently, the state of Georgia has been involved in a similar battle over a KKK group's request to adopt a highway in that state (Ng 2012). As one group's website offered, "We are a people who would rather be hated for who and what we are, than to be loved for a public persona that has no basis in reality." Another Klan leader recently noted, "This is the KKK . . . you know who we are" (*Ku Klux Klan* 2012).

What really situates the KKK in this mildly shadowed region is the silence of their members—making them the more invisible part of the organization. This is perhaps best exemplified by the easily recognized hood historically worn by members. Initially, the hood was more for some members' idea of fun masquerading; indeed, there are historical references to shielding the face in the making of robes and wearing them at parades and other events (Rose 1914). Clearly, though, the hooded robes served a rather practical function in shielding the identity of the members themselves. Secrecy of membership was seen as one of the only ways to protest what some Southerners saw as injustice. Hooded groups known as "wrecking crews" would abduct offenders from their homes and take them to secret locations where they were flogged; in other cases, masked members would carry out even more violent crimes (MacLean 1994). Legal expert Wayne Allen (1991) notes the use of the mask was so central to the KKK that antimask laws in several states trace their roots back to various violent activities of the organization. "Masks and disguises have been a central feature of Klan activity" (822); furthermore, "the Klan regalia of white robe, hood and mask served to simultaneously terrorize victims . . . while concealing perpetrators' identities" (823). Antimask laws have had notable effects on the Klan, making it easier to identify and punish Klanspersons engaged in criminal acts and reducing some of the mystery and allure of the organization. The KKK has claimed that members need anonymity—because without it individual members would be subject to attacks and because it avoids the recipients of Klan charity from owing a debt to someone. Today, the use of hoods or masks to conceal the face has greatly diminished—remaining largely symbolic of former members. However, even today pictures of chapters and members with full masks and robes can be found online, especially on the Anti-Defamation League's website about U.S. extremism (*About the Ku Klux Klan* n.d.), and in a recent Time-Life publication (*Hidden World of Secret Societies* 2012). With or without masks, members are known to carry out their attacks clandestinely (*Ku Klux Klan* 2012).

Hoods are not the only way in which members concealed their identity and affiliation with the Klan. As one KKK website notes, "member names, membership numbers or meeting locations will be not given." There are no pictures or lists of members on websites (though hooded members are depicted in the banner of some sites). Even today, interviews with Klan members may come with requests that real names not be used in order to protect one's job and one's family (Ng 2012). David Chalmers (1987) notes the desire of members to be silent about their membership can be seen historically when Klansmen hastily quit before new laws went into effect in some states that would list members publicly. He adds that secret passwords were used, meeting minutes contained initials but not full names, and items indicating membership (e.g., window stickers) regularly had to be removed to avoid a member being identified and potentially targeted for arrest. Indeed, some online stores associated with KKK groups do sell caps, T-shirts, and other items—though the KKK name or symbol is only visible on some of the items and it seems unlikely that members would wear such items outside KKK-related events.

Historian Nancy MacLean, in her award-winning book *Behind the Mask of Chivalry* (1994), is able to offer a unique glimpse into this organization historically, which provides the basis for the groups found today. Based in large part on the unique case of the Klan in Athens, Georgia, where Klan leaders failed to destroy or hide records, she notes internal documents stress secrecy—even to the extent of encouraging members to lie under oath. At meetings they were not allowed to talk about anything that might discredit the organization if it were to be published. Public silence was vital and a sign of loyalty, and that secrecy discouraged opponents because one did not know which acquaintances might be Klan members. Members were trained about secrecy and loyalty and knew well the price for breaking that obligation (which ranged from expulsion to even death). At one point, a leader of the powerful United Klans of America actually served prison time for refusing to give up the membership list of his organization. Additionally, most members were kept ignorant of some of the more extreme activities of the KKK as a way to further protect them and the organization. Together, this paints a picture of an organization whose members have generally kept silent about their membership in both historic and contemporary periods.

Contributing to its positioning as a mildly shadowed organization, the KKK—especially today—is focused primarily on a rather local/limited audience. Despite some prior success in having a national presence and more of a centralized leadership structure earlier in the twentieth century, the primary audience is in the communities where each group operates. The modern KKK is not one organization; rather it is composed of small independent chapters across the United States. The Anti-Defamation League's website notes that each different Klan group has its own headquarters but is divided into more than forty distinguishable factions. Their website clearly states, "There is no 'one' Ku Klux Klan." They claim that there may be as many as 5,000 members overall, with the greatest strength in parts of the U.S. South and Midwest. Information on KKK faction sites reveals similar statistics, though with typically higher membership numbers. Some of the more prominent KKK groups today are based in Kentucky, Indiana, Arkansas, and Texas. These smaller groups draw most of their members from local surroundings and limit their audience even further given their rather narrow criteria for membership. Although the KKK name may be widely known, the specific splinter factions that are the KKK organizations today are known almost solely in their local communities. Information on their websites suggest they are more likely to partner with other local groups sharing similar concerns than with other KKK groups not proximate to them. In the 1960s, for example, the KKK regularly worked with local law enforcement so the police would look the other way. Some local communities were heavily influenced by the Klan and a number of juries in the various small towns where this movement operated simply would not prosecute those accused (*Ku Klux Klan* 2012). The KKK organizations rarely seek public attention but are more open to some local recognition of their efforts. Of course, efforts may also be made to protect the identity of some local members from others in those communities. In sum, the more local/limited audience for today's KKK organizations helps to further position them as a mildly shadowed organization.

Socialization

As we have noted previously, when members are relatively silent about their membership, socialization can be more challenging. Sometimes this silence comes at least partially out of a recognition that others may react negatively to such membership—which may be a perception formed through anticipatory socialization. As young people, we may hear about problems with street gangs, we understand the stigma associated with admitting one has an addiction and needs a twelve-step group, and regardless of our beliefs we may come to realize that hate groups are viewed negatively by most of society. If a family member belongs to such an organization, he or she may talk about it in limited ways—though neighbors, friends, and other sources are unlikely given the silence members use in talking about the collective. Thus, it may be somewhat difficult to get anything along the lines of a realistic preview of these organizations even if they are more recognized than anonymous.

Nevertheless, socialization is very important to these mildly shadowed organizations because they are clearly interested in attracting new members. Similar to some of what we noted with moderately shaded organizations, having a relatively recognized organization allows for some degree of traditional recruiting (e.g., some use of online tools for recruitment). Yet in this region there is an even stronger preference for showing up to meetings and getting checked out in person. These local/limited organizations will draw from friendly, trusted places (other gangs, families, various churches, etc.) within their community—which can limit numbers and limit diversity. This potential problem is amplified for these mildly shadowed organizations because they may only recruit and consider certain people. Alcoholics Anonymous, for example, says anyone is welcome—but only alcoholics can actually become members and participate in closed meetings. The KKK is even more limited because recruitment is only for free whites of European descent who are also U.S. citizens, at least 18 years of age, Protestant, and do not engage in interracial dating or marriage (which excludes homosexuals, atheists, Catholics, Jews, and the mentally insane to name a few).

Having relatively silent members can complicate the process of information gathering if they remain silent to all—though if members talk internally to other members more so than externally newcomers can still acquire necessary information. Additionally, the relatively visible nature of the organization should help ensure adequate information is shared with the new members. Nevertheless, we may not get formal orientations in most of these organizations. In these mildly shadowed organizations, members are able to assimilate at their own pace and comfort level—deciding on their own at what level they wish to participate (or how engaged they wish to be with the organization). Nevertheless, at least for the nonwork organizations found in this region, there is still an expectation that one will attend key meetings in local communities where most of the organization's work is done (and where its identity is made manifest). That attendance is just one of the ways the collective socializes the member into what may be relatively strong organizational cultures. Various rituals and values related to the secret/private nature of organizational membership may also be an important part of socialization efforts.

Like most organizations, these collectives try to retain members. They generally promote from within (though they are not necessarily very hierarchical). That strong retention effort is especially crucial if ex-members will no longer keep secrets and it is difficult to recruit quality new members. If the socialization effort produces a member who is strongly identified with the organization, that guards against turnover as well. Of course, there may also be some notable differences across organizations in this region and their ability to retain members—especially since some support groups may have members for decades, certain gangs would only permit participants of a certain age, and other organizations rise and fall with changes in the social and political landscape. Overall, the shadowed nature of this region adds to the challenges of successful socialization.

Moderately Shadowed (Region 6): Anonymous, Expressed, and Local/Limited

Even as we move further away from the most transparent regions in our framework, the shadowed regions are not completely dark. For moderately shadowed regions, as with transparent and even most shaded regions, the individual members are relatively more likely to express their membership and belonging to others rather than keep silent about it. However, the relatively anonymous organization and local/limited audience position this region clearly in the shadows. Again, Figure 4 provides a visualization of this region relative to others and lists two example organizations we will describe later: Skull and Bones and Jackie Evans Inc.

For organizations in this region, we tend to find members stating their affiliation with an employer or other collective. Members of these moderately shadowed organizations may still use collective pronouns and other positive language when talking about their organization, and the name of the organization may be mentioned by members when describing themselves or when others ask them what they do. If there are missions, visions, creeds, or other similar codes, members will typically know them and be able to express them to others. Organizational members would be willing to wear items (e.g., clothing or special jewelry) that note their membership. Additionally, they may visibly defend the organization if it is attacked. This expressed identification may also manifest itself in the knowledge members have about the organization and who it is, including an ability to share key information about the organization.

Yet a big part of what makes this region moderately shadowed is that the organizations found here are more anonymous than they are recognized when it comes to communicating their own identity to others. The relatively invisible organizations in this region make strategic efforts to keep the organization and its core identity largely hidden fom most others. The organization may work to keep its own name under the radar even though it almost certainly has one or more names by which it is generally known. The collectives generally found in this region do not typically promote themselves in advertising or anything representing major branding efforts. Logos, recognizable graphics, and signage are usually kept to a minimum if they exist at all. Efforts are made to keep organizational slogans, mission statements, and other aspects largely hidden from outsiders. Physical locations of offices and meetings may be unknown or at least off-limits to any outsiders. Moderately shadowed organizations may not have a strong online presence—and even when they do more identity information is concealed than revealed. This could include, for example, less available contact information, limited publication of identity statements, less visible organizational leadership, and relatively few pictures of the organization and its key staff. Additionally, we might expect little in the way of demographic information about the organization or its partners. These moderately shadowed organizations may also utilize channels that help provide anonymity rather than recognition (restricted online access, offline interactions with known others, private lists, etc.). Organizations in this region may seek some credit for certain actions but will generally avoid attention from others when they can. As we have seen with other partially hidden organizations, this relative anonymity may often be achieved through efforts to keep the organization somewhat decentralized and small in size.

A final key dimension contributing to the shadowed nature of this region is the relatively local/limited audience. Rather than attempting to promote themselves to a large mass/public audience, the collectives operating in this moderately shadowed region tend to operate on a more local stage. They are strategically avoiding that larger audience because they do not want or need widespread public recognition (nor do they generally have to make efforts to actively hide from that audience, which may not know or care much about the organization). In this region, it is local attention that is actively avoided by the organization (which can be even more of a challenge for organizations if others know enough about the organization to wish to know more). These moderately shadowed organizations are thus largely anonymous to both the general public and the local community. Organizations in this region are generally less interested in the mass media (e.g., national/international media who may not be interested in them anyway) and more focused on local media as the ones from whom their identity must be most actively concealed. The organizations operating in this region may not often have extensive resources to manage media in intended ways because of their more limited focus; however, if the goal is to actively conceal the organization's identity from even that more local community, a lack of resources to manage that can be problematic. Interpersonal channels and perhaps even limited communication overall may be vital for moderately shadowed collectives. The organizations found here are likely operating in only one or a limited number of communities and most members likely interact primarily with relatively local others as well.

What types of organizations might we find in this moderately shadowed region, with its relatively anonymous organizations and local/limited audiences—but with members who are still generally able to express their belonging rather than remain silent about it? We can speculate that only a few examples might commonly be found here. Certain locally based fraternal orders or geographically restricted secret societies where the organization has secrets but membership is open would fit (e.g., I can tell you I am a member and express my devotion to that collective, but the core identity of the organization is not known to others). A few street gangs could fit this model if belonging is favorably viewed in their local communities. Perhaps the largest type of organization we may find in this region are those local businesses, clubs, and other groups who conceal their identity because either they do not want to attract unnecessary attention to what they actually do or because any expenditure of resources to promote their identity is unnecessary. This may include many small businesses who do not need to build reputation, who already have the stable organizational relations and/or markets they need, and who do not have to worry much about new members—but whose members are still relatively likely to express their belonging and affiliation with the collective. We can illustrate this with a couple of diverse examples.

Skull and Bones

In some sense, this senior class society at Yale University is not a very well kept secret. Its name is widely known thanks to some of its very prominent members. As one author put it, "So much ink has been spilled about the most secretive and exclusive of Yale University's secret societies that it's an open question as to whether it has any secrets left" (Goldwag 2009, 307). Yet, if we consider the organization's strategic communication about its own identity, it is relatively anonymous in terms of organizational visibility. "Skull and Bones" is the most common of several names describing this collective, including "the Order of Death," "the Order," "the Eulogian Club," and "Lodge 322." It is administered by and incorporated under the name "Russell Trust Association" (named after one of the founders), which lists the New York City headquarters of Brown Brothers Harriman as its address. The society meets twice weekly in a windowless, largely unmarked tomb (building) on High Street in New Haven, Connecticut. The larger order (which would include alumni, known as "patriarchs") also meets occasionally at a private retreat called Deer Island in the St. Lawrence River. There is a society logo of a skull and crossbones, though it is used sparingly and mostly internally. Despite this information that has leaked out over the years, there is relatively little the Order shares about itself—keeping its core rituals a closely held secret. There appears to be very little online communication, favoring interpersonal letters and clandestine meetings. Internal society documents are coded with abbreviated names or have letters replaced with dashes. You will not find websites for Skull and Bones (or any of those other names that are actually part of the organization in question). Thus, there is no known mission/vision, no clear indication of leadership, no way to contact the organization, and no information about its meeting facilities beyond the known location of the building (and island).

My own recent visit to Yale and the tomb of Skull and Bones was enlightening—and confirming about the organization's efforts to retain some anonymity. In contrast to nearly every other building on campus—with their blue Yale signs and building names and visible street addresses—the tomb is almost entirely unmarked (except for a small plaque on the side identifying the building as a "New Haven landmark"). Were it not for a few existing pictures and descriptions of the structure in other published work, one might easily miss the tomb at 64 High Street. Curiously, the building next to it was missing part of its address (showing only a "6" and then an empty spot where some other number once existed), potentially adding to the confusion. The building itself showed up only as an outline in one large campus directory but was missing entirely from the smaller campus maps provided to visitors. When I asked about the tomb's location, the student volunteer at the campus visitor center hesitated and then marked the location on the map, saying (jokingly, I presume), "Don't tell anyone." The building itself has two very large (and very locked) metal front doors and the few windows (on a basement level and on the towers in the back) were too dark to reveal anything in the interior. The tomb sits between a sculpture garden and an art gallery, across the street from various halls on Yale's old campus—plainly in view and yet largely invisible to most. As I made a few notes about the tomb, what seemed to be a small tour group stopped across the street and a guide pointed to the building as one of Yale's secret societies (but without naming it specifically); a bit later, another guide said, "My good friend was in Skulls."

The secrecy surrounding this organization has also led to efforts by outsiders to reveal it and to speculate, sometimes wildly, about who this organization *really* is. Journalist and Yale graduate Alexandra Robbins (2002), in her book *Secrets of the Tomb: Skull and Bones, the Ivy League, and the Hidden Paths of Power*, details some of the many "legends" that surround this secret society—legends that have evolved amid a lack of certainty about the organization. But many of those stories about Skull and Bones are not just the result of outsider speculation. "I learned through my interviews with members of Skull and Bones . . . that the majority of those rumors were carefully planted by Bonesmen themselves" (200). As one Bonesman elaborated, "It is an effective smokescreen" (200). As another part of a communication strategy that promotes its relative anonymity, it actively discourages the media from reporting on them. In writing her book, Robbins was told people would come after her and that her career was in jeopardy for writing about the Order.

Although it has achieved broad name recognition, it has not necessarily sought such a public audience. Its patriarchs may assume roles of broader national importance, but in most ways the relevant audience is primarily a very local/limited one. The society has but one chapter at Yale University in New Haven, Connecticut, in the United States. It recruits from only members of that university (and historically from only certain types within the university). With but a few exceptions, its relevant audience is the Yale campus. Campus and community media are typically the most relevant to it (and are regularly controlled by the Order). The very limited number of members, who meet only on campus or at Deer Island, emphasizes the more local/limited audience here—which also helps keep this organization in the shadows.

Perhaps the most controversial and interesting aspect of this moderately shadowed organization concerns the extent to which its members conceal or reveal their own affiliation with Skull and Bones. There is an oath of secrecy taken by members. The society's activities are known to include a great deal of revealing of one's history and sexual exploits, giving intense feedback to other members, and so on—all of which may have reinforced the oath of secrecy. Yet Robbins (2002) suggests that there are several paradoxes here that show expression of membership occurs alongside the silent affiliation. The society wants a roster of famous graduates but also wants to be invisible. When numerous prominent citizens are well-known members (both Bush presidents; William Howard Taft; James and William Buckley; Dean Witter Jr. and Howard Stanley; Senators John Kerry, David Boren, and John Chafee; Supreme Court Justice Potter Stewart; and Oliver Stone and David Gergen, to name but a few), it is hard to be completely hidden. The vow of silence is important, but members do talk. Membership is something of which members are proud. Furthermore, several patriarchs from various generations talked to Robbins in the writing of her book because, she speculated, they were tired of some of the legends and conspiracy theories. Additionally, "members claim to be secret, insist they want privacy, and then flaunt their membership in this elite group" (47). Thus, there are several ways in which members do express their belonging.

Robbins (2002) reports that senior class members are never supposed to remove their engraved society pin, which would be displayed on the necktie by day and attached to nightclothes while sleeping. Even young tutors (faculty) were sometimes "too proud to hide theirs" even though most faculty members did not wear the pin (68). Following this rule, swimmers would hold their pin in their mouth while competing—with one in the 1880s needing an operation after swallowing the Skull and Bones pin. One of the society's principles is that those who wear the emblem upon their breast shall be considered the best choice for various posts (Sutton 2003). Members expressed at every moment their membership through display of the pin on the necktie (and later on the vest). Within the Yale community, that symbol continues to speak loudly.

Another example surrounds the selection of new members at "tap day." As Robbins (2002) notes, beginning in the 1870s, this was a public event, making it quite apparent who members were. The onlookers would express support through cheers or remain silent when a questionable choice was made. When a senior class member "tapped" a junior for membership, the underclassman had only to look at the pin worn to know what secret society was inviting him for membership (there were several secret societies, though Skull and Bones has almost always been considered the premier of these). The public event ended in the 1950s, partly to avoid the devastation felt by the many qualified members not tapped for a society. Until the late 1900s, the *Yale Daily News* and the *New York Times* would publish the names of the men who were selected for top societies like Skull and Bones. Later, after the public event ended, the campus radio station would broadcast the results. Today, however, names are generally not released (though the opening of membership to slightly more diverse members has drawn added attention)—but for most of its history the organization's practices did much to reveal members.

Robbins (2002) notes several other examples suggesting members do indeed express their membership. One of the Skull and Bones rules for members is that they must leave the room if the words "Skull and Bones" or "322" are mentioned; but that very act of leaving identifies them as Skull and Bones members. Annual group photographs are generally taken that identify members. Special names are given to some new members, but records show members were regularly fined because they sometimes used a special Bones name outside the tomb. Although the tomb building does have a secret tunnel and secret spaces, it does not have secret entrances (despite popular culture claims to the contrary); thus, members are clearly seen entering and leaving the building on campus. Robbins even reports that "[G. W.] Bush did, however, reportedly spend a weekend driving through New York and New Jersey to try to find a tattoo parlor that would brand him with the Skull and Bones logo" (177). Notably, Bush also mentions that he joined Skull and Bones in his autobiography.

Hoover Institute Fellow and Professor Antony Sutton's (2003) book, *America's Secret Establishment: An Introduction to the Order of Skull and Bones*, relies extensively on membership lists provided to him by undisclosed sources. Each member of the Order receives an updated annual catalog of addresses for members. Inside is an alphabetical listing of members and brief information on the following: name and class year with awarded degrees; a brief notation of occupation (i.e., law, education, finance, business); date of birth; current business and private addresses; a list of positions held starting with current position; military and civilian awards and honors; and, finally, a listing of wives and children. These identifying documents are meant for members only but have at times been shared or leaked as they were to Sutton. His book suggests several other ways in which members would reveal names or their membership: during background checks, using full names on internal documents, keeping full membership lists, appearing in class pictures, and wearing the Skull and Bones pin. Combined, these activities suggest members were not silent about membership in several significant ways.

Jackie Evans Inc.
We have all heard of the Girl Scouts, and there is a good chance many of us have bought cookies from club members dressed in their official Girl Scout vest or sash (my immediate family has a Girl Scout member and ex-leader, so we have purchased and consumed more than our fair share of Thin Mints). There is an even better chance we have never heard of the organization that makes those vests and other parts of the Girl Scout uniform. That supplier organization, officially known as Jackie Evans Inc., presents us with a good example (despite inherent limitations surrounding actual data on this business) of a very different type of moderately shadowed organization.

A mere 40 miles up the Jersey Turnpike from the highly visible university where I work, and less than 15 miles west of the globally recognizable Times Square in New York City, is where you will find this shadowed organization. Jackie Evans is one of the few garment manufacturing businesses still found in the Passaic and Paterson areas of the Garden State. This privately owned family clothing manufacturer was founded by Mario Monaco Sr. in 1964, and he co-owns it today with other family members. Jackie Evans employs about ninety people and has annual revenues of five to ten million dollars (see Jackie Evans 2012) from the sale of approximately a million uniforms each year. It has been the primary maker of the required parts of the Girl Scout uniform (vests, sashes) for over a decade. The Girl Scouts in fact are its *one* and *only* client (Macinnes 2010). That unique relationship likely explains why this organization does not promote itself in the community or to the broader public. It does not seek or generally need other clients and thus has little perceived need to brand itself or promote its identity to others. You will not even find the organization's name on the vests it produces. That strategy was challenged back in 2010 when the Girl Scouts threatened to give the uniform contract to a company in China (before intense public and political pressure on the Girl Scouts reversed their intentions), which owners admit would have shut down the company and cost about ninety workers their jobs.

The shadowed nature of this organization is exemplified by the lack of any website or other online presence beyond the numerous directories listing a wide variety of organizations in the area. One will find a phone number and physical address, but little else. A check of the area Chamber of Commerce reveals no membership either. Even more shocking is the physical building itself. If you go to 18 Third Street in Passaic, New Jersey, all you will find is a gray, nondescript concrete building with no windows and only one door with a handle on it. Above it is nothing but the address numbers "18–26"—no company name or other signage of any sort. Stepping inside that door reveals a tiny closet-sized entry area with one door marked "office" and a second labeled "plant"—but still no mention of the organization or its name anywhere (though a few official-looking notices are posted on a single bulletin board). A small, dirty window provides a glimpse back into the plant area where the work is performed. There are cargo vans parked in the front, but none with any labeling of the company. The back side of the building reveals a sizable physical structure stretching to the other side of the block with a loading door—but again no signage or other mention of the organization. On that same block (but along a different street) one finds a number of well-marked businesses. It is hard to imagine that anyone who does not work there would really have any idea what this organization is or what goes on in its plant.

Adding to the shadowed nature is the very limited/local audience of this group. The company is family operated and only exists in the one location in Passaic, New Jersey. It sells to only one company. It has not sought media attention, but when it has been received it has almost always been very local media who provided the primary coverage of events. This happened during the controversy over the Girl Scouts' plans to outsource production of the vests and sashes to China in 2010. It happened again when local politicians used the facility as an example of a manufacturing success story following

President Obama's calls for legal changes to discourage the outsourcing of American jobs (Keep Factory 2012).

It is difficult with only limited data to make claims about members being able to express their membership and affiliation with this organization; however, there is little reason to think that such expression is not occurring. Members are not hiding—in fact media articles related to the China outsourcing plan and the 2012 visits of political leaders following Obama's proposals often showed pictures of factory workers and even specific names of members. The fact that the organization does something as positive as producing uniforms for Girl Scouts also leads to what we can assume is a rather favorable image. In those situations, it is easy to imagine that organizational members would express their belonging to the organization in conversation with relevant others. Some of the few glimpses we get of members suggest a number of them have been with the organization for a long time (over twenty years). Others noted the strong identification with the organization in the face of the potential outsourcing. "They're like family to me," said Dora Amorim, a floor manager who has worked for Jackie Evans Inc. for twenty-five years, following in her mom's footsteps. "They've always treated me right. If they don't keep it here, I will have to find another job" (Macinnes 2010). Thus, it seems safe to assume that members are more expressive about belonging to this organization than they are silent about it.

Socialization

Parts of the socialization process may look rather different across various organizations in this region. This is perhaps best seen in what are often elaborate initiation rites in some of the more secret societies. Secrecy expert Sissela Bok (1982) concludes that initiation ceremonies are remarkably similar across most secret societies and may include elements of disorientation, darkness, various ordeals, and even the appearance of some superior figure. Robbins's (2002) description of the Skull and Bones initiation procedure reveals several similarities to Bok's depiction. Although public information is not available about the initiation rites endured by employees of Jackie Evans, it is a safe bet that these other moderately shadowed organizations do not take such elaborate steps to socialize their members.

Beyond that obvious difference, there are some important similarities. All these organizations appear to recruit from rather closed circles. A secretive society like Skull and Bones tends to favor members of certain families or those who operate in certain circles of influence. We know from news reports that workers in a place like Jackie Evans are also multigenerational and recruitment almost certainly comes from the rather limited local community. This is similar to more mildly shadowed organizations who recruit from friendly, trusted places within their relevant environment—resulting in limited numbers and little diversity given the usual homogeneity of those communities.

This suggests there may be some anticipatory socialization specific to the collectives in question that is communicated from current members to prospective ones. It also suggests little opportunity for any anticipatory socialization outside those closed circles because the anonymous nature of the organization makes it unknown to almost all others. Additionally, neither Skull and Bones nor Jackie Evans is actively advertising for new members and the number of new members is always kept deliberately small.

Having members who are able to express their membership and affiliation with the organization should help, however, with information sharing during socialization in these moderately shadowed organizations. It is easy to identify members inside and outside the organization and even easier to talk about the organization and its norms with others internal to the collective. There are expectations that one shows up for work and for meetings, which are key to getting better socialized into the organization.

Socialization matters here, like it does for most organizations, because it is a way to help ensure strong levels of commitment and identification. There likely is something powerful about being one of only a few members of a somewhat secretive collective—especially when one is still able to express their own affiliation with the organization. That loyalty can obviously reduce member turnover. The secret societies operating here assume one will be a member for life, so retention is key to making sure the identity of the organization remains relatively anonymous. The family-owned and other small businesses operating here also seek long tenure as a way to limit unneeded interaction with the environment.

Mostly Shadowed (Region 7): Anonymous, Silent, and Mass/Public

In many ways this mostly shadowed region shares much in common with the dark region we discussed back in chapter 5. In effect, it may even be closer to the dark region than it is to the other shadowed regions. Of course, there are two main reasons for its shadowed nature: a relatively anonymous organization and a membership that is generally silent about its affiliation. Only the relevance of a broader mass/public audience keeps this region from being entirely dark. Figure 4 depicts this region in relation to other shadowed ones and lists two example organizations described in detail here: U.S. special missions units (e.g., SEAL Team 6) and the hacktivist collective known as Anonymous.

First, the organizations found here are relatively invisible, which means they are more anonymous than they are recognized. By now we know that such organizations generally do not wish to be known to most others. They may have a name—and it may or may not be highly recognizable depending on the specific organization—but the goal is not necessarily to promote or brand that name. In some cases, a front name or pseudonym to help hide the identity of the actual organization may be used. Visual identity elements (logos, graphics) are less common and there may be few if any slogans known to outsiders. For the most part, we would expect any relevant signage to be small and discreet if it exists at physical locations associated with the organization—locations and buildings that are often unknown or invisible to most others. These mostly shadowed organizations may have an online presence, but relatively little is revealed about the organization's identity compared to organizations operating in less shadowed, shaded, or transparent regions. This means generally less contact information is provided, little mention of organizational vision and mission statements exists, and organizational leadership is less visible. For these mostly shadowed collectives, there is relatively little demographic information provided about the organization and others with which it associates. These organizations may utilize secure channels that help conceal identity. As a general rule, they do not seek credit for their actions and attempt to avoid attention from most others.

A second reason this region is mostly shadowed is the members of these collectives are relatively silent about their organizational affiliations. In this region, members generally refrain from talking about their employer or the club/group of which they are a part. The organization's name is rarely if ever used and even individual names may be concealed. One's involvement with these organizations is generally kept hidden from most others for a variety of reasons, including the protection of oneself and one's organization from harm others may wish to inflict. In some cases, involvement is concealed through the use of masks or other disguises. As we have noted previously, organizational members who are silenced tend to use less collective language indicating belonging (e.g., "us," "our," "we," etc.). Organizational mottos, visions, missions, and even secret codes/gestures may be known by members but not generally shared with others external to the organization. Sometimes, this silence stems from a lack of knowledge about the organization's identity—though the silence can also stem from knowing a great deal about why it is important not to be viewed by others as affiliated with an organization. Silencing can also include denials of membership, downplaying of an organization, and little effort to defend or promote the organization to outsiders. Members of organizations in this mostly shadowed region likely avoid providing contact information that reveals their affiliation; thus, use of business cards or similar documents is limited. Members typically do not wear clothing or openly display other items with the organization's name/logo.

The only thing that distinguishes this mostly shadowed region from the entirely dark one is that the relevant audience is more mass/public in general. If an organization's market or relative sphere of influence extends well beyond a limited/local community to more national or global ones, then the mass/public audience is more relevant. The organizations in this region operate on a larger stage or across more diverse locales; furthermore, members may travel more widely and interact with a more diverse audience. More importantly for this mostly shadowed region, identity information has to be concealed from the mass/public audience primarily (which may or may not include concealing it more locally as well). The organizations operating in this region do not want the broader public to necessarily know about them, which may be accomplished through strategic efforts to hide identity information from that audience. It is this mass/public audience that is in mind as the organization works to keep a low organizational profile.

Organizations operating in this mostly shadowed region almost certainly include those involved in terrorism and counterterrorism that plays out on a more national or global stage. These would include many of the various secretive government intelligence organizations found in numerous countries. It would also include the various resistance, freedom, and terrorist movements that have sought a global audience. Major organized crime groups and anonymous activist groups with a more public agenda may operate in this region as well. We close this chapter by examining two representative organizations and socialization processes relevant to collectives operating in this region.

U.S. Special Missions Units

Militaries regularly have special operations forces that go beyond their general capabilities. These combatants frequently carry out clandestine missions in secrecy (Prusaczyk and Goldberg 2002). But the U.S. Special Operations Command (USSOCOM) that oversees such operations in the United States admits, "there has been a substantial investment in low-visibility and clandestine activities," especially since September 11, 2011, which may cross the line between *clandestine* and *covert* actions (see Johnson 2006, 289). Within USSOCOM, the smaller Joint Special Operations Command (JSOC) is an organization specializing in dark operations such as hunting down terrorists—leading some to label it as 'the center of an opaque universe, the dark matter that would shape the global war against al-Qaeda" (Priest and Arkin 2011, 237). The JSOC is generally believed to include three shadowy units, the existence of which is not officially acknowledge by the Pentagon: the Army's First Special Forces Operational Detachment–Delta (typically referred to as the Combat Applications Group within the military but better known as "Delta Force"), the Naval Special Warfare Development Group (DEVGRU, formerly known as SEAL Team 6), and the Air Force's 24th Special Tactics Squadron (Martino 2005). These tier-one counterterrorism organizations are the dark organizations known as U.S. special missions units. As one member of such a unit was quoted as saying, "We're the dark matter. We're the force that orders the universe but can't be seen" (Priest and Arkin 2011, 22). They may be the closest thing to a secret army the United States has ever had.

These units are, of course, not entirely unknown. Failures do get public attention. Most successes go unknown—although the mention of SEAL Team 6 as the organization responsible for the death of Osama bin Laden in 2011 brought them substantial recognition and gratitude in the United States. However, that sort of attention is not something the organization seeks for itself. Its goals are best met when it remains below the radar and out of the public eye. Mann (2011), a member of SEAL Team 6 from 1985 to 1989, said he had rarely even heard its name uttered in public. "Officially, there was no SEAL Team 6 (ST-6) .... Unofficially, ST-6 was the most highly trained warfare unit on the planet" (4). The Department of Defense describes JSOC and USSOCOM in some detail on public websites (though some links for additional information take one to government servers and require password-protected logins), but the fifty-two-page fact book makes no mention of Delta Force, Combat Applications Group, or Army Compartmented Elements (another name for the other two groups just listed). Similarly, there is no mention of SEAL Team 6. The Development Group is listed once (and again on an organizational chart), but nothing more is said about it (U.S. Special Operations Command 2012). One can find headquarters information for JSOC and USSOC, but no such information directly for the special missions units. Contacting the special missions units directly, locating a physical address, or finding other identifying information for these organizations is simply not available to outsiders. They may have a reputation, but do no active advertising and promotion outside the government-military community. Despite the classified information, reports suggest these organizations are divided into various platoons and groups that keep each operational unit relatively small.

The organizational names are thought to be known, but the actual names of these organizations are fluid and perhaps even unknown. SEAL Team 6 was not the sixth team but was actually named that way to confuse Soviet intelligence. Even today the names of these organizations are changed regularly. White House correspondent for the *National Journal* Marc Ambinder (2010) reported that DEVGRU has recently been changed (though we do not know the new label); additionally, Delta Force, or the Combat Applications Group, is now referred to by the military as the Army Compartmented Elements (ACE)—which is a poorly kept secret given information about ACE available online. Ambinder reports that JSOC officials regularly change the names of these units once their identity has been revealed. But again, the general goal of the organization appears to be to keep its identity—its name and its core activities—relatively hidden. Indeed the full mission of these units is classified as a military secret.

Like other special forces, these units often act covertly, which means the identity of the sponsoring organization is not known or acknowledged. Thus, members are not supposed to reveal anything that might identify them as organizational members or even U.S. citizens. These units have been described by military officials as "quiet professionals. They do it, and do it well, but they don't brag about it" (Scahill 2011, n.p.). Current Delta Force and SEAL Team 6 members will not typically reveal that highly classified information to their neighbors or the media. You can find lists of former members online and several book-length accounts, but no presumably accurate list of current members or commanders would be publicly available. Members do not carry cards identifying themselves or talk in ways that might suggest their membership in these special missions organizations. When in uniform, they wear no name or rank identifiers (Priest and Arkin 2011). Identities of members may eventually be discovered when members die, especially when large groups in the organization are killed at one time. Many members may never disclose their membership as a SEAL team member, and those that do eventually reveal it wait until they are no longer members (and comments even then are often seriously restricted given the classified nature of so much of the organization's work).

Eric Haney's book *Inside Delta Force* (2002) provides an unusual glimpse into this special missions organization. He suggests members conceal their identity by wearing civilian clothing and hairstyles; when uniforms are worn, they lack identifying markings (no last names or branch names). Haney went on to produce a popular TV show in recent years based on the book: *The Unit*. But this level of disclosure has not always been welcomed by organizational insiders who value secrecy and see such revelations by members as inappropriate. As a fifteen-year veteran of the organization told the *Tampa Tribune*, "Haney's book revealed too much about the organization's inner workings, potentially putting people and programs at risk. . . . What he has done is break faith with the troops" (Lardner 2006, n.p.). Thus, it seems clear that member silence is highly important and very normative.

These special missions units are limited in number, but they may operate anywhere around the globe with relatively short notice. As part of the U.S. military/defense community, the relevant audience here is more of a mass one than anything especially localized. These special missions units are not completely dark because they are known to be part of the national defense effort and also because they are widely believed to perform their activities in a diverse range of locations. The public knows of them but hardly anything about them or their members. Though these special units work hard to remain concealed, it is more the mass media and national press from which they have to avoid attention. They may not truly order the universe as the earlier quote suggested, but the relevant audience would clearly seem to be more mass/public than anything local/limited.

Anonymous

It seems somehow appropriate that our last organizational example would share the first word from this book's title. This group, which made numerous headlines in 2011 and 2012 as this book was coming together, began back in 2003 on the imageboard 4chan. In that environment, where most posts are anonymous, the idea of Anonymous reflects a collection of unidentified individuals. It has moved from Internet pranks and trolling to also engage in much more politicized actions against governments, corporations, and individuals seen as censoring free speech. They are sometimes seen as the good guys fighting to preserve free speech, expose pedophiles, and help others overthrow corrupt governments. But they have also been depicted in very negative ways as malicious pranksters and hackers with no regard for the law.

There is not widespread agreement on what Anonymous exactly is and whether it is even an organization. A CNN televised special program (*Anonymous* 2012) notes this organization and its members "live in the shadows"—describing it as a leaderless, faceless movement and a "loose collective." It has been labeled a loose federation of programmers (Olson 2011); a loose hacker collective (Greenberg 2011); a loose coalition of hackers, pranksters, and other Internet creatures (Knafo 2012); a loosely organized movement (Greenberg 2012); and a loosely affiliated Internet collective (Federal Agencies 2011). Others argue it is not really a cohesive group or an organization, but then later call it an "ad hoc organization" and a "cyber-lynch mob" (Crenshaw 2011). What is generally agreed upon is that this organization is not like most others—but just because it lacks structure and leadership does not mean it is not essentially engaged in organizing. In fact, "its overall lack of an official power structure is essential to its identity and perhaps its survival" (Knafo 2012, n.p.). Anonymous's own videos (*We Are Legion* n.d.) claim it is an organized effort beyond independent individuals: "We're speaking as one. It's a collective." They clearly speak of themselves as a collective in statements such as, "We are Anonymous. We are Legion. We do not forgive. We do not forget. Expect us."

Media, culture, and communication professor Gabriella Coleman (2011) is one of the leading academic experts on this collective. She notes that "Anonymous is, like its name suggests, shrouded in some degree of deliberate mystery" (n.p.). Thus, it does try to hide key parts of its identity. But she also notes that its core values are access, freedom of speech, and fighting censorship. Anonymous has no official website, though related activity of members can be found on Internet Relay Chat and 4chan (both of which provide substantial anonymity for members) and its own YouTube channel. It has no physical headquarters or central location and thus no phone number or address you can use to contact it. It does have slogans (e.g., "We Are Legion") and even a logo depicting a headless person in a business suit. The organization clearly has an ominous name as well (which makes it *not* anonymous, but perhaps pseudonymous). While use of these devices provides consistency across messages and actions, one can argue that these do more to reinforce the anonymity of the organization than to reveal it. Overall, this collective does a great deal to remain anonymous as an organization.

Its members are also relatively silent about their affiliation with Anonymous. In fact, we know very little about most members of this collective. Their own YouTube video claims they are seventeen to thirty-five-year-olds mostly and that "we have members throughout society." Numbers are almost impossible to know, but one estimate suggested 5,000 online "supporters" after the WikiLeaks cable dump, but a return to about 1,000 a few weeks later (Olson 2011). Others have simply referred to the membership as fluid (Murphy 2011). Members are often called "anons" (Greenberg 2012) and come in two broad types: those who want to change the world and those only in it for the laughs (Knafo 2012). Some have suggested the organization has no official members—which further hides those who silently affiliate with the organization. This ambiguity of membership not only hides the organization but also can create problems. In some ways the organization and its members are so anonymous they cannot always control some members or quickly confirm or deny if any of its members are responsible for certain actions.

Members take several steps to remain hidden. Professor Coleman (2011) notes two of the strong norms in Anonymous are not acting like a leader and not drawing attention to oneself (and violating those norms leads to expulsion). The organization's own web video proclaims that "[we are] one voice—it's not individual voices. That's why we don't show our faces. That's why we don't give our names." Sometimes this is because members do not talk about being a member with outsiders. One member told the Huffington Post his "friends knew nothing of his shadow life in Anonymous" (Knafo 2012). The CNN special *Anonymous* (2012) reveals that the organization's own web videos regular feature disguised voices and masked faces. A *New York Times* piece (Bilton 2011) notes that members hide online and offline. "When members appear in public to protest censorship and what they view as corruption, they don a plastic mask of Guy Fawkes, the 17th century Englishman who tried to blow up the Houses of Parliament." The masks are both symbolic and functional as a way to hide one's identity as a member of the movement. "Anonymous knew if they were going to meet in a visibly public space for the first time, they needed to conceal their identity," says Professor Coleman (cited in Bilton). These masked members could be seen at protests of Scientology churches and more recently at various Occupy events (e.g., Occupy Wall Street). Others have also pointed out that Anonymous members distribute to potential recruits information about how to use and install tools such as TOR, which provide users with substantial anonymity online (Greenberg 2012). Additionally, members actively guard their true names through the use of pseudonyms.

While members attempt to be silent, they are not always able to remain completely hidden. The *Washington Post* reported in September 2011 that the FBI had conducted seventy-five raids and made sixteen arrests in 2011 in connection to illegal hacking linked to Anonymous (Federal Agencies 2011); other major arrests and indictments have followed—based partly on members who were cooperating with authorities in the United States (Sengupta 2012) and partly on some members not effectively using technology to hide their identity (Greenberg 2012). The hidden, online nature of the members means they rarely know the identity of other organizational members (much less who might be working with or for law enforcement). This infiltration, rather than exposing the members widely, has led to steps that may ultimately reinforce their hidden nature. As one veteran member suggested, the organization may return to strategies where members "temporarily unite for a common cause and disband the moment the mission is complete, making them difficult to pin down and even tougher to identify" (Murphy 2012, 22). The creation of an alternative chat network and suborganizations like MalSec (Malicious Security) may also better hide the identity of the organization and its members. Others have suggested efforts to take the organization down will only serve to enhance recruitment and reinforce the "culture of strong anonymity" that characterizes this collective (Greenberg 2012, 184).

There seems little doubt that Anonymous operates with a mass/public audience in mind. Existing primarily on the Internet helps remove geographical restrictions and thus facilitates this broader focus. The organization's own video notes its "geo-political impact." The Huffington Post describes them as a force in worldwide affairs (Knafo 2012), Wikipedia notes the region it serves is global, and even NATO "named Anonymous as an important new actor on the 'international stage'" (n.p.). As further evidence of the large public stage on which this organization strategically operates, one only need look at this long, but incomplete, list of countries where Anonymous activities have been performed: Algeria, Brazil, Chile, Colombia, Ecuador, Egypt, England, Finland, Iran, Libya, Mexico, New Zealand, Peru, Philippines, Spain, Syria, United States, and Yemen. This widespread presence and the public attention that accompanies it is perhaps the only thing that separates an organization such as this from the very darkest regions of all.

Socialization
The anticipatory socialization for these mostly shadowed organizations is likely limited in several ways. Relatively few individuals may be members of organizations in these regions, and even those who are generally do not disclose such information sometimes even to family, so there are fewer opportunities for people to come into contact with mostly shadowed organizational members during their formative years. Of course there are media portrayals of these mostly shadowed organizations, providing both positive and negative—but not necessarily realistic—depictions of these organizations and what it might be like to be part of them. Also, there may be some early exposure to the occupations involved (e.g., military, hacker, resistance fighter) given the skills of family members and socially influential others, but this too is likely quite limited.

Actual recruitment into such organizations may occur somewhat differently than is typically found in more shaded and transparent collectives—and may vary notably even within this region. Though details are classified, recruitment into the special missions units we have discussed is thought to occur entirely from within SEAL units for DEVGRU and within Army Ranger units for Delta Force. Internal recruitment documents may mention Delta Force or other mission units by name, but such posts are not thought to be made outside the military borders. A group like Anonymous would also not advertise broadly; only those people already frequenting 4chan, certain chatrooms, or message boards are likely to become members. We would not expect large organized crime or global terrorist groups to advertise publicly either. For organizations in this mostly shadowed region, a crucial factor in recruitment is not only someone with requisite skills and interests but also someone who can keep the organization's identity and his/her membership in it hidden. The recruits need to be people who do not seek personal recognition, can keep classified or secret information concealed, and are able to stay out of trouble with the authorities.

Clearly, there may be notable differences in the job training required of members. Our two example organizations help illustrate that given the formal rigors of special missions unit training versus the relative informality of joining a group like Anonymous (though members of either group must likely be quite skilled at their craft). Information seeking as part of the socialization process becomes somewhat limited in mostly shadowed organizations. At best, members may only be able to talk to organizational insiders. As we saw in the dark regions, in organizations where identity must be concealed, cultures likely develop that discourage information sharing more broadly. If new members cannot readily acquire information about the culture and/or their job, there may be less effective socialization. One outcome (among many) of such a situation is a reduced ability to effectively conceal identity information.

Retention is another aspect of the socialization process very relevant to these mostly shadowed organizations. In general organizations can better maintain member silence (and avoid other leaks about the organization's identity) when individuals remain members. This may be why these collectives make members very aware of the consequences of breaking silence. Professor Gabriella Coleman (2011) notes that members will be kicked out of groups like Anonymous if they violate norms of not acting like a leader and not drawing attention to oneself. However, it is sometimes the ex–organizational member or disgruntled former member who starts revealing secrets that shed too much undesired light on the organization—making retention especially important here.

Casting a Long Shadow

In this chapter we have examined three shadowed regions where we might find relatively hidden organizations. These regions share much in common with the very darkest region in terms of how the organization and its members communicate identity to various audiences, but each has one characteristic that keeps it out of complete darkness and positions it more in the shadows. In the mildly shadowed region, the organization's identity is still relatively recognized even though members are more silent than expressed and the relevant audience is a local/limited one. The collectives we might find here would include various locally operated and visible offline support groups where members conceal their belonging (e.g., twelve-step groups), certain online support groups that are restricted in the scope of their efforts, various visible hate groups—both online and offline—that target a more limited audience, and even some local street gangs if those groups are able to be open about who they are even while concealing their members. Additionally, certain forms of dirty work and even some fraternal orders or secret societies could fit here—as long as they are visible organizations operating locally while their members attempt to stay hidden.

The moderately shadowed region is distinguished by organizations who make themselves anonymous and whose relevant audience is still a rather local/limited one; however, in this region, members are more likely to express their belonging/affiliation than keep it silenced. The collectives in this region are of only a few types: locally based fraternal orders, geographically restricted secret societies, and a small number of gangs if belonging is highly valued in that community. Probably the largest category in this region are those local businesses and other groups who conceal their identity because either they do not want to attract unnecessary attention or because any expenditure of resources to promote their identity is unnecessary—and yet their members are still relatively likely to express their affiliation with those collectives. Finally, the mostly shadowed region is characterized by relatively anonymous organizations and relatively silent members but a relevant audience that is mass/public, which keeps them from being entirely dark. The organizations operating in this region might include various secretive government/military intelligence organizations found in numerous countries; the myriad resistance, freedom, and terrorist movements that have sought a global audience; major organized crime groups; and anonymous activist groups with a more public agenda.

Although all the shadowed regions share certain features in common, their differences are also crucial to consider. The extent of the shadowing matters here, and the specific organizations we examined help to illustrate that point. A mostly shadowed organization may have more in common with a dark organization than with a mildly shadowed organization. Clearly, there are some variations within each region also (regularly pertaining to the motives behind the efforts to hide the organization's identity), but differences across them are more relevant. Finally, by looking at the socialization dynamics most relevant to each of these regions, we can begin to better understand some of the opportunities and challenges faced by organizations operating in these spaces.

8   Classified Conclusions, Implications of Invisibility, and a Faceless Future

Up to this point, we have reviewed relevant literature on hidden organizations and issues related to organizational identity and anonymity in order to develop a framework for thinking more broadly about organizations. That framework, which examines how organizations and their members communicate identity to various audiences, suggests eight different regions where organizations operate. These regions can be grouped into four categories: transparent, shaded, shadowed, and dark. For each of these regions and categories, we have examined key characteristics, suggested representative organizations, and explored how socialization processes occur. Figure 5 illustrates the eight regions, their representative organizations, and the four broader categories as they relate to one another. But up to this point we have had little opportunity to draw any broader conclusions and observations, discuss scholarly and practical implications of these ideas, or suggest directions for continued work in this area. These are the issues we tackle in this final chapter.

Classified Conclusions

The conclusions offered here are not classified in the sense that one needs some formal security clearance to read them, but they do relate closely to our efforts to provide a framework that inevitably classifies organizations. Our efforts to create a new framework for describing organizations on the basis of

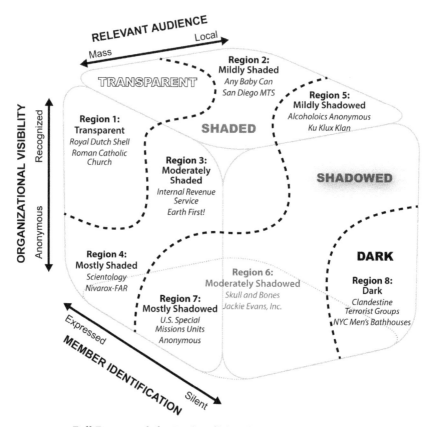

FIGURE 5. Full Framework for Regionalizing Organizations with Representative Collectives for Each.

how they and their members communicate identity to various audiences also allow us to draw a few broader conclusions and make some general observations. First, not only do these hidden collectives exist, but they are usefully and appropriately described as "organizations." They do not necessarily share common goals, similar structures, or comparable means of coordination, but they are all social collectives that have goals, some type of organizing structure, and some mechanisms for coordination. When we think of organizations as only corporations and businesses, and perhaps even nonprofits and governments—but treat secret societies, fraternal orders, support/hate groups, gangs, and various other social movements as something less than or different than organizations—we are excluding collectives in our midst that also organize. When we focus on what is big, formal, legal, visible, and/ or well known, we can too often miss or even dismiss those organizations that are smaller, informal, criminal, less visible, and/or largely unknown. Such oversight by organizational scholars seems ill-advised, especially in light of the substantial data suggesting the likely benefit in analyzing these hidden collectives as highly consequential organizations.

Second, the development of this framework serves to emphasize both similarities and differences among the array of organizations in the contemporary landscape. Whether you agree or disagree with the controversial claim that "corporations are people," we probably can agree that organizations are like people: they come in all sizes and shapes, some are nicer than others, and some seek fame and recognition while others value their privacy and obscurity. The framework offered here focuses on a set of characteristics related to ideas like recognition and obscurity—qualities that have not commonly been included in more macro considerations of organizational types. By describing organizations in terms of their visibility we begin to notice variation between those who are anonymous and those who are recognizable. By characterizing organizations in terms of their members' communicated level of identification we see differences between those who express that belonging versus those who keep affiliations silent. By emphasizing the relevant audience for an organization, we start to notice distinctiveness in those who target a more mass/public audience relative to those seeking more local and limited others. This emphasis and the framework that captures it is not intended as a replacement for other ways of describing and classifying organizations; instead, it is a supplement and complement that adds valuable additional information about an even wider array of contemporary organizations. The fact that we have not only theoretically possible regions and categories but also actual organizations that seem to represent those spaces suggests the potential utility of this new framework.

A third observation is that the value of the proposed framework is illustrated by the potentially unexpected organizations that surface in some regions. Indeed, not only do organizations vary but even those in the same shaded, shadowed, or dark region may differ from one another. Admittedly, finding Alcoholics Anonymous and the KKK in the same shadowed region or the IRS and Earth First! in the same shaded region may at first seem a little surprising. The claim that Scientology and an obscure Swiss watch manufacturer share the same shaded region while Skull and Bones is in the same shadowed region as a family-owned business making Girl Scout uniforms will no doubt strike some readers as bordering on the ridiculous. However, on closer examination there are reasonable explanations for these seemingly odd combinations. For example, we have mentioned some of the overlap in earlier chapters where boundaries between secret societies, terrorist groups, and organized crime have regularly blurred. Alcoholics Anonymous and the KKK have both at times been considered secret societies. The group Anonymous has even been said to "look like the non-state insurgents the U.S. has faced in Iraq and Afghanistan—small groups of non-state actors using asymmetric means of warfare to destabilize and disrupt existing political authority" (Rosenzweig 2011, 3).

As an alternate explanation for these unexpected combinations, we have to remember that we have been disciplined to think about organizations in narrow ways that emphasize structure, size, profit-orientation, industry, and so forth. Comparing them in novel ways is almost certain to reveal similarities and differences along these new dimensions. We have attempted to make the case here that a focus on the communication of identity is of substantial contemporary importance to organizations in an age where identity issues are central. Foregrounding how organizations and their members communicate and conceal their identity to various others should provide an alternate view of organizations that facilitates useful comparisons and contrasts.

Another explanation for some of the unanticipated representatives in the different regions relates back to motivations. Motives matter for why organizations wish to be identified or remain anonymous and why members either express or silence their own identification with the organization. We may find similar communication strategies between Jackie Evans Inc. and Skull and Bones—but the motives behind the relative anonymity of the organizations would seem to differ dramatically. Similarly, the motives that lead IRS members to be relatively silent about their organizational membership appear quite different from the reasons an Earth First! member attempts to hide his/her membership. At least in certain regions, different motives behind the communicative choices explain a great deal. I have highlighted different motivations here to illustrate this variety, but I also contend there are a number of organizations in each region who do share those varied motives.

Of course, differences could also result from the sizable variation that exists even within the space of any one region. An organization that is extremely anonymous with very silent members may be rather different from an organization in the same region that is only slightly more anonymous than recognized and whose members are barely more silent than expressive about their affiliations. Some regions and organizations operating within them may have more in common with regions in a completely different category (e.g., mostly shadowed organizations may have more in common with dark organizations than with other shadowed collectives). Even with efforts to loosely describe regions as relatively more or less regarding each of the three dimensions, the end result still resembles the eight possibilities created by a 2 x 2 x 2 scheme—allowing for substantial variation even within regions. Clearly, some organizations are found near the shared borders of various regions while others are best positioned more centrally or even at the far edges of a specific region or category.

More important than accounting for the interesting combinations of organizations in various regions, we have to ask if this framework shines any useful light on the shaded, shadowed, and dark organizations that have previously received so little attention relative to more transparent collectives. As a possibility, could knowledge of how U.S. special missions teams recruit members, communicate during missions, and successfully avoid recognition help us better understand how groups like Anonymous or even global terrorist organizations engage in such practices? Could knowledge of a bathhouse's strategies to remain relatively dark provide insights into the tactics that certain gangs, extremist groups, and various criminal organizations might also use to hide themselves and their members? Could the selective use of certain communication channels and other successful interaction strategies of twelve-step groups that reveal the organization but conceal the members help us understand how certain secret societies and hate groups use communication channels and other interaction tools to accomplish their goals as well? I contend the answer to these questions is often yes. The scope of what we can infer may be limited to key communication processes and identity-related dynamics, but this framework will be useful if it helps us make insightful comparisons and contrasts—especially if it enables us to identify organizations to whom we may have some entrée that can then be used to infer qualities of less accessible collectives.

As another observation about this classification framework, obviously an effort has been made to develop useful claims about the various regions and categories and then to offer representative organizations that might generally fit each. At the end of the day, though, some notion of correct classification of organizations is not what is of primary importance for us here. Ultimately, readers and their subsequent empirical exploration will make better accuracy assessments. Our primary goal here is more theoretical and heuristic: increasing our recognition of relatively hidden organizations, proposing novel ways for thinking about them, specifying scholarly based regions and categories in which such organizations may be found, suggesting potential but not definitive representatives for those regions, and providing an overall framework to better compare and contrast them to a wider range of collectives in our global society.

A couple of additional conclusions can be drawn related to the communication strategies observed here. We already know a great deal about the efforts organizations use to make themselves recognizable; thus, we will not elaborate on those. Drawing on our examination of the representative organizations presented in the prior three chapters, there appear to be several strategies used by organizations to make themselves more anonymous: small size, single location or decentralized structure, minimal or no online presence (no website), limited or no physical signage, limited or no logos or other visual identity information, locations off well-traveled routes, obscure or rarely mentioned names, limited or no contact information, limited or no mention/ pictures of leadership, no leadership staff at all, front/false names or identities, vague information about "who we are," secret or changing locations, isolated/remote physical location, no tours or access for nonmembers, windowless buildings, lack of any physical building/headquarters, no mission/ vision/identity statements, no provision of products/services to the public or to more than a few others, no information about meetings, use of interpersonal and offline channels, use of online channels that afford some degree of anonymity, disinformation about the organization's identity, threats and lawsuits against those seeking to uncover identity, privately (not publicly) owned, no use of name on products/services/materials, limited or no branding of name, few partnerships with others or membership in any associations, no official acknowledgment of the organization's existence, complete lack of visible activity, and changing names. Although most of these seem to lend themselves to strategic choices on the part of the organization, we should also recognize that some could be more accidental or coincidental. Though not of relevance to our efforts here, we also note that sometimes organizations are anonymous because of a lack of effort or failed efforts to be more recognizable. Additionally, some organizations may disguise their core identity through uses of strategic ambiguity and certain types of organizational mimicry (see recent work by Heiss, Monge, and Fulk 2012 on crisis pregnancy centers).

Similarly, we know about general efforts that might be used to display one's identification, but there are also strategies organizations and organizational members might take to silence member identification or affiliation with the organization. Based on what we have presented from the representative organizations, these strategies include the following: no pictures of members, no membership lists or email lists, no membership card (or not carrying one), silence about membership in the organization, members saying they work for someone else (a larger organization or front organization), members having little knowledge/information to share with others, limited or no display of material with organizational name/logo in public, members' discretion in activities, only working with trusted others who will not reveal identity, providing information on how to avoid and deal with law enforcement, avoiding any claim of individual responsibility for actions, providing and using anonymous online channels, working with media to help conceal member names/pictures, use of only first names or initials, closed meetings, limited use of collective language, hoods/masks, uniforms with no name or other identifying information, blending in with others, not acting like a leader/spokesperson, disguising one's voice, fake/false identification information, remaining a lifelong member, or sometimes even leaving the organization entirely (voluntarily or involuntarily) or through ending one's life (by homicide or suicide). Again, most of these are strategic efforts, but some could result without much conscious choice. Furthermore, some members may express their identity but do so in ways that still fail to identify them as organizational members—though that would not typically represent a strategy to be silent about member identification (even if the effect is the same).

Implications of Invisibility

What are the implications of being invisible as an organization and/or keeping silent about one's sense of belonging to an organization? What other ramifications emerge from this attempt to describe organizations based on how they and their members communicate identity to various audiences? We can discuss a range of practical, scholarly, and ethical implications stemming from the proposed framework offered here.

Practical/applied

The strategies to make an organization anonymous and/or keep member identification quiet (or, conversely, strategies to avoid being anonymous and/or silent) are quite relevant to several organizational groups. Organizational leadership, when it exists, may have to identify desirable strategies for achieving identity goals. It may be the job of corporate communication professionals and public relations experts—or select individuals and even volunteers in organizations lacking such resources—to actually implement those specific strategies into the organization's planned communication. In terms of organizational messages that conceal one's identity, there are choices that avoid communication, others that provide false information, some that lack message consistency, other messages that state one's hidden nature, and the obscure/vague communication that may be a function of strategic ambiguity (Eisenberg 1984). Organizational members, perhaps with organizational guidance, can also make choices about how to best conceal (or reveal) their level of identification with the organization from among the numerous strategies identified here. Also to be considered in these choices is the role of autocommunication, which refers to the creation and consumption of organizational messages by its own members (see Cheney et al. 2004). The crafting of messages that conceal and reveal the organization and/or its members communicates not only to external audiences but also to internal ones as those messages clarify expectations, reinforce loyalties, and further establish identity.

Before selecting specific communication strategies to use, it would be useful for most organizations to do some self-assessment about their own goals relative to communication of identity. Top leadership and key management personnel should strategize about their desired level of organizational visibility, asking questions such as the following: What are we doing now? Do we wish to be dark, shadowed, shaded, transparent, or something else? Which strategies are concealing us in less than helpful ways? Which strategies are concealing us effectively? A framework such as the one proposed here is useful not only for potentially thinking about how a wide array of organizations might relate to one another but also for helping independent organizations identify their own relative location among the various regions. The framework might also be useful for assessment of an organization's members and their desired levels of communicated identification.

It is also quite likely that various external stakeholders may have opinions about the organization's communicative choices that seem to reveal or conceal that organization from these audiences. This framework and the previously discussed strategies could help them identify and challenge those communication efforts they deem problematic. For example, in some regions audiences such as the national media or the general public may not care much about concealing strategies that create problems for access and a lack of general transparency. Conversely, other more local audiences such as shareholders or certain community leaders may reject the somewhat hidden nature of the organization and demand greater visibility. The framework presented here may provide them with language to describe the organization's identity goals and its specific strategies to achieve them—and with that knowledge comes greater ability to question or reinforce the status quo. It may be that different types of stakeholders (more or less definitive) and various types of audiences (mass/public or local/limited) can all make use of the framework presented here, even if they vary in their assessment of the organization's actual strategies.

Organizations and industries may find such a framework useful in thinking about guidelines and policies related to the communication of identity—though any such formulations should carefully consider the effectiveness and appropriateness of such efforts (which we will examine later in the chapter). Organizations, industry associations, various professional groups (e.g., International Association of Business Communicators), and far less formal groups who establish community norms may be in a position to offer informed standards, guidelines, and policies. The framework provided here can guide what might be reasonable choices for such statements. My own research into this topic suggests that, in general, there is a lack of policy related to issues of identity and anonymity in organizations (Scott and Choi 2009). I have argued elsewhere that organizations do not usually think much about anonymity as a policy issue, in part because it goes against assumptions about openness and directness (Bronco 2004). However, if we foreground issues of how identity gets communicated by organizations and their members, there may be a renewed urgency to offer guidelines about such issues as who does the concealing, what are the consequences for concealing or revealing identity information wrongly, how do we protect against unintended concealing and revealing, and how do we decide who members are allowed to talk with about identity issues. This is not to suggest that some organizations do not already have policies about dealing with the media, for example; however, policies related to the specifics of how organizations and their members conceal and reveal identity to various audiences is largely nonexistent.

The framework proposed here may also be viewed as having legal ramifications. Legally, various governments and other legislative bodies may wish to consider laws related to a range of issues such as acceptable signage, adequate contact information, use of masks, and requirement of member identification cards. Do we as a society care if adequate contact information is not provided for some organizations? Is there a concern with a lack of clear names or an absence of signage? Do we accept the wearing of masks in otherwise legal behavior? Should members of various stigmatized or otherwise hidden organizations be expected to have something that identifies them as members at least to law enforcement? In general, laws in this country have generally been supportive of anonymity as part of one's free speech rights (Bronco 2004); however, it is unclear exactly how the law treats some hidden organizations. For the informal economy, certain hate groups, and some secret activities at the fringes of what is considered legal, laws could be useful. This is complicated by organizations with a global focus or without a clear physical location, because it may not be apparent what laws and jurisdictions apply. Again, a consideration of effectiveness and appropriateness would be relevant here in assessing benefits versus costs associated with hidden organizations.

Scholarly

As we have already suggested, theory and research on identification, identity, and anonymity should be influenced by a broader consideration of hidden organizations. With regard to the work on organizational identification, at least two key implications surface. First, theory and research suggest that the attractiveness of the organization's image contributes to identification and that people's desire for self-enhancement may motivate a sense of oneness with prestigious organizations. However, with more hidden organizations, image attractiveness and prestige are often unknown. This suggests that theory needs to better account for the possibility that *internal* image and prestige may be more salient. Additionally, it is possible that some members will identify with an organization and express that identification because of the hidden image or because it lacks public recognition. This suggests expanded motives for identification with relatively hidden collectives. Second, the model here gives primary attention to the expression of or silencing of identification—emphasizing that the key is not just being cognitively identified but also the choice to either conceal or reveal that through our communication with others. In part this demands we pay more attention to communication-based views of identification in all organizations, including these hidden ones (see Scott, Corman, and Cheney 1998). But we also need more sophisticated and nuanced efforts to better understand what communicative expressions and silence convey. Expressed identification is relatively straightforward except in those instances where a false or fake identification is being expressed (as may occur in undercover work). More challenging are efforts to understand when silence reflects a lack of belonging and when it is actually a way of displaying that identification (by continuing to hide the identity of organizational members). Existing models of organizational silence (Morrison and Milliken 2000) can provide some guidance, though such efforts have not yet been well incorporated into identification research.

The work here also has implications for identity-related issues such as reputation. Elsewhere I have suggested several observations related to the intersection of reputation and hidden organizations that go beyond much of the existing reputation literature (Scott forthcoming). For example, because it is more difficult for others to assess a hidden organization's reputation when so much information is concealed, attributions or assessments may be made by the evaluator on the basis of other clues. At least some hidden organizations may strategically seek to avoid reputations and awareness by tightly managing communication with external audiences. For some, the hidden/secretive nature of the organization may be the basis for reputation—and in many instances a less than positive reputation may result if one is aware of the organization but suspicious about the lack of information surrounding it. Having said that, hidden organizations will have more favorable reputations in contexts where secrecy is valued. The reduced information makes reputation not only more difficult to establish in these hidden organizations but also very difficult to protect when attacked. To the extent that a reputation is promoted, these collectives may do so among rival groups or in certain industries, but they prefer not to be in the general public's eye. In some cases, organizations will hide behind front organizations to avoid their own negative reputations or to help build the reputation of the organization backing them. In summary, hidden organizations regularly have a *reputation* problem: they must create enough of a favorable reputation to attract needed resources (money, members, clients, etc.), but they have to do so without disclosing core information that could reveal the organization. We as scholars in this area have a different type of reputation problem in that our theorizing and research has barely considered these hidden organizations.

The framework proposed here may have implications for our research on anonymity, secrecy, and privacy as well. Most notably, these concepts that have usually been applied to the individual level are clearly appropriate at the organizational level. As we have seen, it is useful to talk about organizations that make themselves anonymous or somewhat anonymous through conceal-ment of identity information. Similarly, organizations have secrets—includ-ing secrets about who they really are (i.e., their identity)—as well as core information about themselves that they wish to keep private. Additionally, the anonymity literature may benefit from the various strategies organiza-tions use to be anonymous and the various forms the anonymity may take. It is quite possible that Marx's (2004, 2006) list of identity markers could be extended when considering ways in which organizations reveal and conceal who they are. Rarely is the organization truly anonymous in the sense it has no name; but we see numerous other ways in which some degree of anonym-ity is achieved that should expand our thinking about what anonymity is and how it may be accomplished.

Given our arguments about the existence of hidden organizations, another implication is that we may need to re-examine many of our organizational theories—which are almost all developed and tested in relatively transparent organizations. We have already illustrated how certain socialization dynam-ics may change with certain shaded, shadowed, and dark organizations. Addi-tionally, a focus on hidden organizations might suggest new types of crises (e.g., revealing of a hidden organization's members) or novel crisis responses (e.g., maintaining one's anonymity despite calls for transparency) that the cri-sis communication literature has so far largely neglected. Because an "identity crisis" for more shadowed and dark organizations is not about not knowing who you are or even others not knowing who you are, but about unintended others knowing who you are, our current theory and research in this area needs to be extended.

As another example, conflict and negotiation literature may need expan-sion to better consider additional sources of tensions (e.g., being unable to fully identify hidden organizations involved in a dispute) and appropri-ate conflict management strategies when hidden organizations are involved (which could include greater use of mediated channels or mediators who can protect the identity of the organization and its members). Furthermore, theories of networks and interorganizational relationships have rarely talked about hidden linkages or motivations to establish ties with shaded, shadowed, or dark organizations. Perhaps we need to talk about not only strong and weak ties but hidden ones as well; perhaps we need to consider not only bridging and bonding ties but also forms of "dark" capital based on relations with hidden collectives. Indeed, organizations and their members may very well have needs, both legitimate and illegitimate, to quietly establish relations with various hidden groups (to sell products in underground economies, to provide help to organizational members with socially stigmatized problems, to work for controversial political changes, etc.), which has important potential implications for networks and interorganizational theory and research. Of course, these are only a few of many possible examples where an emphasis on hidden organizations creates a need to reconsider and likely expand some of our current theories about organizations and communication.

This interest in hidden collectives should also renew interest in other hidden forms surrounding various organizations. We have not really addressed the hidden organizations that work behind many other organizations. Public relations agencies and talent management groups, for example, may work behind the scenes to promote an organization, but they themselves stay largely invisible in that work. Although we have not focused on the hidden workers that regularly exist in even fairly transparent organizations, attention to them is certainly warranted—and it is possible that better comprehension of certain forms of hidden work may also help us understand hidden organizations that also hide their members. Although there has certainly been attention paid to board members, hidden owners, and silent partners, renewed focus on them as largely hidden aspects of most organizations seems warranted. Additionally, an examination of hidden organizations also suggests the need to look at hidden audiences and hidden markets for one's products/services and as a pool for various resources.

Ethical

A separate section for ethics does not imply that the practical and scholarly implications of this work should not also be concerned with ethics; however, I do wish to draw special attention to ethical concerns and implications of hidden organizations. Without careful thought, one could dismiss these hidden organizations as ones that must conceal themselves because they are engaged in illegitimate, immoral, and often illegal activities. Indeed, one could look at organized crime, street gangs, and terrorist organizations to make this point. A focus on parts of the underground economy, the sex industry, and various hate groups may only add to such claims. Yet we may judge other hidden organizations as more legitimate, moral, and legal when we talk about counterterrorism units, anonymous support groups, and benevolent fraternal orders. Furthermore, the range of backstreet small businesses that remain hidden to most are seen as a vital part of most economies. The point is we should be very hesitant to label hidden organizations as somehow less ethical than transparent ones. Even though one motivation for hiding is to provide cover for wrongdoing, other motivations for hiding are about protecting the rights of people and organizations, resisting corrupt systems, and even being responsible with one's resources.

One useful way to think through some of the possible ethics related to hidden organizations and how they and their members communicate identity is to consider what is called "communication competence." Organizational scholars have certainly written about this (see Jablin and Sias 2001), though the most useful treatment for our purposes comes from communication professors Brian Spitzberg and Bill Cupach (1984). Those authors contend that we can judge the competence of communication in terms of whether it meets two criteria: (1) effectiveness in accomplishing its goal, and (2) social appropriateness, which relates closely to an ethical dimension. Thus, if want to judge the competence of an organization's communication about its identity, we have to consider the extent to which it is both effective and appropriate in the choice it makes to reveal or conceal its identity.

Table 3 suggests the range of possibilities here. The competent hidden organization is one whose identity should remain concealed and the organization is successful in keeping it concealed. Similarly competent are those organizations whose identity should be revealed and who are successful in revealing it. In both cases, an appropriate strategic choice is made about concealing or revealing and the organization communicates in ways that accomplish that goal. In other cases, an organization may effectively conceal or reveal its identity—but if that goal is viewed as inappropriate (i.e., that organization should not be concealed or not be revealed), then we have an unethical situation made worse by successfully accomplishing the unethical communication goal. In some cases an organization may be appropriate about its desire to be revealed or concealed, but for whatever reason it

TABLE 3. Effectiveness and Appropriateness of Communicative Strategies Related to Concealing and Revealing of Identity

	Effective—Goal Accomplished	
Goal	*Appropriate Goal*	*Inappropriate Goal*
Reveal Identity	Competent—identity is revealed and should be revealed	Effective, but inappropriate—identity is revealed but should be concealed
Conceal Identity	Competent—identity is concealed and should be concealed	Effective, but inappropriate—identity is concealed but should be revealed
	Ineffective—Goal Not Accomplished	
Goal	*Appropriate Goal*	*Inappropriate Goal*
Reveal Identity	Appropriate, but ineffective—identity should be revealed but organization fails to do so	Incompetent—identity is not revealed and should not be revealed
Conceal Identity	Appropriate, but ineffective—identity should be concealed but organization fails to do so	Incompetent—identity is not concealed and should not be concealed

cannot effectively accomplish that goal (thus, an organization that should be concealed ends up being more revealed, or an organization that should be revealed stays relatively concealed). Finally, we get to the most incompetent communication where the goal is inappropriate and the organization is not able to accomplish that goal—which may actually make the consequences here less problematic than when an inappropriate communication goal does get accomplished. Thus, this table displays several situations where the choice to conceal (or reveal) may be unethical if it is viewed as inappropriate. It also illustrates that the concealing of identity is only competent when such concealment is both appropriate and effectively accomplished by the organization. Again, the assessments of appropriateness and a full treatment of ethicality are well beyond our goals here; but it is vital that we consider ethical implications of the choices organizations and their members make when communicating about their identity.

A discussion of ethics also raises potentially unique ethical challenges for more hidden organizations. For example, how far should an organization go to protect its identity and the identity of its members? If our identity is fundamentally who we are as organizations or even organizational members, and if the concealment of that identity is fundamental as well, then we could expect those involved to go to great lengths to hide their identity as a form of self-preservation. We know some organizations have used lawsuits to protect their identity, but exactly what our rights are and what they should be seems unclear. We also know that organized crime and intelligence agencies have killed and imprisoned individuals who threatened to reveal too much about an organization's covert activities. Such issues rarely surface when we are focused solely on relatively transparent collectives; but as we enter the regions where shaded, shadowed, and dark organizations are found, we can expect even greater efforts made to effectively conceal identity. Many of those choices raise important ethical questions.

As another example, what are our responsibilities to potentially reveal a hidden organization? Should we ever "out" a hidden organization and reveal its identity to an audience rather than let it decide when to reveal itself? This is an ethical question that researchers, journalists, and others may increasingly face as we encounter hidden organizations. Part of that determination likely rests on assessments of the appropriateness of the identity concealment. There is, of course, some precedent for such decisions as the media have often concealed identities in the interest of national security; additionally, groups like AA have been successful in working with the media to avoid publication of members. Decisions about how to handle the more ambiguous cases demand better understanding of how these hidden organizations relate to their audiences and society at large. We turn now to consider this and other opportunities for future research.

Faceless Future

Future work in organizational studies must pay greater attention to the more invisible and unrecognized collectives all around us, so in that sense the focus of our future efforts really should be on those relatively faceless organizations. Hopefully, the framework presented here provides organizational scholars with something of a map that reveals all sorts of interesting and largely undiscovered places for future inquiries. Some of these we have already visited quite a bit, with the transparent region a very popular scholarly research destination. We can also find several forays into the mildly and moderately shaded regions. Organizational scholars have been generally reluctant to venture into most of the other regions in sustained ways. But now, with this framework as a different map (and with apologies to fellow *Star Trek* enthusiasts), we are prepared for a new frontier, ready to explore strange new organizations, to seek out new collectives, and to boldly go where few organizational scholars have gone before.

Future research into these faceless, hidden organizations can also work to address limitations in the current theorizing provided here. Clearly one of those concerns is the inadequate attention to the more dynamic, constitutive processes by which identities are created and shared. Our focus here has been to initially examine the communicative choices by the organization and its members and the relevant audience for the organization in question. Although such choices are not made without awareness of prior communication or expectations about future interactions, focusing only on the organization here is limiting (even if a reasonable first step). A more complete effort to understand hidden organizations would have to look at both audience and third-party messages as well. Part of this study could be an examination of reactions from relevant audiences and even the general public to communicated identity messages. We could also examine messages about the identity of the organization and its members as put forth by various stakeholders with opinions about who the organization is and what its core values are. In other words, the communication of identity is a complex, dynamic process involving multiple communicators. Additionally, identity is not solely something we communicate—it is constituted by that communication. The very interactions in which we engage serve to construct and reconstruct identities in ways that may make them more or less hidden.

Even the very notion of what it means to be hidden (in the various shaded, shadowed, or dark forms described here) likely depends on the assessments of others. Considered very simply, a truly hidden organization is one where both the organization and the relevant audience(s) agree about its concealed nature (we could get more specific and discuss if perceptions are aligned in terms of the degree to which they are hidden as well). In the opposite case, an organization and its relevant audience(s) may agree that an organization is not hidden. In both of these instances, assessing just the strategic communication of the organization is adequate because it aligns with the audience's perception. However, consider instances when an organization sees itself as relatively hidden, but the public or some other relevant audience feels it knows the organization relatively well; or, conversely, sometimes an organization may feel it is generally revealed but the relevant audiences perceive it to be largely hidden. In these latter instances, considering only the communication of identity by the organization would be limiting given that other communicators do not see the organization's identity similarly. As we know, reactions to and consequences of being hidden can depend as much, if not more, on the perceptions of various stakeholders. Thus, future research would be wise to address this limitation by more actively including the role of the relevant audiences and their perceptions into research about hidden organizations.

Future work may also benefit from moving beyond the focus on communication about an organization's or member's current identity. It is possible that organizations and/or their members may at times conceal some historical version of who they were (wishing to hide some scandalous version of the organization perhaps before it changed names, or hoping to hide a failed spinoff company), or ex-members will remain silent about some prior organizational membership even long after the organization has dissolved (perhaps because of ramifications today related to their own identity). The passing of time itself likely serves to hide some organizations or at least their prior identities—and yet our revealing and concealing of those collectives today may be informative. Considerations of these more temporal elements may even lead us to think about what we conceal and reveal about future organizations (planned ventures or initial efforts to establish new collectives) and our membership in them—as we make strategic choices that sometimes serve to hide or hype organizations in preorganizational stages.

In presenting this framework for thinking more broadly about organizations, we have emphasized theoretically possible regions and categories and then attempted to support the validity of those with representative organizations for each. Although we have drawn on existing literature, surface-level analysis of websites, and some personal experience, we have made no real attempt to do original research here. Such an undertaking goes beyond what was possible for this book, but it represents a very reasonable next step. Although the framework itself does not offer specific propositions to be tested, it does suggest several directions for future research. For example, we discussed several differences in socialization processes across regions. Future research could do more data-based studies comparing socialization processes across transparent, shaded, shadowed, and dark organizations. Also, the three dimensions on which the framework is based and the characteristics found in the relative ends of each dimension need some empirical validation to assess the relative importance of each for contributing to an organization's hidden nature. Work that examines the relative importance of each characteristic could also be used to create measures of organizational anonymity and/or organizational visibility, silent member identification and/or expressed member identification, and local/limited audience and/or mass/public audience. Scores on such indices could be used to situate specific organizations in various regions of the framework. Those scores could also be related to a wide range of other organizational, communication, and identity variables—potentially allowing researchers to assess the relationship between those key process variables and the communication of identity by organizations and their members. It would be of broad interest to know, for example, how revealing and concealing of information are related to organizational performance and even survival.

As we reviewed in chapter 2, researching hidden organizations is filled with challenges. Not only are they hidden, and thus often hard to access safely, but also they are regularly moving targets with sometimes unknown members operating in remote or hard-to-reach locations. Despite that, there are methods that can be used to study these organizations so that we can conduct more original research in the future. When access is attained, fieldwork and participant observation techniques could yield incredible insight. For online organizations, virtual ethnographies may be quite appropriate. Especially for those organizations where members are relatively identified, traditional surveys (questionnaires/interviews) may still be feasible. When the organization itself is recognized and visible, interviews with top leadership and analysis of documents is more feasible. In many cases it is a combination of such methods in the form of a case study that may be most useful—especially given the limited research data we have on many of these organizations.

Some researchers have already made substantial headway into studying certain aspects of the darker organizations that are often least accessible. These include communication network studies to detect secretive and non-secretive groups (Baumes et al. 2004), comparing dark networks to more common ones (Xu and Chen 2008), analyzing criminal networks (Sparrow 1991; Xu et al. 2004), and detecting enemies using network analysis (Levchuk, Chopra, and Pattipati 2005). Other interesting methods and techniques have also been proposed, including content crawlers of the dark web to help find content on forums and other tools buried deeply and usually inaccessible to traditional crawling techniques (Fu, Abbasi, and Chen 2010), analyzing hyperlink structures and content of extremist websites (Zhou et al. 2005), examining web content and interactivity comparisons of extremist groups to government sites (Qin et al. 2007), and even efforts to detect identity through spectral analysis of recorded vocal interactions (Bradley 2010). Although this work is not generally published in organizational studies journals, this may change as these fields gain greater experience with the network analytic and other methods described here.

In addition to topics and methods, we should also discuss some other procedures and tactics that may be useful in conducting and disseminating research on hidden organizations. We must think creatively about ways to access such organizations through tapping diverse networks and establishing relations with others who may have that access. As an example, I have graduate students active in hacker communities and an underground music network who are potential points of access. We may also need to provide anonymous tools for willing others to use as they interact with researchers without revealing their identity. For the organizations we can access, we still have to be smart about protecting ourselves. Those that involve terrorism and organized crime, for example, could pose real threats to many researchers—and in those cases the need for quality research is trumped by the greater need for individual safety. For nearly all hidden organizations, research activity represents a potential way in which their identity or the identity of members may be exposed. If one's goal is to infiltrate and bring down the hidden organization by revealing it to others, then such identity disclosures are not a concern; however, such ambitions are generally inappropriate for scholarly research (and would, in fact, do much to damage the possibility of other scholarly inquiry into these collectives). Thus, additional steps should be taken to protect organizational and member identity if that is their wish. For example, data should not be recorded in ways that if subpoenaed or intercepted would reveal such information. Interestingly, this can be at odds with the institutional review board (IRB) policies at research universities, which are supposed to protect the identity of human participants but sometimes do not (see Scott 2005). More specifically, typical IRB policies about access, permission, and consent may very well need modification with research into various hidden collectives. Finally, the work on these organizations may benefit from alternate ways of distributing this scholarship. Indeed, the timely nature of the work and the practical implications of the research lend it more to outlets other than scholarly journals with their somewhat limited readership and relatively slow publication procedures. For example, Arizona State

University's Center for Strategic Communication (http://csc.asu.edu/), which explains its purpose as "applying knowledge of human communication to issues of countering ideological support for terrorism," has emphasized white papers to key stakeholders interested in their scholarly findings. Drawing on models such as this, where research on hidden organizations can have both an immediate practical impact and a presence in scholarly journals, seems ideal.

Secret Journey

Perhaps it is appropriate that I conclude this volume approximately where I began it. It was in uptown Manhattan where President John F. Kennedy spoke these words:

> The very word "secrecy" is repugnant in a free and open society; and we are as a people inherently and historically opposed to secret societies, to secret oaths and to secret proceedings. We decided long ago that the dangers of excessive and unwarranted concealment . . . far outweighed the dangers which are cited to justify it. (1961, n.p.)

Many do not realize that those words delivered to the American Newspaper Publishers Association were actually part of a speech asking them to *keep* secrets in times of peril, to *not* disclose information that might reach the enemy, and to *suspend* freedoms of the press during periods of clear and present danger. Even today, much of humanity still wrestles with a distrust of secrecy along-side a recognition of its importance in certain contexts. We try to reconcile our strong desire for transparency with our fundamental need to maintain privacy. We struggle to make sense of the often-conflicting functions of anonymity as a tool that allows some to avoid accountability for terrible acts and yet others to protect themselves and their basic rights when threatened.

Perhaps not surprisingly, then, the organizational landscape is also filled with similar tensions when it comes to the concealing and revealing of iden-tity. We see demands that terrorist groups take responsibility for cowardly acts but then observe covert and clandestine actions in retaliation. We read about WikiLeaks revealing classified information from organizations thought to be too secretive, and then watch one of the most hidden organizations in the world (Anonymous) come to their defense. We celebrate firms with the best global reputations and then criticize many of the same corporations for devoting too many resources to their own branding. We praise groups like

Narconon and Applied Scholastics for the wonderful work they do but are equally suspicious of the organization behind those front groups: Scientology. We dismiss and ridicule many secret societies but cannot resist movies, books, and other popular accounts of them. We openly criticize elements of the underground economy and many organizations in the sex industry—and then secretly take advantage of the products and services they provide.

Contradictions such as these are just some of many reasons why we as global citizens, members of various collectives, and scholars of organizations must seek to better understand the anonymous agencies, backstreet businesses, covert collectives, and other hidden organizations of the twenty-first century. Like any journey into the unknown, there are dangers in such exploration; but I suspect the adventure that awaits us will be filled with substantial excitement and important insight. It is my hope that the ideas shared in this book will help guide our quest as we expand our thinking to include these diverse, intriguing, and consequential organizations in the contemporary landscape.

References

2006 best places to launch a career: Shell Oil Company. 2006. *Businessweek.* Retrieved November 2, 2011 from http://www.businessweek.com/careers/bplc/companies _36.htm.

Abimbola, T., and C. Vallaster. 2007. Brand, organizational identity and reputation in SMEs: An overview. *Qualitative Market Research: An International Journal* 10:341–348.

About the Ku Klux Klan—Extremism in America. N.d. Anti-Defamation League. Retrieved January 26, 2012 from http://www.adl.org/learn/ext_us/kkk/default .asp.

Abrahms, M. 2008. What terrorists really want: Terrorist motives and counterterrorism strategy. *International Security* 32(4):78–105.

Acharya, A., and S. Marwah. 2011. Nizam, la tanzim (system, not organization): Do organizations matter in terrorism today? A study of the November 2008 Mumbai attacks. *Studies in Conflict and Terrorism* 34:1–16.

Ahrne, G., and N. Brunsson. 2011. Organization outside organizations: The significance of partial organization. *Organization* 18:83–104.

Albert, S., B. Ashforth, and J. Dutton. 2000. Organizational identity and identification: Charting new waters and building new bridges. *Academy of Management Review* 25:13–17.

Albert, S., and D. A. Whetten. 1985. Organizational identity. *Research in Organizational Behavior* 7:263–295.

Alcoholics Anonymous. 1952. *Twelve Steps and Twelve Traditions.* New York: Alcoholics Anonymous World Services.

Alcoholics Anonymous. 2012. A.A. Fact File. Retrieved on January 20, 2012 from http://aa.org/pdf/products/m-24_aafactfile.pdf.

All U.S. companies. 2011. Manta. Retrieved May 19, 2011 from http://www.manta.com /mb.

Alleged Continuity IRA leader named in Carroll murder trial. 2012. BBC News Northern Ireland, February 2. Retrieved February 10, 2012 from http://www.bbc.co.uk /news/uk-northern-ireland-16851715.

Allen, M. W., S. J. Coopman, J. L. Hart, and K. L. Walker. 2007. Workplace surveillance and managing privacy boundaries. *Management Communication Quarterly* 21:172–200.

Allen, W. R. 1991. Klan, cloth, and constitution: Anti-mask laws and the First Amendment. *Georgia Law Review* 25:810–860.

Alvesson, M. 2004. Organization: From substance to image? In *Organizational identity: A reader*, ed. M. J. Hatch and M. Schultz, 161–182. Oxford: Oxford University Press.

Ambinder, M. 2010. Delta Force gets a name change. *The Atlantic*, October 12. Retrieved on October 20, 2012 from http://www.theatlantic.com/politics /archive/2010/10/delta-force-gets-a-name-change/64310/.

Amine, L., and P. Magnusson. 2007. Cost-benefit models of stakeholders in the global counterfeiting industry: A marketing point of view. *Multinational Business Review* 15:1–22.

Anheier, H. K. 2010. Secret societies. In *International Encyclopedia of Civil Society*, ed. H. K. Anheier and S. Toepler, pt. 19, 1355–1358. New York: Springer Science.

Anonymous. 1998. To reveal or not to reveal: A theoretical model of anonymous communication. *Communication Theory* 8:381–407.

Anonymous. 2012. CNN Presents. Retrieved January 31, 2012 from http://www.youtube .com/watch?v=henUw1irtU4.

Apollonio, D. E., and L. A. Bero. 2007. Creating industry front groups: The tobacco industry and "Get Government Off Our Back." *American Journal of Public Health* 97:419–427.

Aprill, E. P. 2011. Once and future gift taxation of transfers to section 501(c)(4) organizations: Current law, constitutional issues, and policy considerations. *New York University Journal of Legislation and Public Policy* 15:289–327.

Argenti, P., and B. Druckenmiller. 2004. Reputation and the corporate brand. *Corporate Reputation Review* 6:368–374.

Armond, P. D. 2001. Netwar in the Emerald City: WTO protest strategy and tactics. In *Networks and netwars: The future of terror, crime and militancy*, ed. J. Arquilla and D. Ronfeldt, 201–238. Santa Monica, CA: Rand.

Arquilla, J., and D. Ronfeldt. 2001. Afterword (September 2001): The sharpening fight for the future. In *Networks and netwars: The future of terror, crime and militancy*, ed. J. Arquilla and D. Ronfeldt, 201–238. Santa Monica, CA: Rand.

Arquilla, J., D. Ronfeldt, and M. Zanini. 1999. Networks, netwar and information age terrorism. In *Countering the new terrorism*, ed. A. Lesser, B. Hoffman, J. Arquilla, D. Ronfeldt, and M. Zanini, 39–84. Santa Monica, CA: Rand.

Ashforth, B. E., and S. A. Johnson. 2001. Which hat to wear: The relative salience of multiple identities in organizational contexts. In *Social identity processes in organizational contexts*, ed. M. A. Hogg and D. J. Terry, 31–48. Philadelphia: Psychology Press.

Ashforth, B. E., and G. E. Kreiner. 1999. "How can you do it?": Dirty work and the challenge of constructing a positive identity. *Academy of Management Review* 24:413–434.

Ayling, J. 2009. Criminal organizations and resilience. *International Journal of Law, Crime and Justice* 37:182–196.

Ball, C. 2009. What is transparency? *Public Integrity* 11(4):293–307.

Balmer, J. M. T. 2001. From the Pentagon: A new identity framework. *Corporate Reputation Review* 4:11–21.

Balser, D. B. 1997. The impact of environmental factors on factionalism and schism in social movement organizations. *Social Forces* 76:199–228.

Bamford, J. 2001. *Body of secrets: Anatomy of the ultra-secret National Security Agency from the cold war through the dawn of a new century.* New York: Doubleday.

Bamford, J. 2008. *The shadow factory: The ultra-secret NSA from 9/11 to the eavesdropping on America.* New York: Doubleday.

Bandsuch, M., L. Pate, and J. Thies. 2008. Rebuilding stakeholder trust in business: An examination of principle-centered leadership and organizational transparency in corporate governance. *Business and Society Review* 113:99–127.

Barker, J. R. 1998. Managing identification. In *Identity in organizations: Building theory through conversations*, ed. D. Whetten and P. Godfrey, 257–267. Thousand Oaks, CA: Sage.

Barnes, N. G., A. M. Lescault, and J. Andonian. 2012. *Social media surge by the 2012 Fortune 500: Increase use of blogs, Facebook, Twitter and more.* Retrieved October 19, 2012 from http://www.umassd.edu/cmr/socialmedia/2012fortune500/.

Barnett, B. A. 2007. Hate group community-building online: A case study in the visual content of Internet hate sites. In *Proceedings of the 65th Annual Conference of the New York State Communication Association*, October 19–21, ed. S. Dincki and B. Kelly, 1–15. Kerhonsken, NY: n.p.

Baumes, J., M. Goldberg, M. Magdon-Ismail, and W. Wallace. 2004. *Discovering hidden groups in communication networks.* 2nd NSF/NIJ Symposium on Intelligence and Security Informatics, Tucson, AZ.

Becker, K. F. 2004. *The informal economy.* Stockholm: Swedish International Development Agency.

Behar, R. 1991. The thriving cult of greed and power. *Time,* May 6, 52–60.

Beit-Hallahmi, B. 2003. Scientology: Religion or racket? *Marburg Journal of Religion* 8:1–45.

Belanger, F., and R. E. Crossler. 2011. Privacy in the digital age: A review of information privacy research in information systems. *MIS Quarterly* 35:1017–1041.

Benoit, W. L. 1997. Image repair discourse and crisis communication. *Public Relations Review* 23:177–186.

Bertelli, A. M. 2006. Motivation crowding and the federal civil servant: Evidence from the U.S. Internal Revenue Service. *International Public Management Journal* 9:3–23.

Best places to work in Switzerland. 2011. Retrieved December 19, 2011 from http://worldradio.ch/wrs/news/wrsnews/swiss-companies-among-best-places-to-work.shtml.

Best, R. A., Jr., and A. Feickert. 2006. *CRS Report for Congress: Special operations forces (SOF) and CIA paramilitary operations: Issues for congress.* Washington, DC: Congressional Research Service, Library of Congress.

Bilton, N. 2011. Masked protesters aid Time Warner's bottom line. *New York Times*, August 29, 4.

Birchfield, R. 2010. Reputation is everything. *New Zealand Management* 57(8):25–29.

Black, E. 1988. Secrecy and disclosure as rhetorical forms. *Quarterly Journal of Speech* 74:133–150.

Blau, P. M., and W. R. Scott. 1962. *Formal organizations: A comparative approach.* San Francisco: Chandler (reissued as a Business Classic, Stanford University Press, 2003).

Blauvelt, T. K. 2011. March of the Chekists: Beria's secret police patronage network and Soviet crypto-politics. *Communist and Post-Communist Studies* 44:73–88.

Boatright, R. G. 2007. Situating the new 527 organizations in Interest Group Theory. *Forum* 5(2):1–23.

Boele, R., H. Fabig, and D. Wheeler. 2001. Shell, Nigeria and the Ogoni: A study in unsustainable development: I. The story of Shell, Nigeria and the Ogoni people—Environment, economy, relationships: Conflict and prospects for resolution. *Sustainable Development* 9:74–86.

Bok, S. 1982. *Secrets: On the ethics of concealment and revelation.* New York: Pantheon Books.

Bonini, S., D. Court, and A. Marchi. 2009. Rebuilding corporate reputations. *McKinsey Quarterly* 3:75–83.

Borkman, T. 2006. Sharing experience, conveying hope: Egalitarian relations as the essential method of alcoholics anonymous. *Nonprofit Management and Leadership* 17:145–161.

Bostdorff, D. M. 2004. The Internet rhetoric of the Ku Klux Klan: A case study in web site community building run amok. *Communication Studies* 55:340–361.

Bovenkerk, F. 2011. On leaving criminal organizations. *Crime, Law and Social Change* 55:261–276.

Bradley, R. T. 2010. Detecting the identity signature of secret social groups: Holographic processes and the communication of member affiliation. *World Futures* 66:124–162.

Brammer, S., and S. Pavelin. 2004. Building a good reputation. *European Management Journal* 22:704–713.

"Bronco" a.k.a. Scott, C. R. 2004. Benefits and drawbacks of anonymous online communication: Legal challenges and communicative recommendations. In *Free speech yearbook*, ed. S. Drucker, 41: 127–141. Washington, DC: National Communication Association.

Brown, T., P. Dacin, M. Pratt, and D. Whetten. 2006. Identity, intended image, construed image, and reputation: An interdisciplinary framework and suggested methodology. *Journal of the Academy of Marketing Science* 34:95–106.

Burkell, J. A. 2006. Anonymity in behavioral research: Not being unnamed, but being unknown. *University of Ottawa Law and Technology Journal* 3:189–203.

Burns, T., and G. M. Stalker. 1961. *The management of innovation.* London: Tavistock.

Caiani, M., and L. Parenti. 2009. The dark side of the Web: Italian right-wing extremist groups and the Internet. *South European Society and Politics* 14:273–294.

Cain, R. 1994. Managing impressions of an AIDS service organization: Into the mainstream or out of the closet? *Qualitative Sociology* 17(1): 43–61.

Campbell, A. 2009. Over 70% of the largest small businesses have a website. Retrieved June 1, 2011 from http://www.sellingtosmallbusinesses.com/70-percent-largest-small-businesses-have-website/.

Campbell, D. 2010. More than 40% of domestic violence victims are male, report reveals. *The Guardian,* September 4. Retrieved June 9, 2011 from http://www.guardian.co.uk/society/2010/sep/05/men-victims-domestic-violence.

Carmeli, A., G. Gilat, and J. Weisberg. 2006. Perceived external prestige, organizational identification and affective commitment: A stakeholder approach. *Corporate Reputation Review* 9:92–10.

Carpenter, M. A., and A. D. Stajkovic. 2006. Social network theory and methods as tools for helping business confront global terrorism: Capturing the case and contingencies presented by dark social networks. In *Corporate strategies under international terrorism and adversity,* ed. G. G. S. Suder, 7–19. Northampton, MA: Edward Elgar.

Carper, W. B., and W. E. Snizek. 1980. The nature and types of organizational taxonomies: An overview. *Academy of Management Review* 5:65–75.

Castells, M., and A. Portes. 1989. World underneath: The origins, dynamics, and effects of the informal economy. In *The informal economy: Studies in advanced and less developed countries,* ed. A. Portes, M. Castells, and L. Benton, 11–37. Baltimore: Johns Hopkins University Press.

Center for Applied Research in the Apostolate. 2011. Frequently requested church statistics. Retrieved on October 28, 2011 from http://cara.georgetown.edu/CARAServices/requestedchurchstats.html.

Chalmers, D. M. 1987. *Hooded Americanism: The history of the Ku Klux Klan.* Durham, NC: Duke University Press.

Chan, C. S. 2004. The *Falun Gong* in China: A sociological perspective. *China Quarterly* 179:665–683.

Cheney, G. 1983a. On the various and changing meanings of organizational membership: A field study of organizational identification. *Communication Monographs* 50:342–362.

Cheney, G. 1983b. The rhetoric of identification and the study of organizational communication. *Quarterly Journal of Speech* 69:143–158.

Cheney, G. 1991. *Rhetoric in an organizational society: Managing multiple identities.* Columbia: University of South Carolina Press.

Cheney, G. 2000. Thinking differently about organizational communication: Why, how, and where. *Management Communication Quarterly* 14:132–141.

Cheney, G., and L. T. Christensen. 2001. Organizational identity: Linkages between internal and external communication. In *The new handbook of organizational communication: Advances in theory, research, and methods*, ed. F. M. Jablin and L. L. Putnam, 231–269. Thousand Oaks, CA: Sage.

Cheney, G., L. T. Christensen, T. E. Zorn Jr., and S. Ganesh. 2004. *Organizational communication in an age of globalization: Issues, reflections, practices.* Prospect Heights, IL: Waveland.

Christensen, L.T., and G. Cheney. 2000. Self-absorption and self-seduction in the corporate identity game. In *The expressive organization: Linking identity, reputation, and the corporate brand*, ed. M. Schultz, M. J. Hatch, and M. H. Larsen, 246–270. Oxford: Oxford University Press.

Christensen, L. T., M. Morsing, and G. Cheney. 2008. *Corporate communications.* Los Angeles: Sage.

Clandestine services: FAQs. 2010. Central Intelligence Agency, June 29. Retrieved on June 8, 2011 from https://www.cia.gov/offices-of-cia/clandestine-service/faqs.html.

Coleman, G. E. 2011. Anonymous: From the Lulz to collective action, April 6. Retrieved January 31, 2012 from http://mediacommons.futureofthebook.org/tne/pieces/anonymous-lulz-collective-action.

Conant, J. 2008. *The irregulars: Roald Dahl and the British spy ring in wartime Washington.* New York: Simon & Schuster.

Conquergood, D. 1994. Homeboys and hoods: Gangs and cultural space. In *Group communication in context: Studies of natural groups*, ed. L. R. Frey, 23–55. Hillsdale, NJ: Lawrence Erlbaum.

Coombs, W. T. 2012. *Ongoing crisis communication: Planning, managing, and responding.* 3rd ed. Thousand Oaks, CA: Sage.

Corman, S. R. 2011. Has al-Qaeda become a toxic brand? Retrieved on October 6, 2011 from http://comops.org/journal/2011/08/09/has-al-qaeda-become-a-toxic-brand/.

Corman, S. R., A. Trethewey, and H. L. Goodall Jr., eds. 2008. *Weapons of mass persuasion: Strategic communication in the struggle against violent extremism.* New York: Peter Lang.

Cornelissen, J. P., S. A. Haslam, and J. M. T. Balmer. 2007. Social identity, organizational identity and corporate identity: Towards an integrated understanding of processes, patternings and products. *British Journal of Management* 18:1–16.

Costoya, M. M. 2007. *Civil society actors: The case of the movement to change international trade rules and barriers.* Civil Society and Social Movements Program Paper No. 30. Geneva: United Nations Research Institute for Social Development.

Cote, K. 2011. Germany's shocking neo-Nazi killers: How did they go undetected? *Time World*, November 17. Retrieved February 10, 2012 from http://www.time.com/time/world/article/0,8599,2099616,00.html.

Crenshaw, A. 2011. Crude, inconsistent threat: Understanding Anonymous. Retrieved January 31, 2012 from http://www.irongeek.com/i.php?page=security/understanding-anonymous.

Crenshaw, M. 1988. Theories of terrorism: Instrumental and organizational approaches. In *Inside terrorist organizations*, ed. D. C. Rapoport, 13–31. New York: Columbia University Press.

Crowley, M. 2009. Corporate governance, Royal Dutch Shell, terrorism, and reputational risk. *Finance Industry* 11:35–47.

Cruz, J. 2012. *Community through invisibility: Market women's organizing in post-conflict Liberia.* Paper presented at Annual Conference of the National Communication Association, Orlando, FL.

Cult of the Dead Cow. 2011. About: Team bio. Retrieved October 17, 2011 from http://w3.cultdeadcow.com/cms/team_bio.html.

Czarniawska, B. 1997. *Narrating the organization: Dramas of institutional identity.* Chicago: University of Chicago Press.

D'Antonio, W. V. 1994. Autonomy and democracy in an autocratic organization: The case of the Roman Catholic Church. *Sociology of Religion* 55:379–396.

Davis, G. F. 2009. The rise and fall of finance and the end of the society of organizations. *Academy of Management Perspectives* 23(3): 27–44.

Davis, S. L. 1997. *Unbridled power: Inside the secret culture of the IRS.* New York: HarperBusiness.

Dawson, T. 2011. *What should corporate identity development cost?* Retrieved on May 19, 2011 from http://www.pullinc.com/what-should-corporate-identity-development-cost/.

de Geus, A. 1997. *The living company: Habits for survival in a turbulent business environment.* Boston: Harvard Business School Press.

de Grazia, R. 1980. Clandestine employment: A problem of our times. *International Labour Review* 119:549–563.

Del Pero, M. 2003. The role of covert operations in U.S. cold war foreign policy. In *Secret intelligence in the twentieth century*, ed. H. Bungert, J. G. Heitmann, and M. Wala, 68–82. London: Frank Cass.

Delph, E. 1978. *The silent community.* Beverly Hills, CA: Sage.

DeLuca, K. 1999. *Image politics: The new rhetoric of environmental activism.* New York: Guilford Press.

Denning, D. E. 2001. Activism, hacktivism, and cyberterrorism: The Internet as a tool for influencing foreign policy. In *Networks and netwars: The future of terror, crime and militancy*, ed. J. Arquilla and D. Ronfeldt, 239–288. Santa Monica, CA: Rand.

Drozdova, K., and M. Samoilov. 2010. Predictive analysis of concealed social network activities based on communication technology choices: Early-warning detection of attack signals from terrorist organizations. *Computational and Mathematical Organization Theory* 16:61–88.

Dufresne, R. L., and E. H. Offstein. 2008. On the virtues of secrecy in organizations. *Journal of Management Inquiry* 17:102–106.

Dukerich, J. M., and S. M. Carter. 2000. Distorted images and reputation repair. In *The expressive organization: Linking identity, reputation, and the corporate brand,* ed. M. Schultz, M. J. Hatch, and M. H. Larsen, 97–112. Oxford: Oxford University Press.

Dukerich, J. M., R. Kramer, and J. M. Parks. 1998. The dark side of organizational identification. In *Identity in organizations: Building theory through conversations*, ed. D. A. Whetten and P. C. Godfrey, 245–256. Thousand Oaks, CA: Sage.

Dutton, J. E., and J. M. Dukerich. 1991. Keeping an eye on the mirror: Image and identity in organizational adaptation. *Academy of Management Journal* 34:517–554.

Dutton, J. E., J. M. Dukerich, and C. V. Harquail. 1994. Organizational images and member identification. *Administrative Science Quarterly* 39:239–263.

Egelhoff, W. G., and F. Sen. 1992. An information-processing model of crisis management. *Management Communication Quarterly* 5:443–484.

Egley, A., Jr., J. C. Howell, and J. P. Moore. 2010. Highlights of the 2008 National Youth Gang Survey. *U.S. Department of Justice OJJDP Fact Sheet*. Retrieved on May 20, 2011 from https://www.ncjrs.gov/pdffiles1/ojjdp/229249.pdf.

EHS Today Staff. 1999. OSHA ranked lowest with IRS in customer satisfaction survey. *EHS Today*, December 22. Retrieved on February 6, 2012 from http://ehstoday.com/news/ehs_imp_32848/.

Einstein, M. 2011. The evolution of religious branding. *Social Compass* 58:331–338.

Eisenberg, E. M. 1984. Ambiguity as strategy in organizational communication. *Communication Monographs* 51:227–242.

Eisenberg, E. M., and G. M. Witten. 1987. Reconsidering openness in organizational communication. *Academy of Management Review* 12:418–426.

Elsbach, K. D., and R. M. Sutton. 1992. Acquiring organizational legitimacy through illegitimate actions: A marriage of institutional and impression management theories. *Academy of Management Journal* 35:699–738.

Elwood, W. N., K. Greene, and K. K. Carter. 2003. Gentlemen don't speak: Communication norms and condom use in bathhouses. *Journal of Applied Communication Research* 31:277–297.

Emerson, S. 2002. *Fund-raising methods and procedures for international terrorist organizations*. Testimony before the House Committee on Financial Services Subcommittee on Oversight and Investigations. Retrieved on October 21, 2012 from http://www.au.af.mil/au/awc/awcgate/congress/021202se.pdf.

Emery, F., and E. Trist. 1965. The causal texture of organizational environments. *Human Relations* 18:21–32.

Engell, R. 2011. *"I'm positive. So what?" HIV illness narratives from Zimbabwe and the United States*. Unpublished paper, Department of Anthropology, Mount Holyoke College, South Hadley, MA.

Enste, D. H. 2010. Shadow economy: The impact of regulation in OECD-countries. *International Economic Journal* 24:555–571.

Erickson, B. 1981. Secret societies and social structure. *Social Forces* 60(1):188–210.

Etzioni, A. 1961. *A comparative analysis of complex organizations*. New York: Free Press.

Eyre, A. 1994. Religious cults in twentieth century America. *American Studies Today*

Online, 1. Retrieved June 7, 2011 from http://www.americansc.org.uk/Online /cults.htm.

Fang, L. 2009. Exclusive: Attacks on health reform orchestrated by yet another shadowy corporate front group—"CMPI." Retrieved on October 21, 2012 from http:// thinkprogress.org/economy/2009/11/18/69874/cmpi-front-group/.

Federal agencies pursue Anonymous. 2011. *Washington Post*, September 11.

Ferreira-Tiryaki, G. 2008. The informal economy and business cycles. *Journal of Applied Economics* 11:91–117.

Final Salute to Comdt-General Tom Maguire. 1994. *Saoirse*, 2. Retrieved February 12, 2012 from http://indiamond6.ulib.iupui.edu/cdm4/document.php?CISOROOT= %2FIrishNews&CISOPTR=2746&REC=16&CISOBOX=Continuity.

Fiss, P. C. 2011. Building better causal theories: A fuzzy set approach to typologies in organizational research. *Academy of Management Journal* 54:393–420.

Fombrun, C., and V. Rindova. 2000. The road to transparency: Reputation management at Royal Dutch/Shell. In *The expressive organization: Linking identity, reputation, and the corporate brand*, ed. M. Schultz, M. J. Hatch, and M. H. Larsen, 77–96. Oxford: Oxford University Press.

Fong, M. L. 1981. *The sociology of secret societies: A study of Chinese secret societies in Singapore and Peninsular Malaysia*. Kuala Lumpur: Oxford University Press.

Foreign Terrorist Organizations. 2012. U.S. State Department. Retrieved on May 19, 2011 from http://www.state.gov/j/ct/rls/other/des/123085.htm.

Foreman, D. 1985. *Ecodefense: A field guide to monkeywrenching.* Chico, CA: Abbzug Press.

Freeman, R. E. 1984. *Strategic management: A stakeholder approach.* Boston: Pitman.

Frequently asked questions. 2010. Small Business Administration. Retrieved October 27, 2010 from http://www.sba.gov/sites/default/files/sbfaq.pdf.

Frumkin, P. 2002. *On being nonprofit: A conceptual and policy primer.* Cambridge, MA: Harvard University Press.

Fu, T., A. Abbasi, and H. Chen. 2010. A focused crawler for dark web forums. *Journal of the American Society for Information Science and Technology* 61:1213–1231.

Galagher, J., L. Sproull, and S. Kiesler. 1998. Legitimacy, authority, and community in electronic support groups. *Written Communication* 15:493–530.

Gambetta, D. 2009. *Codes of the underworld: How criminals communicate.* Princeton, NJ: Princeton University Press.

Gang violence on the rise on Indian reservations. 2009. *National Public Radio*, August 25. Retrieved on June 8, 2011 from http://www.npr.org/templates/story/story .php?storyId=112200614.

Gardham, D. 2009. Northern Ireland shootings: A profile of the Continuity IRA. *The Telegraph*, March 11. Retrieved February 10, 2012 from http://www.telegraph .co.uk/news/uknews/northernireland/4968775/Northern-Ireland-shootings-A-profile-of-the-Continuity-IRA.html.

Gerxhani, K. 2004. The informal sector in developed and less developed countries. *Public Choice* 120:267–300.

Gioia, D. A., M. Schultz, and K. G. Corley. 2000. Organizational identity, image and adaptive instability. *Academy of Management Review* 25:63–81.

Gist, N. P. 1938. Structure and process in secret societies. *Social Forces* 16:349–357.

Global Terrorism Database. 2011. START. Retrieved on June 8, 2011 from http://www .start.umd.edu/gtd/.

Godfrey, P. C. 2011. Toward a theory of the informal economy. *Academy of Management Annals* 5:231–277.

Goffman, E. 1959. *The presentation of self in everyday life.* New York: Anchor.

Goldwag, A. 2009. *Cults, conspiracies, and secret societies: The straight scoop on Freemasons, the Illuminati, Skull and Bones, Black Helicopters, The New World Order, and many, many more.* New York: Vintage.

Gossett, L. M. 2002. Kept at arm's length: Questioning the organizational desirability of member identification. *Communication Monographs* 69:385–404.

Grant, K. 2009. Metropolitan Transit System named "Best of the Best" nationwide. *SDMetro,* October 6. Retrieved December 6, 2011 from http://sandiegometro .com/2009/10/metropolitan-transit-system-named-%E2%80%98best-of-the-best%E2%80%99-nationwide/.

Grant, R. M. 2005. Organizational restructuring within the Royal Dutch/Shell Group. In *Cases to accompany contemporary strategy analysis,* ed. R. M. Grant, 117–142. 5th ed. Malden, MA: Blackwell.

Greenberg, A. 2011. Anonymous faces identity dilemma over Sony hack. *Forbes,* May 5, 4.

Greenberg, A. 2012. *This machine kills secrets: How WikiLeakers, cypherpunks, and hacktivists aim to free the world's information.* New York: Dutton.

Green-Hamann, S., K. C. Eichhorn, and J. C. Sherblom. 2011. An exploration of why people participate in Second Life social support groups. *Journal of Computer-Mediated Communication* 16:465–491.

Grey, C. 2009. Security studies and organization studies: Parallels and possibilities. *Organization* 16:303–316.

Gross, R. C. 2009. *Different worlds: Unacknowledged special operations and covert action.* Unpublished report, U.S. Army War College, Carlisle, PA.

Grunig, J., and T. Hunt. 1984. *Managing public relations.* New York: Holt, Rinehart & Winston.

Gude, H., S. Robel, and H. Stark. 2012. The clandestine life of the neo-Nazi terror cell. *Spiegel Online International.* Retrieved February 10, 2012 from http://www.spiegel .de/international/germany/0,1518,808275,00.html.

Gunaratna, R., and A. Oreg. 2010. Al Qaeda's organizational structure and its evolution. *Studies in Conflict and Terrorism* 33:1043–1078.

Gutwirth, J. 1999. From the word to the televisual image: The Televangelists and Pope John Paul II. *Diogenes* 47:122–133.

Habibullah, M. S., and Y. K. Eng. 2006. Crime and the underground economy in Malaysia: Are they related? *Journal of Global Business Management* 2:138–155.

Hall, D. T., and B. Schneider. 1972. Correlates of organizational identification as a function of career pattern and organizational type. *Administrative Science Quarterly* 17:340–350.

Hammers, C. 2009. An examination of lesbian/queer bathhouse culture and the social organization of (im)personal sex. *Journal of Contemporary Ethnography* 38:308–335.

Haney, E. 2002. *Inside Delta Force: The story of America's elite counterterrorist unit.* New York: Delacorte Press.

Hannan, M. T., L. Polos, and G. R. Carroll. 2007. *Logics of organization theory: Audiences, codes, and ecologies.* Princeton, NJ: Princeton University Press.

Hart, K. 2007. Bureaucratic form and the informal economy. In *Linking the formal and informal economy: Concepts and policies,* ed. B. Guha-Khasnobis, R. Kanbur, and E. Ostrom. Oxford: Oxford University Press.

Hartzog, R. 2010. *Genealogy research: Complete list of fraternal organizations.* Retrieved May 18, 2011 from http://www.exonumia.com/art/society.htm.

Harwood, W. S. 1897. Secret societies in America. *North American Review* 164:617–624.

Hatch, M. J., and M. Schultz. 2000. Scaling the Tower of Babel: Relational differences between identity, image, and culture in organizations. In *The expressive organization: Linking identity, reputation, and the corporate brand,* ed. M. Schultz, M. J. Hatch, and M. H. Larsen, 11–35. Oxford: Oxford University Press.

Hatch, M. J., and M. Schultz. 2003. Bringing the corporation into corporate branding. *European Journal of Marketing* 37:1041–1064.

Hatch, M. J., and M. Schultz. 2010. Toward a theory of brand co-creation with implications for brand governance. *Brand Management* 17:590–604.

Hate group numbers up by 54% since 2000. 2009. Southern Poverty Law Center. Retrieved March 2, 2009 from http://www.splcenter.org/news/item.jsp?aid=366.

Hazelrigg, L. 1969. A reexamination of Simmel's "The Secret and the Secret Society": Nine propositions. *Social Forces* 47(3):323–330.

Heckethorn, C. W. 1965. *The secret societies of all ages and countries.* Vols. 1 and 2. New Hyde Park, NY: University Books.

Heinonen, U. 2008. The hidden role of informal economy: Is informal economy insignificant for Phnom Penh's development? In *Modern myths of the Mekong,* ed. M. Kummu, M. Keskinen, and O. Varis, 123–132. Helskinki: Helsinki University of Technology.

Heiss, B. M. R., P. Monge, and J. Fulk. 2012. *Predatory mimicry in the crisis pregnancy center movement: Ambiguous form communication as an evolutionary strategy.* Paper presented at the annual convention of the International Communication Association, Phoenix, AZ.

Heller, M. 2008. Corporate brand building at Shell-Mex Ltd in the Interwar Period. In *Working Papers.* CGR Working paper 23. Queen Mary, University of London, School of Business and Management, Centre for Globalisation Research, London, England.

Hellman, C., and R. Huang. N.d. List of known terrorist organizations. *Center for Defense Information.* Retrieved February 10, 2012 from http://www.cdi.org/terrorism/terrorist-groups.cfm.

Heymann, L. 2011. Naming, identity, and trademark law. *Indiana Law Journal* 86:381–446.

Hidden world of secret societies: An illustrated history of the most mysterious organizations. 2012. New York: Life Books.

Hollander, J. 2001. The language of privacy. *Social Research* 68(1):5–28.

Hudson, B. A. 2008. Against all odds: A consideration of core-stigmatized organizations. *Academy of Management Review,* 33:252–266.

Hudson, B. A., and G. A. Okhuysen. 2009. Not with a ten-foot pole: Core stigma, stigma transfer, and improbable persistence of men's bathhouses. *Organization Science* 20:134–153.

Illia, L., and F. Lurati. 2006. Stakeholder perspectives on organizational identity: Searching for a relationship approach. *Corporate Reputation Review* 8:293–304.

International Sign Association. 2008. *U.S. Sign Industry Size and Impact Study.* Retrieved on May 19, 2011 from http://www.signs.org/IndustryResources/SignIndustry Statistics/USSignIndustrySizeandImpactStudy/tabid/644/Default.aspx.

Jaakson, K. 2010. Engagement of organizational stakeholders in the process of formulating values statements. *Atlantic Journal of Communication* 18(3):158–176.

Jablin, F. M. 2001. Organizational entry, assimilation, and disengagement/exit. In *The new handbook of organizational communication*, ed. F. M. Jablin and L. L. Putnam, 732–818. Thousand Oaks, CA: Sage.

Jablin, F. M., and P. M. Sias. 2001. Communication competence. In *The new handbook of organizational communication*, ed. F. M. Jablin and L. L. Putnam, 819–864. Thousand Oaks, CA: Sage.

Jackie Evans Inc. 2012. Manta. Retrieved February 2, 2012 from http://www.manta .com/c/mmn3r9y/jackie-evans-inc.

Jenkins, P. 2003. *Images of terror: What we can and can't know about terrorism.* New York: Aldine de Gruyter.

Johnson, M. 2006. The growing relevance of Special Operations Forces in U.S. military strategy. *Comparative Strategy* 25:273–296.

Jones, C. 2006. Al-Qaeda's innovative improvisers: Learning in a diffuse transnational network. *Cambridge Review of International Affairs* 19:555–569.

Jones, C., and E. H. Volpe. 2011. Organizational identification: Extending our understanding of social identities through social networks. *Journal of Organizational Behavior* 32:413–434.

Kanter, B., and A. H. Fine. 2010. *The networked nonprofit: Connecting with social media to drive change.* San Francisco: Jossey-Bass.

Katz, D., and R. L. Kahn. 1966. *The social psychology of organizations.* New York: Wiley.

Keep factory jobs home. 2012. *Herald News.* Retrieved February 2, 2012 from http:// www.northjersey.com/news/opinions/138462159_Keeping_factory_jobs__.html.

Keller, K. L. 2000. Building and managing corporate brand equity. In *The expressive organization: Linking identity, reputation and the corporate brand*, ed. M. Schultz, M. J. Hatch, and M. H. Larsen, 115–137. Oxford: Oxford University Press.

Kennedy, J. F. 1961. *The President and the Press*, April 27. Address delivered to the American Newspaper Publishers Association, New York. Retrieved February 9, 2012 from http://cuttingthroughthematrix.com/transcripts/JFK_Video_Speech .html.

Kerr, D. 1997. The Continuity IRA. *Ulster Nation*. Retrieved February 11, 2012 from http://www.ulsternation.org.uk/continuity_ira.htm.

Kerwood, H. A. 1995. Where do just-in-time manufacturing networks fit? A typology of networks and a framework for analysis. *Human Relations* 48:927–950.

King, A. 2009. The special Air Service and the concentration of military power. *Armed Forces and Society* 35:646–666.

Kinyanjui, M. N. 2010. *Social relations and association in the informal sector in Kenya*. Social Policy and Development Paper No. 43. Geneva: United Nations Research Institute for Social Development.

Kitzmiller, F. 2011. Gangs aren't always easy to see. *NewsHerald.com*. Retrieved May 20, 2011 from http://www.streetgangs.com/news/010311_gang_identification.

Kleemans, E. R. 2007. Organized crime, transit crime, and racketeering. *Crime and Justice* 35:163–215.

Klement, F. L. 1984. *Dark lanterns: Secret political societies, conspiracies, and treason trials in the Civil War*. Baton Rouge: Louisiana State University Press.

Knafo, S. 2012. *Anonymous and the war over the Internet*. Retrieved January 31, 2012 from http://www.huffingtonpost.com/2012/01/30/anonymous-internet-war_n_1233977. html and from http://www.huffingtonpost.com/2012/01/31/anonymous -war-overinternet_n_1237058.html.

Knight, P. 1998. *Profits and principles—does there have to be a choice?* London: Royal Dutch/Shell Group.

Kopp, P. 1999. *Organized crime: Strategies and countermeasures*. White paper published by Vienna International Center.

Kreiner, G. E., B. E. Ashforth, and D. M. Sluss. 2006. Identity dynamics in occupational dirty work: Integrating social identity and system justification perspectives. *Organization Science* 17:619–636.

Ku Klux Klan: A secret history. 2012. Documentary film. History Channel broadcast, January 26.

Landman, A. 2009. Attack of the living front groups: PR Watch offers help to unmask corporate tricksters. PR Watch, August 28. Retrieved June 9, 2011 from http:// www.prwatch.org/node/8531.

Lardner, R. 2006. Delta Force vets dismiss claims of "The Unit" writer. *Tampa Tribune*, April 11. Retrieved on December, 1, 2011 from http://web.archive.org /web/20060424151026/http://news.tbo.com/news/metro/MGBMS7AKVLE.html.

Leggatt, H. 2009. Nearly half of small businesses have no website. Retrieved October 24, 2010 from http://www.bizreport.com/2009/01/nearly_half_of_small_ businesses_have_no_website.html.

Levchuk, G., K. Chopra, and K. Pattipati. 2005. NetSTAR: Methodology to identify enemy network structure, tasks, activities, and roles. Presented at the 10th

International Command and Control Research and Technology Symposium: The Future Of C2, McLean, VA.

Lewis, L. 2005. The civil society sector. *Management Communication Quarterly* 19:238–267.

Lewis, L. K. 2007. An organizational stakeholder model of change implementation communication. *Communication Theory* 17:176–204.

Liebeskind, J. 1997. Keeping organizational secrets: Protective institutional mechanisms and their costs. *Industrial and Corporate Change* 6:623–663.

Lieven, A. 2011. The enemy's enemy. *New Statesman,* May 16, 24–27.

Lindelauf, R., P. Borm, and H. Hamers. 2008. The influence of secrecy on the communication structure of covert networks. *Social Networks* 31(2):126–137.

List of Intelligence Agencies. 2011. Wikipedia. Retrieved on June 8, 2011 from http://en.wikipedia.org/wiki/List_of_intelligence_agencies.

Little, K. L. 1949. The role of the secret society in cultural specialization. *American Anthropologist* 51:199–212.

Livesey, S. M. 2001. Eco-identity as discursive struggle: Royal Dutch/Shell, Brent Spar, and Nigeria. *Journal of Business Communication* 38:58–91.

Livesey, S. M., and K. Kearins. 2002. Transparent and caring corporations? A study of the sustainability reports by The Body Shop and Royal Dutch/Shell. *Organization and Environment* 15:233–258.

Losby, J. L, J. F. Else, M. E. Kingslow, E. L. Edgcomb, E. T. Malm, and V. Kao. 2002. *Informal economy literature review.* Unpublished working paper. Aspen Institute, Washington, DC.

Lu, Y., X. Luo, M. Polgar, and Y. Cao. 2010. Social network analysis of a criminal hacker community. *Journal of Computer Information Systems* 51(2):31–41.

Lucock, C., and M. Yeo. 2006. Naming names: The pseudonym in the name of the law. *University of Ottawa Law and Technology Journal* 3:53–108.

Lunde, P. 2004. *Organized crime: An inside guide to the world's most successful industry.* New York: DK Publishing.

Lydon, D. 2004. The Mafia, the Triads and the IRA: A study of criminal and political secret societies. Retrieved on October 21, 2012 from http://www.internetjournalof criminology.com/Lydon%20-%20The%20Mafia%20the%20Triads%20and%20 the%20IRA.pdf.

Macinnes, A. 2010. Passaic textile company could face closure if Girl Scouts end contract. Retrieved February 2, 2012 from http://www.northjersey.com/news/102810 _Passaic_textile_company_could_lose_90_jobs_if_Girl_Scouts_end_contract. html.

MacKenzie, N., ed. 1967. *Secret societies.* New York: Holt, Rinehart & Winston.

MacLean, N. K. 1994. *Behind the mask of chivalry: The making of the second Ku Klux Klan.* New York: Oxford University Press.

Mael, F. A., and B. E. Ashforth. 1992. Alumni and their alma mater: A partial test of the reformulated model of organizational identification. *Journal of Organizational Behavior* 13:103–123.

Mael, F. A., and B. E. Ashforth. 1995. Loyal from day one: Biodata, organizational identification, and turnover among newcomers. *Personnel Psychology* 48:309–333.

Mangus, R. J. 2009. *Obama win fuels Ku Klux Klan membership.* Retrieved January 26, 2012 from http://www.nowpublic.com/world/obama-win-fuels-ku-klux-klan-membership.

Mann, D. 2011. *Inside SEAL Team Six: My life and missions with America's elite warriors.* New York: Little, Brown.

Marquis, C., and M. W. Toffel. 2011. *The globalization of corporate environmental disclosure: Accountability or greenwashing?* Harvard Business School Organizational Behavior Unit Working Paper No. 11–115. Retrieved on October 21, 2012 from http://www.exed.hbs.edu/assets/Documents/globalization-environmental-disclosure.pdf.

Marret, J. 2008. Al-Qaeda in Islamic Maghreb: A glocal organization. *Studies in Conflict and Terrorism* 31:541–552.

Martino, L. 2005. From covert through overt to covert again: The parabola of U.S. Special Operation Forces. *CeMiSS Quarterly* 3(3):37–45.

Martins, J., and A. Ligthelm. 2004. *Level of entrepreneurship in the informal retail sector of South Africa.* Pretoria: University of South Africa, Bureau of Market Research.

Marx, G. T. 2004. Internet anonymity as reflection of broader issues involving technology and society. *Asia-Pacific Review* 11:142–166.

Marx, G. T. 2006. Varieties of personal information as influences on attitudes toward surveillance. In *The new politics of surveillance and visibility*, ed. K. Haggerty and R. Ericson, 79–110. Toronto: University of Toronto Press.

Mayntz, R. 2004. *Organizational forms of terrorism: Hierarchy, network, or a type sui generis?* Unpublished paper. Max Planck Institute for the Study of Societies, Cologne, Germany.

McDonald, H. 2010. One in seven Northern Ireland nationalists sympathise with dissident terrorists. *The Guardian*, October 6. Retrieved February 10, 2012 from http://www.guardian.co.uk/uk/2010/oct/06/one-in-seven-nationalists-support-terrorists.

McDonald, H. 2011. Continuity IRA member rules out peace moves. *The Guardian*, July 14. Retrieved February 10, 2012 from http://www.guardian.co.uk/uk/2011/jul/14/continuity-ira-member-rules-out-peace-moves.

McKelvey, B. 1982. *Organizational systematics: Taxonomy, evolution, classification.* Berkeley: University of California Press.

McPhee, R. D., and M. S. Poole. 2001. Organizational structures and configurations. In *The new handbook of organizational communication: Advances in theory, research, and methods*, ed. F. M. Jablin and L. L. Putnam, 503–543. Thousand Oaks, CA: Sage.

Messer, J. G. 1994. Emergent organization as a practical strategy: Executing trustee functions in Alcoholics Anonymous. *Nonprofit and Voluntary Sector Quarterly* 23:293–307.

Meyer, M. W. 1977. *Theory of organizational structure.* Indianapolis: Bobbs-Merrill.

Meyer, S. 2006. Trafficking in human organs in Europe: A myth or an actual threat? *European Journal of Crime, Criminal Law and Criminal Justice* 14(2):208–229.

Michael, K. 2008. The paradigm shift in transnational organized crime. LEGL960: Issues in Transnational Organised Crime. Retrieved June 21, 2011 from http://works.bepress.com/kmichael/195.

Miles, R. E., and C. Snow. 1978. *Organizational strategy, structure and process.* New York: McGraw-Hill.

Miller, B. M. 2010. Community stakeholders and marketplace advocacy: A model of advocacy, agenda building, and industry approval. *Journal of Public Relations Research* 22:85–112.

Mintzberg, H. 1979. *The structuring of organizations.* Englewood Cliffs, NJ: Prentice-Hall.

Mishal, S., and M. Rosenthal. 2005. Al Qaeda as a dune organization: Toward a typology of Islamic terrorist organizations. *Studies in Conflict and Terrorism* 28:275–293.

Mitchell, R. K., B. R. Agle, and D. J. Wood. 1997. Toward a theory of stakeholder identification and salience: Defining the principle of who and what really counts. *Academy of Management Review* 22:853–886.

Moffitt, S. L. 2010. Promoting agency reputation through public advice: Advisory committee use in the FDA. *Journal of Politics* 72:880–893.

More than 100 German far-right suspects at large. 2012. Retrieved on October 21, 2012 from http://www.france24.com/en/20121021-more-100-german-far-right-suspects-large.

Morgan, G. 1986. *Images of organizations.* Beverly Hills, CA: Sage.

Morrill, C., M. N. Zald, and H. Rao. 2003. Covert political conflict in organizations: Challenges from below. *Annual Review of Sociology* 29:391–415.

Morrison, E. W., and F. Milliken. 2000. Organizational silence: A barrier to change and development in a pluralistic world. *Academy of Management Review* 25:706–725.

Mozes, T., and G. Weimann. 2010. The e-marketing strategy of Hamas. *Studies in Conflict and Terrorism* 33:211–225.

Mulinge, M. M., and M. M. Munyae. 1998. The persistent growth in size and importance of the informal economy in African countries: Implications for theorizing the economy and labor markets. *African Sociological Review* 2:20–45.

Murphy, S. 2011. Agents provocateurs. *New Scientist* 211:46–49.

Murphy, S. 2012. Leak it for the people. *New Scientist* 214:22.

Muzellec, L. 2006. What is in a name change? Re-joycing corporate names to create corporate brands. *Corporate Reputation Review* 8:305–321.

Natarajan, M., and M. Belanger. 1998. Varieties of upper-level drug dealing organizations: A typology of cases prosecuted in New York City. *Journal of Drug Issues* 28(4):1005–1026.

National Bank Operating Subsidiary List. 2009. U.S. Department of Treasury. Retrieved on June 9, 2011 from http://www.helpwithmybank.gov/national-banks/operating-subsidiaries/national-banks-subsidiaries-a-m.html#d.

Ng, C. 2012. KKK group applies to adopt Georgia highway. *ABC News,* June 11. Retrieved October

23, 2012 from http:// abcnews.go.com/US/kkk-group-applies-adopt-georgia-highway/ story?id=16542326.

Nosco, P. 1993. Secrecy and the transmission of tradition: Issues in the study of the "underground" Christians. *Japanese Journal of Religious Studies* 20:3–29.

Nothnagle, A. 2011. Neo-Nazi terror gang leaves trail of blood across Germany. *Open Salon*, November 14. Retrieved February 10, 2012 from http:// open.salon.com/blog/lost_in_berlin/2011/11/14/neonazi_terror_gang_leaves _trail_of_blood_across_germany.

Olson, P. 2011. Anonymous speaks. *Forbes*, February 14, 38.

Ownby, D. 1993. Chinese *Hui* and the early modern social order: Evidence from eighteenth-century Southeast China. In *"Secret societies" reconsidered: Perspectives on the social history of modern South China and Southeast Asia*, ed. D. Ownby and M. S. Heidhues, 34–67. Armonk, NY: M. E. Sharpe.

Ownby, D., and M. S. Heidhues, eds. 1993. *"Secret societies" reconsidered: Perspectives on the social history of modern South China and Southeast Asia*. Armonk, NY: M. E. Sharpe.

Padanyi, P., and B. Gainer. 2003. Peer reputation in the nonprofit sector: Its role in nonprofit sector management. *Corporate Reputation Review* 6:252–265.

Paetzold, R. L., R. L. Dipboye, and K. D. Elsbach. 2008. A new look at stigmatization in and of organizations. *Academy of Management Review* 33:186–193.

Palmer, E. N. 1944. Negro secret societies. *Social Forces* 23:207–212.

Paoli, L. 2002. The paradoxes of organized crime. *Crime, Law and Social Change* 37:51–97.

Parsons, T. 1956. Suggestions for a sociological approach to the theory of organizations. *Administrative Science Quarterly* 7:63–85, 225–239.

Passas, N., and M. E. Castillo. 1992. Scientology and its "clear" business. *Behavioral Sciences and the Law* 10:103–116.

Peckham, M. 1998. New dimensions of social movement/countermovement interaction: The case of Scientology and its Internet critics. *Canadian Journal of Sociology* 23:317–347.

Peña, S. 1999. Informal markets: Street vendors in Mexico City. *Habitat International* 23:363–372.

Perrow, C. 1986. *Complex organizations: A critical essay*. 3rd ed. New York: Random House.

Petronio, S. 2002. *Boundaries of privacy: Dialectics of disclosure*. Albany: SUNY Press.

Petrou, M. 2011. Germany's Brown Army Faction? *Macleans.ca*, December 7. Retrieved February 10, 2012 from http://www2.macleans .ca/2011/12/07/a-brown-army-faction/.

Podolny, J. M., and K. L. Page. 1998. Network forms of organization. *Annual Review of Sociology* 24:57–76.

Portes, A., and W. Haller. 2005. The informal economy. In *Handbook of economic sociology*, ed. N. Smelser and R. Swedberg, 403–428. 2nd ed. New York: Russell Sage Foundation.

Powell, W. W. 1990. Neither market nor hierarchy: Network forms of organization. *Research in Organizational Behavior* 12:295–336.

Pratt, M. G. 1998. To be or not to be? Central questions in organizational identification. In *Identity in organizations: Building theory through conversations*, ed. D. A. Whetten and P. C. Godfrey, 171–207. Thousand Oaks, CA: Sage.

Pratt, M. G. 2000. The good, the bad, and the ambivalent: Managing identification among Amway distributors. *Administrative Science Quarterly* 45:456–493.

Pratt, M. G., and P. O. Foreman. 2000. Classifying managerial responses to multiple organizational identities. *Academy of Management Review* 25:18–42.

Priest, D., and W. M. Arkin. 2011. *Top secret America: The rise of the new American security state.* New York: Little, Brown.

Prusaczyk, W. K., and G. M. Goldberg. 2002. Organizational, psychological and training aspects of Special Operations Forces. US Army Medical Department. *Medical Aspects of Harsh Environments* 2:1166–1193.

Putnam, L. L., N. Phillips, and P. Chapman. 1996. Metaphors of communication and organization. In *Managing organizations: Current issues*, ed. S. R. Clegg, C. Hardy, and W. R. Nord, 125–158. London: Sage.

Qin, J., Y. Zhou, E. Reid, G. Lai, and H. Chen. 2007. Analysing terror campaigns on the Internet: Technical sophistication, content richness and web interactivity. *International Journal of Human-Computer Studies* 65:71–84.

Quintano, C., and P. Mazzocchi. 2010. Some alternative estimates of underground economies in 12 new UE member states. *International Economic Journal* 24:611–628.

Rains, S. A. 2005. What's in a name: Two studies examining the impact of anonymity on perceptions of source credibility and influence. Unpublished doctoral dissertation, University of Texas at Austin.

Rains, S. A., and C. R. Scott. 2007. Receiver responses to anonymous communication. *Communication Theory* 17:61–91.

Randol, S. 2003. Terrorism and the United States: A pragmatic and theoretical approach. *Scholars* (Spring 2003). Retrieved on May 24, 2011 from http://faculty.mckendree.edu/scholars/2003/randol.htm.

Rankin, K. 2008. IRS faces thinning ranks: Oversight board report highlights alarming turnover. *Accounting Today* 26(9):1, 16.

Rawlins, B. L. 2009. Give the emperor a mirror: Toward developing a stakeholder measurement of organizational transparency. *Journal of Public Relations Research* 21:71–99.

Raymond, J. G., D. M. Hughes, and C. J. Gomez. 2001. *Sex trafficking of women in the United States: International and domestic trends.* Unpublished report. Coalition Against Trafficking in Women, Amherst, MA.

Reitman, J. 2011. *Inside scientology: The story of America's most secretive religion.* New York: Houghton Mifflin Harcourt.

Reuter, P. 1983. *Disorganized crime: The economics of the visible hand.* Cambridge, MA: MIT Press.

Rich, P. 1992. The organizational taxonomy: Definition and design. *Academy of Management Review* 17:758–781.

Robbins, A. 2002. *Secrets of the tomb: Skull and Bones, the Ivy League, and the hidden paths of power*. New York: Little, Brown.

Rodin. 2008. Seeds of victory: Why we can't succeed without a multigenerational movement. Retrieved December 23, 2011 from http://www.earthfirstjournal.org/article.php?id=382.

Ronfeldt, D., and J. Arquilla. 2001. What next for networks and netwars? In *Networks and netwars: The future of terror, crime and militancy*, ed. J. Arquilla and D. Ronfeldt, 311–361. Santa Monica, CA: Rand.

Rose, S. E. F. 1914. *The Ku Klux Klan or invisible empire*. New Orleans: L. Graham.

Rosenzweig, P. 2011. Lessons of WikiLeaks: The U.S. needs a counterinsurgency strategy for cyberspace. *The Heritage Foundation Backgrounder, No. 2560*, 1–6. Retrieved on October 21, 2012 from http://papers.ssrn.com/sol3/papers.cfm?abstract_id=1884336.

Rudy, D., and A. Greil. 1988. Is Alcoholics Anonymous a religious organization?: Meditations on marginality. *Sociological Analysis* 50:41–51.

Sales, N. A. 2007. Secrecy and national-security investigations. *Alabama Law Review* 58:811–884.

Scahill, J. 2009. The secret U.S. war in Pakistan. *The Nation*, December 21/28,11–18.

Scahill, J. 2011. JSOC: The black ops force that took down Bin Laden. *The Nation*, May 2. Retrieved December 1, 2011 from http://www.thenation.com/blog/160332/jsoc-black-ops-force-took-down-bin-laden.

Schlosser, E. 2003. *Reefer madness: Sex, drugs, and cheap labor in the American black market*. Boston: Houghton Mifflin.

Schmitt, E., and T. Shanker. 2011. *Counterstrike: The untold story of America's secret campaign against Al-Qaeda*. New York: Times Books.

Schneider, F. 2002. *Size and measurement of the informal economy in 110 countries around the world*. Paper presented at workshop of Australian National Tax Centre, Canberra, Australia.

Schneider, F., A. Buehn, and C. E. Montenegro. 2010. New estimates for the shadow economies all over the world. *International Economic Journal* 24:443–461.

Schneider, F., and D. H. Enste. 2000. Shadow economies: Size, causes and consequences. *Journal of Economic Literature* 38(1):77–114.

Schoeneborn, D., and A. G. Scherer. 2012. Clandestine organizations, al Qaeda, and the paradox of invisibility: A response to Stohl and Stohl. *Organization Studies* 33:963–971.

Schubert, M. A., and T. J. Borkman. 1991. An organizational typology for self-help groups. *American Journal of Community Psychology* 19:769–787.

Schultz, M., M. J. Hatch, and M. H. Larsen. 2000. *The expressive organization—Linking identity, reputation, and the corporate brand*. Oxford: Oxford University Press.

Scott, C. R. 1997. Identification with multiple targets in a geographically dispersed organization. *Management Communication Quarterly* 10:491–522.

Scott, C. R. 2005. Anonymity in applied communication research: Tensions between IRBs, researchers, and human subjects. *Journal of Applied Communication Research* 33:242–257.

Scott, C. R. Forthcoming. Hidden organizations and reputation. In *Handbook of communication and corporate reputation*, ed. C. E. Carroll. Oxford: Wiley-Blackwell.

Scott, C. R., and S. Choi. 2009. *Communication policies in the workplace: Tensions surrounding identifiability and anonymity of technology users*. Paper presented at the annual convention of the International Communication Association, Chicago, IL.

Scott, C. R., S. R. Corman, and G. Cheney. 1998. Development of a situated-action theory of identification in the organization. *Communication Theory* 8:298–336.

Scott, C. R., S. A. Rains, and M. Haseki. 2011. Anonymous communication: Unmasking findings across fields. In *Communication Yearbook*, ed. C. T. Salmon, 35:299–342. New York: Routledge.

Scott, S. G., and V. R. Lane. 2000. A stakeholder approach to organizational identity. *Academy of Management Review* 25:43–62.

Seabright, M. A., and J. Delacroix. 1996. The minimalist organization as a postbureaucratic form: The example of Alcoholics Anonymous. *Journal of Management Inquiry* 5:140–154.

Selepak, A. 2010. Skinhead Super Mario Brothers: An examination of racist and violent games on white supremacist web sites. *Journal of Criminal Justice and Popular Culture* 17(1):1–47.

Sen, S., and P. M. Nair. 2004. *A report on trafficking in women and children in India 2002–2003*. New Delhi: Institute of Social Sciences, National Human Rights Commission, and UNIFEM.

Sengupta, S. 2012. The soul of the new hacktivist. *New York Times*, March 17. Retrieved June 11, 2012 from http://www.nytimes.com/2012/03/18/sunday-review/the-soul-of-the-new-hacktivist.html.

Shalit, R. 1999. *The name game: Welcome to the vicious world of corporate name-creation, where $75,000 buys you a suffix and competing shops slur each other over the virtues of Agilent and Avilant*. Retrieved May 19, 2011 from http://www.salon.com/media/col/shal/1999/11/30/naming/.

Shapiro, J. N. 2005. *Organizing terror: Hierarchy and networks in covert organizations*. Working paper, Stanford University.

Shell oil reviews. 2011. Glassdoor.com. Retrieved November 2, 2011 from http://www.glassdoor.com/Reviews/Shell-Oil-Reviews-E5833.htm.

Shelley, L. I., and J. T. Picarelli. 2002. Methods not motives: Implications of the convergence of international organized crime and terrorism. *Police Practice and Research* 3:305–318.

Siebert, W. H. 1898. *The underground railroad: From slavery to freedom*. New York: Russell & Russell.

Simmel, G. 1906. The sociology of secrecy and of secret societies. *American Journal of Sociology* 11:441–498.

Simmons, J. 2008 Employee significance within stakeholder-accountable performance management systems. *TQM Journal* 20:463–475.

Simon, H. 1996. *Hidden champions: Lessons from 500 of the world's best unknown companies*. Boston: Harvard Business School Press.

Simon, H. 2009. *Hidden champions of the twenty-first century. Success strategies of unknown world market leaders.* Bonn, Germany: Springer.

Smith, J. 2012a. America's most reputable companies. Retrieved on October 21, 2012 from http://www.forbes.com/sites/jacquelynsmith/2012/04/04/americas-most- reputable-companies/.

Smith, J. 2012b. The world's most reputable companies. Retrieved on October 21, 2012 from http://www.forbes.com/sites/jacquelynsmith/2012/06/07/the-worlds-most-reputable-companies/2/.

Smith, M. 1998. *Station X: The codebreakers of Bletchley Park.* London: Channel 4 Books.

Snyder, J. L., and M. D. Cistulli. 2011. The relationship between workplace e-mail privacy and psychological contract violation, and their influence on trust in top management and affective commitment. *Communication Research Reports* 28:121–129.

Solet, D. M. 2001. *Strategies of influence: How corporate power directs and constrains the FDA.* Unpublished paper, Harvard Law School, Cambridge, MA.

Southerland, M. D., and G. W. Potter. 1993. Applying organization theory to organized crime. *Journal of Contemporary Criminal Justice* 9:251–267.

Spaeth, T. N.d. *What does it cost?* Retrieved May 19, 2011 from http://www.identityworks.com/issues/issues7.htm.

Sparrow, M. K. 1991. The application of network analysis to criminal intelligence: An assessment of the prospects. *Social Networks* 13:251–274.

Spittal, R., and R. Abratt. 2009. The impact of geographic expansion on intended identity of an organization. *Journal of General Management* 35:65–78.

Spitzberg, B. H., and W. R. Cupach. 1984. *Interpersonal communication competence.* Beverly Hills, CA: Sage.

Stevens, J. 2010. America's secret ICE castles. *The Nation,* January 4, 13–17.

Stohl, C., and M. Stohl. 2007. Networks of terror: Theoretical assumptions and pragmatic consequences. *Communication Theory* 17:93–124.

Stohl, C., and M. Stohl. 2011. Secret agencies: The communicative constitution of a clandestine organization. *Organization Studies* 32:1197–1215.

Stohmeier, G. 2009. The Pope in the public eye: Distortions as a result of communication deficiency. *Journal of Media Research* 4:37–48.

Strategic Name Development's proprietary research uncovers 9 reasons for company naming changes in the U.S. 2007. *Strategic Name Development,* July 30. Retrieved on May 19, 2011 from http://www.namedevelopment.com/articles/company-naming-changes.html.

Sturcke, J. 2009. Explainer: Real IRA and Continuity IRA. *The Guardian,* March 10. Retrieved February 10, 2012 from http://www.guardian.co.uk/uk/2009/mar/10/real-ira-continuity.

Sutton, A. C. 2003. *America's secret establishment: An introduction to the Order of Skull and Bones.* Walterville, OR: Trine Day.

Tadelis, S. 2003. Firm reputation with hidden information. *Economic Theory* 21:635–651.

Tajfel, H., and J. C. Turner. 1986. The social identity theory of intergroup behavior. In *Psychology of intergroup relations*, ed. S. Worchel, 7–24. Chicago: Nelson-Hall.

Tapscott, D., and D. Ticoll. 2003. *The naked corporation: How the age of transparency will revolutionize business.* New York: Free Press.

Taylor, P. A. 2005. From hackers to hacktivists: Speed bumps on the global highway? *New Media and Society* 7:625–646.

Tefft, S. K. 1992. *The dialectics of secret society power in states.* Atlantic Highlands, NJ: Humanities Press.

Tewksbury, R. 2002. Bathhouse intercourse: Structural and behavioral aspects of an erotic oasis. *Deviant Behavior: An Interdisciplinary Journal* 23:75–112.

Thießen, U. 2010. The shadow economy in international comparison: Options for economic policy derived from an OECD panel analysis. *International Economic Journal* 24:481–509.

Thomas, G. 1999. *Gideon's spies: The secret history of the Mossad.* New York: Thomas Dunne.

Thomas, T. L. 2003. Al Qaeda and the Internet: The danger of "cyberplanning." *Parameters* 33:112–123.

Thompson, J. D. 1967. *Organizations in action.* New York: McGraw-Hill.

Thorne, K. 2005. Designing virtual organizations? Themes and trends in political and organizational discourses. *Journal of Management Development* 24:580–607.

Times Square advertising business annual estimate. 2005. *Digital Signage.* Retrieved on June 13, 2011 from http://webpavement.blogspot.com/2005/05/times-square-advertising-business.html.

Tirreau, S., and G. Kerforn. 2004. Hate speech and hate crime in France. In *Hate on the net: Virtual nursery for in real life crime*, ed. S. Bronkhorst and R. Eissens, 9–12. Amsterdam: International Network Against Cyber Hate.

Tompkins, P. K., and G. Cheney. 1983. Account analysis of organizations: Decision making and identification. In *Communication and organizations: An interpretive approach*, ed. L. L. Putnam and M. E. Pacanowsky, 123–146. Beverly Hills, CA: Sage.

Tompkins, P. K., and G. Cheney. 1985. Communication and unobtrusive control in contemporary organizations. In *Organizational communication: Traditional themes and new directions*, ed. R. D. McPhee and P. K. Tompkins, 179–210. Beverly Hills, CA: Sage.

Tonge, J. 2004. "They haven't gone away, you know": Irish republican "dissidents" and "armed struggle." *Terrorism and Political Violence* 16:671–693.

Top component maker pulls back the curtain. 2007. *MarketWatch*, November 10. Retrieved December 16, 2011 from http://www.marketwatch.com/story/nivarox-top-component-maker-pulls-back-the-curtain.

Top rated charities. 2011. American Institute of Philanthropy. Retrieved May 19, 2011 from http://www.charitywatch.org/toprated.html.

Top workplaces 2011. 2011. *Austin American Statesman*, November 15. Retrieved

December 1, 2011 from http://shopping.statesman.com/SS/Page.aspx?secid=11114
8&pagenum=1&facing=true.

Toth, J. I., and E. Sik. 2002. Hidden economy in Hungary, 1992–1999. In *The social impact of informal economies in Eastern Europe*, ed. R. Neef and M. Stanculescu, 219–230. Aldershot, UK: Ashgate.

Tucker, D. 2008. Terrorism, networks, and strategy: Why the conventional wisdom is wrong. *Homeland Security Affairs* 4(2):1–18.

Underwood, P. C. 2009. *New directions in networked activism and online social movement mobilization: The case of Anonymous and Project Chanology.* Unpublished thesis, College of Arts and Sciences, Ohio University, Athens, OH.

Urban, H. B. 2006. Fair game: Secrecy, security, and the Church of Scientology in Cold War America. *Journal of the American Academy of Religion* 74:356–389.

Urban, M. 2010. *Task Force Black: The explosive true story of the secret special forces war in Iraq.* New York: St. Martin's.

U.S. Special Operations Command. 2012. *U.S. Special Operations Command fact book.* Retrieved December 1, 2011 from http://www.socom.mil/news/documents/usso com_fact_book_2012.pdf.

Valdez, A. 2003. Toward a typology of contemporary Mexican-American youth gangs. In *Gangs and society: Alternative perspectives*, ed. L. Kontos, D. Broutherton, and L. Barrios, 12–40. New York: Columbia University Press.

Vallier, I. 1971. The Roman Catholic Church: A transnational actor. In *Transnational Relations and World Politics*, ed. R. O. Keohane and J. S. Nye, 129–152. Cambridge, MA: Harvard University Press.

Van de Bunt, H. 2010. Walls of secrecy and silence: The Madoff case and cartels in the construction industry. *Criminology and Public Policy* 9:435–453.

Van den Bosch, A. L. M., M. D. T. de Jong, and W. J. L. Elving. 2006. Managing corporate visual identity: Differences between profit and not-for-profit, and manufacturing and service organizations. *Journal of Business Communication* 43:138–157.

Van der Wal, Z., G. de Graaf, and K. Lasthuizen. 2008. What's valued most? Similarities and differences between the organizational values of the public and private sector. *Public Administration* 86:465–482.

Von Nordenflycht, A. 2010. What is a professional service firm? Toward a theory and taxonomy of knowledge-intensive firms. *Academy of Management Review* 35:155–174.

Walker, K. 2010. A systematic review of the corporate reputation literature: Definition, measurement, and theory. *Corporate Reputation Review* 12:357–387.

Wallis, R. 1977. *The road to total freedom: A sociological analysis of scientology.* New York: Columbia University Press.

Walsh, J. 2010. Street vendors and the dynamics of the informal economy: Evidence from Vung Tau, Vietnam. *Asian Social Sciences* 6:159–165.

Ward, T. J. 2011. The shared trajectories of Al Qaeda and the Ku Klux Klan. *International Journal on World Peace* 28(4):33–58.

Warning over number of crime gangs. 2011. Retrieved May 20, 2011 from www.herald.ie/ breaking-news/national-news/warning-over-number-of-crime-gangs-2591439.html.

We are legion: The story of the Hacktivists—Trailer. N.d. Retrieved February 2, 2012 from http://www.youtube.com/user/TheAnonMessage#p/f/36/gn9-8oObG.

Webb, J. W., L. Tihanyi, D. R. Ireland, and D. G. Sirmon. 2009. You say illegal, I say legitimate: Entrepreneurship in the informal economy. *Academy of Management Review* 34:492–510.

Wedgewood, C. H. 1930. The nature and functions of secret societies. *Oceania* 1:129–145.

What are the main dissident Irish republican groups? 2011. *Guardian*, April 23. Retrieved February 10, 2012 from http://www.guardian.co.uk/uk/2011/apr/23/ irish-dissident-republican-groups.

Wheeler, D., H. Fabig, and R. Boele. 2002. Paradoxes and dilemmas for stakeholder responsive firms in the extractive sector: Lessons from the case of Shell and the Ogoni. *Journal of Business Ethics* 39:297–318.

Wheeler, V., and N. Brooks. 2010. LA gangs take over UK streets. *The Sun*, April 15. Retrieved online June 8, 2011 from http://www.thesun.co.uk/sol/homepage/ news/2932813/London-gangs-are-aligning-themselves-to-LA-based-Bloods-and-Crips.html.

Whetten, D. A., and P. C. Godfrey, eds. 1998. *Identity in organizations: Building theory through conversations.* Thousand Oaks, CA: Sage.

Whittaker, D. J., ed. 2001. *The terrorism reader.* London: Routledge.

Williams, C. C. 2008. A critical evaluation of competing representations of the relationship between formal and informal work. *Community, Work & Family* 11:105–124.

Williams, C. C., and S. Nadin. 2010. Entrepreneurship and the informal economy: An overview. *Journal of Developmental Entrepreneurship* 15:361–378.

Williams, C. C., and J. Windebank. 2004. The heterogeneity of the underground economy. *International Journal of Economic Development* 6(2):1–23.

Williams, P. 2001. Transnational criminal networks. In *Networks and netwars: The future of terror, crime and militancy,* ed. J. Arquilla and D. Ronfeldt, 61–97. Santa Monica, CA: Rand.

Wise, D., and T. B. Ross. 1964. *The invisible government.* New York: Random House.

Wise, D., and T. B. Ross. 1967. *The espionage establishment.* New York: Random House.

Witmer, D. F. 1997. Communication and recovery: Structuration as an ontological approach to organizational culture. *Communication Monographs* 64:324–349.

Woodward, D. G., P. Edwards, and F. Birkin. 1996. Organizational legitimacy and stakeholder information provision. *British Journal of Management* 7:329–347.

Woodward, J. 1958. *Management and technology.* London: Her Majesty's Printing Office.

Woodward, J. 2011. A new way of communicating for the Vatican. Retrieved December 16, 2011 from http://www.prsa.org/SearchResults/view/9256/105/A_new_way_of _communicating_for_the_Vatican.

World's most admired companies. 2012. *Fortune*, March 19. Retrieved on June 14, 2012 from http://money.cnn.com/magazines/fortune/most-admired/2012/full_list/.

Xia, M. 2008. Organizational formations of organized crime in China: Perspectives from the state, markets, and networks. *Journal of Contemporary China* 17(54):1–23.

Xu, J., and H. Chen. 2008. The topology of dark networks. *Communications of the ACM* 51(10):58–65.

Xu, J., B. Marshall, S. Kaza, and H. Chen. 2004. Analyzing and visualizing criminal network dynamics: A case study. In *Proceedings of the 2nd NSF/NIJ Symposium on Intelligence and Security Informatics (ISI '04)*, Tucson, AZ.

Young, L. B. 2011. Personal construct theory and the transformation of identity in Alcoholics Anonymous. *International Journal of Mental Health Addiction* 9:709–722.

Zanini, M., and S. J. A. Edwards. 2001. The networking of terror in the information age. In *Networks and netwars: The future of terror, crime and militancy*, ed. J. Arquilla and D. Ronfeldt, 29–60. Santa Monica, CA: Rand.

Zhou, Y., E. Reid, J. Qin, H. Chen, and G. Lai. 2005. U.S. extremist groups on the web: Link and content analysis. *IEEE Intelligent Systems* 20:44–51.

Zohar, A., and T. Borkman. 1997. Emergent order and self-organization: A case study of Alcoholics Anonymous. *Nonprofit and Voluntary Sector Quarterly* 26:527–552.

Index

Interest, 49. *See also* Front
organizations
Central Intelligence Agency, 13, 19–20,
44–46. *See also* Secret government
agencies
Chalmers, D. M., 168–169, 171
Chaos Computer Club, 20, 50
Cheka, 46
Chen, H., 40, 82, 215
Cheney, G., 2, 9, 24, 53, 55–56, 61, 63, 75,
91, 94, 110, 113–114, 204, 207
Chinese Triads, 11, 31
Christensen, L. T., 2, 24, 53, 55, 75, 110
Citizens for the Integrity of Science, 49.
See also Front organizations
Clandestine: CIA links, 13, 45; defined,
13, 39; general, 9, 42, 127, 141, 159, 187,
217; meetings, 168, 177; organizations,
36–40, 43, 56, 107, 121–125, 187. *See also*
Covert; Dark (Region 8); Terrorist
organizations
Classification of organizations:
conclusions about, 197–203; eight
new regions, 98–99; four new
categories, 99–101; general, 18, 20–21,
40, 81, 83; new framework, 82–99,
198; previous general classifications,
21–23; specific organizational types,
10, 12, 29, 33. *See also* Framework for
regionalizing organizations
Codes of the Underworld, 32. *See also*
Criminal organizations
Coleman, G. E., 190–192, 194
Columbian drug cartels, 31
Combat Applications Group. *See* Delta
Force
Communication: anonymous, 66–69;
audience, 93–99, 111, 130, 205, 207;
competence, 210–211; corporate, 2,
5, 204; crises, 103, 111, 208; general,
23, 53–54, 60, 73, 86, 90, 113, 166, 178,
201, 209; in specific organizations,
29, 32–33, 35–36, 38, 40–41, 43, 45, 97;

interpersonal, 73, 85, 96–97, 115, 118,
120, 133, 150, 164, 176–177, 202; lack
of, 36, 51, 55, 64, 68, 88, 121, 123, 144,
163, 176–177, 182, 204; of identity by
organizations, 24, 27, 35, 46, 53–56,
58, 60, 74–75, 83–88, 93–100, 102–104,
110, 113, 129, 133–134, 136, 163, 175, 177,
198, 200, 203–205, 213–215; of identity
by members, 24, 27, 54, 60, 63–65, 74,
83, 89–100, 102–104, 129, 136, 144, 150,
163, 198–200, 203–204, 215; offline,
18, 42, 164, 175, 192, 195, 202; pronoun
use, 109, 133, 135, 149, 175; strategic,
27, 39, 63, 93, 163, 177–178, 200, 202,
204, 213. *See also* Communication
channels; Disclosure; Motivations;
Organizational identification;
Organizational identity;
Socialization; specific regions
Communication channels: anonymous,
17, 41–42, 51, 69, 146, 167, 175, 191–192,
202–203, 216; encrypted CMC, 42,
118, 146; general, 19, 51, 73, 86–87,
109, 140, 162, 201, 208; in specific
organizations, 41–42, 48, 146; mass-
mediated, 68–69; online tools, 7–8,
11, 17–19, 42, 47–48, 85–86, 95, 109, 112,
118, 124, 126, 144, 147, 150, 152, 157, 164,
167, 169, 171, 173, 175, 185, 189, 195, 215;
social media, 8, 17, 90, 96, 111, 114, 135,
167; website use, 7–8, 16, 42, 47, 50,
85–86, 90, 109–112, 116, 119, 125–126,
133–138, 142–147, 149, 151, 154–156,
165–167, 170–172, 188, 215. *See also*
Communication
Communication Privacy Management
Theory, 73
Communication problem, 32, 51. *See also*
Criminal organizations
Concealing identity, 21, 26, 39, 54–55,
58–60, 66, 68, 70–71, 79, 84–90,
94–95, 97, 115, 118–121, 128, 132, 141,
147, 150–152, 155, 159, 163–164, 167,